658.4013 C3376a

Case studies in performance
  management

CASE STUDIES IN PERFORMANCE MANAGEMENT

CASE STUDIES IN PERFORMANCE MANAGEMENT

A Guide from the Experts

TONY ADKINS

WILEY

John Wiley & Sons, Inc.

Published by John Wiley & Sons, Inc., Hoboken, New Jersey.
Published simultaneously in Canada.

For general information on our other products and services, or technical support, please contact our Customer Care Department within the United States at 800-762-2974, outside the United States at 317-572-3993 or fax 317-572-4002.

Wiley also publishes its books in a variety of electronic formats. Some content that appears in print may not be available in electronic books.

For more information about Wiley products, visit our Web site at http://www.wiley.com.

Library of Congress Cataloging-in-Publication Data

Case studies in performance management : a guide from the experts /
[edited by] Tony Adkins.
    p. cm.
  Includes index.
  ISBN-13: 978-0-471-77659-8 (cloth)
  ISBN-10: 0-471-77659-9 (cloth)
 1. Activity-based costing—Case studies.   2. Managerial accounting—Case studies.
3. Cost accounting—Case studies.   4. Performance—Management—Case studies.
5. Industrial management—Cost effectiveness—Case studies.   I. Adkins, Tony (Tony C.)
HF5686.C8C295 2006
658.4′013—dc22   2005029726

*Dedicated to my wife, Judy, for her unselfish support and
dedication to our family
To our three children, Justin, Brendan, and Colin
Thanks!—Go Cougs!*

CONTENTS

PREFACE

It has always fascinated me how energetic, passionate, and in some cases fanatical people get over a topic like performance management and cost management. Over the years I have seen discussions that could have doubled as death matches over whether you should use a verb/noun description of an activity in an ABC model.

I have always tried to boil it down to something simple. To me, performance management is optimizing your organization's performance. If you are successful at using activity-based costing to understand your cost management, you are probably surfacing that information in a way that it can be used to make decisions. Many organizations use a scorecard for that. It could be a true "Balanced Scorecard," as Robert S. Kaplan and David P. Norton describe in their book, *The Balanced Scorecard: Translating Strategy into Action* or a simple metrics report. Implementations that end in success typically use their cost information, in some way, for planning and budgeting. They may not have matured to a completely integrated system that automates their capacity information and their budget execution, but at a minimum, they take a greater understanding of their costs into their budgeting process.

Recently the fanaticism has been over methodology and modeling approach, top-down versus bottom-up, consumption based versus driver based, time- or event-based versus traditional ABC. All of these approaches are valid; however, there is no one-size-fits-all. In the foreword of this book, Gary Cokins outlines some of these approaches. I have implemented ABC models with small and large companies in over 15 countries, and they have all used multiple approaches in their cost model. Some costs are driven with traditional drivers, some are driven with a rate-based driver, and some simply use traditional allocations. None of these methodologies is new; ABC implementations have been using all of them since the mid- to late 1980s. There is expertise out there to help companies decide on a best fit for them.

The key, which you will see in many of these cases, is to evaluate your needs with a pilot project and design the model around your own needs.

This book is a collection of case studies taken from actual companies. The names of the companies have been changed in the interest of anonymity. This book is for anyone who wants to gain a better understanding of performance and cost management and how activity-based costing is the basis for understanding an organization's cost structure.

Tony Adkins
March 2006

ACKNOWLEDGMENTS

Since beginning to work with activity-based costing models in 1994, I have had the good fortune to work and learn from some of the best companies and minds in the world of cost management. When I joined ABC Technologies in 1996 and met my good friend Gary Cokins, I began to see the excitement that companies experience when they realized that they finally had found a way to understand their organization's cost and manage their performance.

In growing my understanding of cost management, there have been many who have helped me either through mentorship, thanks Gary, or by working side by side with me while implementing activity-based costing/management and scorecards at some of the world's best-run companies.

I cannot imagine where I would be today without my first experience shadowing the great Tim Carey in Hong Kong on my first real ABC consulting engagement. I do not know if it was the work on the cost model or the times in the Irish pub in Kowloon, but I will never forget that experience.

It is important for me to acknowledge the people who help me grow and mature at ABC Tech; in particular, I can't forget Chris Pieper, Mohan Nair, Bob Rubitschun, John Rutledge, Chris Dorrenbacher, Tom Puccetti, and Nancy Coderre, who always stood behind me and allowed me to travel the world and work with great organizations.

In addition, I want to thank those at SAS Institute who have made this endeavor possible: Jonathan Hornby, Dan Minto, Christiana Lycan, Julie Platt, and all of the people in SAS Publications, without whose help this would have been impossible.

I am fortunate to have had the backing and input of the experts who contributed to each case by evaluating it and providing their insight. I was humbled by the fact that these great authors, consultants, and friends agreed to assist me by contributing to this work. Thanks to Gary Cokins, Tom Kang, John Miller, Ashok Vadgama, Jonathan Hornby, John Antos, Alan Stratton, Jeffrey Thomson, Don Bean, and Professor Ed Blocher.

Finally, I cannot forget Sheck Cho, Natasha Andrews, and Helen Cho and everyone at John Wiley and Sons for their willingness to work with me on the project and their flexibility and insight into the manuscript.

Tony Adkins
March 2006

ABOUT THE CONTRIBUTORS

John Antos is president of Value Creation Group, Inc., an internationally recognized consulting group providing innovative strategic and operational solutions in areas such as activity-based management/costing/budgeting, strategic planning, balanced scorecard, outsourcing, performance management, reengineering, quality and value management. Mr. Antos has been president, chief financial officer, treasurer, and controller of various companies. He is the coauthor of *Activity Management for Services Industries, Government Entities, & Nonprofit Organizations* and *Driving Value Using Activity Budgeting* (both from John Wiley & Sons).

Don Bean is product manager, Activity-Based Management Solutions, at SAS Mr. Bean sets the strategic direction for SAS Activity-Based Management solutions. He has spearheaded product management and development efforts for activity-based analysis, scorecarding, and financial management solutions at ABC Technologies, which was acquired by SAS in March 2002. He is recognized globally as an expert in activity-based management, appearing as a speaker for BetterManagement Live seminars in North America, Europe and Asia. Before joining ABC Technologies, Mr. Bean spent 10 years in sales and product management with Control Data and FaxBack.

Edward Blocher is a professor at the University of North Carolina, Chapel Hill. He is the coauthor of *Cost Management: A Strategic Emphasis, Third Edition* and *Cases and Readings in Cost Management, Third Edition* (both with Irwin/McGraw-Hill). His articles have appeared in *The Journal of Cost Management, Strategic Finance*, and *Issues in Accounting Education*. He received his B.A. from Rice University, his MBA in Business Administration from Tulane University, and his Ph.D. from the University of Texas.

Gary Cokins is the lead Strategist, Performance Management Solutions, with SAS, the world's largest privately owned software vendor. He is an internationally recognized expert, speaker, and author in advanced cost management and performance improvement systems. He began his career as a strategic planner in FMC's Link-Belt Division and then served as financial controller and operations manager. In 1981 Mr. Cokins began his management consulting career with Deloitte & Touche. Next with KPMG Peat Marwick, he was trained on ABC by Harvard Business School professors Robert Kaplan and Robin Cooper. He is the author of several books: *Performance Management: Finding the Missing Pieces (to Close the Intelligence Gap)*, *Activity-Based Cost Management: An Executive's Guide* (both with John Wiley & Sons), *Activity-Based Cost Management Making It Work: A Manager's Guide to Implementing and Sustaining an Effective ABC System* (McGraw-Hill), and *Activity-Based Cost Management in Government* (Management Concepts).

Songyu He is a product marketing manager for SAS Activity-Based Management, the world's leading software for activity-based costing and profitability management. In that position, he drives product marketing by ensuring SAS understands the costing and profitability analysis needs of companies in major industries, such as retail/CPG, banking, telecom, and others. He has also been the director of International Business Development with ABC Technologies and helped many organizations across Asia Pacific deploy activity-based management systems.

Jonathan Hornby is the director, Performance Management, Worldwide Marketing, SAS. In that position, he ensures that SAS understands and delivers management solutions that help customers achieve their desired goals with a clear understanding of cost. Doing this involves close collaboration with business thought leaders from management schools to commercial and public sector organizations. Mr. Hornby works closely with SAS research and development, strategy, and implementation teams globally. Prior to joining SAS, he had 15 years of business experience in the financial sector in activity-based management, process reengineering, performance analysis, and marketing.

Thomas M. Kang is president and chief operating officer at CSMG, where he leads the company's strategic planning and operations. Prior to joining CSMG, Mr. Kang spent 10 years at Mobil Corporation, in strategic planning, business performance evaluation, operations management, systems implementation, and organizational reengineering. While at Mobil, he led a global initiative on the implementation of strategic business evaluation models involving market segmentation/evaluation/improvement/investment techniques; today those models are still in use.

John A. Miller is director of Client Services, Arkonas Management Consulting Services. He is an internationally recognized expert and leading authority in the area of activity-based management and related performance measurement and process improvement initiatives. He is the author of *Implementing Activity-Based Management in Daily Operations* (John Wiley & Sons), which has been published in four languages. Mr. Miller has over 35 years of experience, a large portion of which has been in industry, where he held the positions of chief financial officer for a publicly held New York Stock Exchange manufacturing company and for a privately owned independent exploration and production oil and gas company. In addition, he has held positions of corporate director for Strategic and Operations Planning for two other large, publicly held Fortune 500 companies. As a former partner at Arthur Andersen & Co. and founder of his own consulting firm, Mr. Miller has led and conducted activity-based costing, performance measurement, and process improvement consulting projects for the government and in a wide variety of industries in the private sector. As a subject matter expert at Andersen, Mr. Miller was part of the Cost Management Competency Center, responsible for the development of Andersen's worldwide cost management consulting practice, including the development of ABM methodologies, tools, and training

Alan Stratton, CMA, CPA, is a product strategist and subject matter expert at SAS. He is also a board member and an active participant at CAM-I, a consortium leading development of management methods and techniques in cost, process, and performance management. He is the coauthor of *An ABB Manager's Primer: Straight Talk on Activity-Based Budgeting and Planning, Second Edition*, and *An ABC Manager's Primer: Straight Talk on Activity-Based Costing* (Institute of Management Accountants), the leading introduction to activity-based costing/management (ABC/M) and capacity measurement and improvement. Mr. Stratton's articles have appeared in *Management Accounting*, *Journal of Cost Management*, *Corporate Controller*, *CMA Magazine*, and *As Easy as ABC*. Prior to joining SAS, he was an independent ABC/M consultant, director of Customer Advocacy at ABC Technologies, and held financial management positions at Cost Technology, National Semiconductor, Atari, General Instrument, and GTE.

Jeff Thomson is vice president, Research at the Institute of Management Accountants (IMA), the world's leading association for management finance and accounting professionals. He recently retired as chief financial officer, Business Sales at AT&T, where he was responsible for an $18 billion revenue stream.

While at AT&T, he was responsible for the first successful activity-based costing implementation at a major telecom (a $30 million billing center responsible for all billing functions associated with multibillion-dollar corporate accounts).

Ashok Vadgama is the president of CAM-I, a global consortium for leadership in cost, process, and performance management. Previously he was the manager for Data Management at Motorola Semiconductor Product sector in Austin, Texas. He has extensive experience in implementing integrated financial and business process modeling systems and driving strategic initiatives in the United States, Europe, Asia, and Mexico. He has held various positions in finance and operations in multinational companies in the United States and United Kingdom. Mr. Vadgama is a visiting lecturer at Northwestern University and the University of Texas. He was also an editor for the *Corporate Controller* journal and *Handbook of Cost Management* (Warren, Gorham and Lamont). He is the coauthor of *Data . . . The DNA of Business Intelligence* (Bookman Publishing). His articles have been published in various finance periodicals.

FOREWORD

GARY COKINS

With this book, Tony Adkins has made an important contribution to the body of knowledge of managerial accounting. It offers examples of problem solving that could have only been applied by using the progressive power of information technology that was only recently developed and mastered in the 1990s. Have there been other books written about activity-based costing and management? Of course. I even authored a few. So have several of the contributors to this book. But the majority of material written about activity-based management (ABM)—the increasingly accepted term for measuring costs with activity-based costing math but also changing things with the insights gained—described outcomes from before ABM software was advanced to the stage to accommodate much more flexible modeling, including multistage cost assignments, multidimensional viewing, and scoring costs with attributes (i.e., value-added versus non–value-added), to name a few.

Tony is proof of a hypothesis I have long held that it is easier for an individual (like Tony) with strong capabilities in information technology (IT) to learn managerial accounting than it is for an accountant to learn IT. Before flexible modeling with ABM principles, accountants were restricted to the traditional thinking of debits and credits and departmental step-down cost allocations of support departments, succeeded by 1980s primitive two-step cost allocation of work activities. With the 1980s ABM thinking, accountants still continued to routinely commit the sin of violating the cause-and-effect relationships (still using broad-brushed cost allocating averages, although less broad) with which twenty-first-century ABM technology enabled compliance.

Tony's employment in the 1990s with the world's leading ABM commercial software provider gave him the opportunity to work with a group of similarly talented professionals with IT backgrounds who were all at the same time observing organizations that could finally discard the yoke of restrictive costing practices and truly model the transformation of resource expense inputs (e.g., salaries, supplies, travel, etc.) into their calculated costs so that the costs realistically represented the economics of the organization. Costing is modeling. It was an experience for Tony not that dissimilar in exhilaration as that enjoyed by junior architects working at Frank Lloyd Wright's Taliesin offices or young scientists working at Thomas Edison's "idea factory." The knowledge of better ways to model costs accelerated as organizations that had purchased ABM software were applying it to their organization's real-world problems.

ABM'S DARK AGES?

But along with successes using ABM in the 1990s there also came limited results and in some cases failures. And perhaps due to misguided lofty expectations that ABM would be some form of a magic pill that could solve all problems, rumors circulated that ABM was ineffective. People would periodically ask me, "Is ABM still going on?" as if it had passed on as another short-lived management fad. The implication was that ABM system implementations were either scaling down or being abandoned—or that those organizations that had not yet implemented ABM had examined it and chosen to not likely implement it near term.

The problem was not with ABM principles but rather with how ABM was being implemented. It will be tough to stop the use of ABM-principled accounting because it correctly answers eternal questions that managers will forever be asking. What do things cost? Where do we make or lose money? What will be the future impact on spending from possible planned changes?

Before I provide further background about this important issue of growing the adoption rate of ABM and sustaining ABM environments once up and running, let me give you with the answer up front. ABM is indeed alive and well. This book provides evidence of real implementations with real significant results to prove it. In fact, in my opinion, Tony's book chronicles arguably the most successful adoption of an accounting initiative related to cost management and performance management. The rate of adoption of ABM systems, however, is simply going slower than many of us who implemented its earlier versions in the 1990s thought it would. But it has continuously ascended since I got involved with it.

I am honored that Tony invited me to write the foreword for his book. The past few years I have had the privilege to present seminars around the world on the broader topic of performance management that includes ABM, strategy maps, and balanced scorecards, just to name a few of its components. (I describe performance management as one of Tony's contributors in Chapter 1.) As background, I was fortunate to have gotten involved with the ABM movement as a consultant with KPMG Peat Marwick in the mid-1980s and then was trained by Professors Robert S. Kaplan and Robin Cooper of the Harvard Business School. Bob and Robin were pioneers in researching, documenting, and applying ABM.

Once you are exposed to the logic of and superior visibility from ABM, you wonder, "Why doesn't everybody use this practice?" But now that roughly 25 years have passed since Kaplan formally introduced ABM, I too have wondered what accounts for its slower-than-expected adoption. In my travels abroad I routinely ask this question of trusted practitioners in the field. The initial explanations included lack of good data or the complexity or inability of software to replicate the ABM principles. But, as mentioned, those obstacles were resolved in the early 1990s, when "end-to-end" integrated commercial ABM software had matured and ABM implementers learned to use ABM rapid prototyping with iterative remodeling methods to get quick results with sufficient accuracy.

A deeper explanation surfaced: that the mentality of accountants, who often drive ABM implementation projects, have done more damage than good for the ABM movement. That is, not only is accountants' unnecessary concern for precision and exactness (which by the way is a myth) a hindrance because of the resulting oversized and overengineered ABM models that retarded learning and buy-in, but their concern for their accounting data to reconcile with generally accepted accounting principles (GAAP) regulatory reporting may even have been a worse obstacle.

More recently I heard opinions about ABM's slow adoption rate that support one of the unspoken laws of management: If your senior leadership cannot articulate the basic principles of an improvement initiative, then employees will never achieve or sustain the initiative. And if the leadership is weak, success may be low. I believe this may better explain why the adoption rate of ABM has been so gradual.

But as I attend various business conferences and continue to spend time with organizations that have been using ABM for several years, I am very impressed with the depth of problems it is being used for. For example, telecommunication companies and banks are moving beyond measuring customer profitability to further measure customer lifetime value—treating existing and future customers like an investment in a portfolio—in order for their sales and marketing people to better deploy resources for differentiated customer treatments and segmented marketing campaigns with varying deals and offers in proportion to the value of the customer or sales prospect. Granular ABM data are integral in those calculations.

So does ABM not work? Sure it does. But implementers need to be prudent and economical. Any improvement initiative like ABM will always be judged by management based on a cost versus benefits test. If you keep the administrative effort to operate ABM low and the benefits from using the data for decision analysis high, ABM systems will be adopted and sustained. My sense is that in this next decade or two, ABM will become as widely accepted as standard cost accounting is today. But some hurdles for ABM to overcome lie ahead.

CONFUSION WITH ACCOUNTING

It is understandable that people with nonfinancial backgrounds and training have difficulties understanding accounting—and for many of them, accounting is outside their comfort zone. But there is a gathering storm in the community of management accountants, where a need for so-called advanced accounting techniques (e.g., resource consumption accounting, time-based activity-based costing) is confusing even the trained accountants—even seasoned ABM practitioners. What is the problem?

The fields of law and medicine build on each decade because their body of knowledge is codified. In a sense financial accounting's GAAP, although varying from country to country, also has codified rules and principles (but with lots of loopholes) to support external reporting for regulatory agencies and bankers. Unfortunately, unlike financial accounting with its codification, managerial accounting has no such framework or set of universal standards. Accountants are left to their own devices, which are typically the methods and treatments at their organization that they inherit from their prior managers whom they succeeded. Accountants burn the midnight oil with lots of daily problems to solve, so getting around to improving (or reforming) the accounting information for their managers and employees is not a frequent routine. And the escalation of global compliance reporting, such as with Sarbanes-Oxley, is major distraction from investing time to evaluate improvements to an organization's managerial accounting system.

But in managerial accounting, although rules are many, principles are few. Sadly, many accountants apparently missed the schoolday class that defined the purpose of managerial accounting as to provide data that influences people's behavior and supports good decision making. Of course, how to apply cost information for decision support can lead to heated debates. For example, what is the incremental cost for one additional order? For starters, that answer depends on several assumptions, but if the debaters agree on them, then the robustness of the costing system and the resulting accuracy requirement to make the correct decision for that question might justify an advanced costing methodology.

Another accounting principle is precision is a myth: There is no such thing as a correct cost, because something's cost is determined (i.e., calculated) based on assumptions that an organization has latitude to make. It is this latitude that is causing increasing confusion among accountants. If we step back for a better view, we can see that an organization can refine its managerial accounting system over time through various stages of maturity. Changes to managerial accounting methods and treatments are typically not continuous, but occur as periodic and punctuated reforms.

If we travel back through time and revisit the weeks in which an organization's managerial accounting system was initially architected, we first realize that it is a spin-off or variant of the ongoing financial accounting system already in place. The nature of the organization's purpose and the economic conditions it faces govern the initial financial accounting system design. So, for example, if the organization's output is nonrecurring with a life cycle, such as constructing a building or executing a consulting engagement, then project accounting is the more appropriate method—a very high form of direct costing. Similarly, if the organization is a manufacturer of unique one-time engineer-to-order products, then the firm likely will begin with a job-order cost accounting scheme.

In contrast, if the product made or service delivered is recurring, as consequently will also be employee work activities, then the initial accounting method may take on a standard costing approach, where the repeating material requirements and labor time effort of work tasks is first measured and then the equivalent costs for both direct material and labor are assumed as constant and applied in total based on the quantity and volume of output: products made or services delivered. Of course, the actual expenses paid each accounting period to third parties and employees will always differ from these costs that were calculated "at standard," so there are various methods of cost variance analysis (e.g., volume variance, labor rate or price variance, etc.) to report what actually happened relative to what was expected.

The overarching point here is that an organization's initial condition—the types of products and services it makes and delivers as well as its expense structure—governs its initial costing methodology.

ENTER A NEW CHARACTER: SHARED AND INDIRECT EXPENSES

For organizations that were founded with recurring products and work, typically with longer product life cycles, none of them can last long term as only a one-trick pony. Inevitably proliferation of different types of products (e.g., colors, sizes, ranges) or standard service lines evolves to remain a viable organization. Increases in the diversity and variation (i.e., heterogeneity) of outputs quickly results in complexity that causes the need to add people and system resources to manage that complexity. Gradually these support expenses are no longer insignificant or immaterial, and the organizational managers begin requesting visibility of these costs, not only as part of the organization's monthly expenses but also as they are associated with each product or standard service line—the calculated costs.

This need by managers to view output costs, not just input expenses incurred, ultimately leads an organization to experience one of those punctuated reform changes along the accounting system's stages of maturity—full absorption costing with so-called overhead cost allocations.

Of course, this is where concepts such as support department–to–support department step-down overhead expense allocation, and in the 1980s its more granular method, activity-based costing, evolved. And many readers know the story from here. Many organizations now realize that their predecessor accountants' past choice was a convenient cost allocation factor that simplistically relies on broad-based averages (i.e., number of output units produced or labor input hours) as the factor or basis for the cost allocation. Hence, using that method, the true cost of each product or standard service line does not reflect the true consumption of the portion of the indirect resources that each product or service is uniquely consuming.

What then are the consequences? Because the descriptive view of expenses incurred (i.e., money spent in a historical past period) is a permanent event, any error to allocate them into calculated costs is a zero-sum error game. Some products will be overcosted, and all of the other products *must* be undercosted. Hence, the cost data being used by managers and employee team for decisions or profit margin–validated pricing is somewhat (and in many cases grotesquely) flawed and misleading. Increasingly more organizations are coming to this realization; however, they are intimidated by the perceived heights that they would need to scale to return to the levels of cost accuracy they once enjoyed. Inevitably they come to grips with their predicament. Should they reform their accounting method using activity-based management principles? Or take no action and remain with the status quo, hoping that the lack of transparency of indirect costs, their drivers, and the degree of misleading information will not too adversely result in bad decision making? In either case, both are choices accountants are making. That is, to change or not to change—both are choices, where either one could be wrong.

THE PLOT THICKENS: ANOTHER SET OF BARRIERS

Imagine the frustration of the Lewis and Clark expedition in the early 1800s to complete their task for President Thomas Jefferson to explore, survey, and map the western territories of the United States to the next sea (the Pacific Ocean). When they entered the Rocky Mountain range, each time they successfully scaled a peak, they did not see that expected body of water to end their westward journey but rather an endless view of more mountain peaks, all also needing to be scaled.

The situation is not that dire for those accountants who have already reformed their accounting system with some activity-based assignment principles, but they are facing another set of mountain ranges. These mountains come with names such as time-driven ABC, pull-ABC, Grenzplankostenrechnung (GPK), resource consumption accounting (RCA), throughput accounting (courtesy of Eli Goldratt and his "theory of constraints [TOC]" followers), or explicit resource dynamics. Must the accountants take a next step up the maturity curve? Is it a total choice or a blend retaining some of the practices they have in place?

The important point to appreciate here is that when you consider this managerial accounting "stages of maturity" framework I earlier referenced, progressing to a next higher stage does not necessarily equate to being better off. Each progressive advance, which again is typically a disruptive and punctuated reform change to an organization's existing managerial accounting method, should be evaluated as to whether it is worth the change. That is, the test for advancing is if the incremental benefits in the form of better information exceeds the incrementally higher investment and administrative effort to collect, calculate, and deploy the information. Regardless of which stage of costing with ABM principles an organization chooses as best for it, they are all valid. In practice, some companies develop hybrid ABM practices that have elements of several of the ABM variants that I describe next.

STAGES OF MATURITY: HOW MUCH BETTER?

I do not want to reduce the importance of ABM, but it is simply full absorption costing. However, ABM traces the expenses as they are consumed by processes into their cost objects the correct way rather than violating a key rule of cause-and-effect relationships as accountants do when they revert to convenient broadly averaged allocation factors lacking causality. Costing is simply modeling how resource capacity expenses (e.g., salaries, supplies, energy, etc.) are consumed by outputs, products, service lines, sales or distribution channels, and customers. Products, services, channels, and customers place demands on work activities, and the work activities draw on the resource capacity—the expenses. As a consequence, the costs flow the opposite direction. Costs are a measure of effect—a universal property of cost accounting.

If the accountants are respectful in designing a good multistage ABM cost assignment network, they will include a "business sustaining" final cost object, at the same level as products and customers, in order to trace those organizational expenses that have nothing to do with making a product or delivering a service to a customer, such as the annual company picnic or when the accountants close the books each month. Doing this prevents fictitiously overstating the costs of products, services, and customers while still fully absorbing 100% of the expenses.

The easiest ABM approach is to push the costs with tracing assignment relationships from resources to activities and then into final activity costs based on drivers. Some call this a top-down approach. Push ABM is relatively simple to calculate after you realize that full absorption costing is simply modeling—and the key to calculating reasonably accurate costs has less to do with the numbers (after all, you begin with each period's precise actual expenses accumulated in the general ledger accounting system) and is primarily influenced by the design and architecture of the cost assignment system.

Are there any deficiencies with calculating output costs with conventional push ABM? Yes. Is the impact critical? It depends.

Now we must begin a brief primer to describe the various set of "mountain ranges" facing accountants who have already successfully implemented push ABM. As there are already magazine articles and some books dedicated to these alternative pull (i.e., bottom-up) methodologies, this book is not the place to explain the differences beyond push ABM in great detail, but I will give a brief overview.

PUSH (TOP-DOWN) VERSUS PULL (BOTTOM-UP) ABM

First, make no mistake: Descriptive (historical period) costing is simply a physical representation of the equivalent spending of resource expenses converted into the same costs of processes and the resulting outputs that consume the work activities that belong to the processes. I morbidly refer to descriptive costing as a "cost autopsy," because the period's spending is recorded as transactions so a period's total expenses are known exactly. What is not known is where the spending expenses went. What were costs of the processes (and the work activities that belong to the processes) and the cost of the outputs that consumed the processes, such as products and customers? Once you have those costs, by measuring (or estimating in some areas) the time effort and quantity of the activity drivers, the output costs are calculated. Again, this is classic full absorption costing—but done the correct way (at least a more correct way than applying broad averages). The total costs of the processes and their subsequent outputs must exactly total the resource spending—hence all the period's expenses are directly or indirectly traced.

In contrast to descriptive costing, predictive costing has a reverse problem to solve. Instead of costing outputs, which descriptive costing does, predictive costing determines what level resource (capacity) spending would be required to validly meet estimated demand—the known amount you have for descriptive costing. In effect, predictive costing is for expense planning.

But predictive costing is much trickier than descriptive costing. For future periods, the volume and mix of demand will never exactly replicate that of past periods, so (presuming that many equipment and employees have specific or dedicated capabilities and skills) the consequence is that there will always soon be too many resources that you will not need (excess capacity) and not enough resources that you will need (capacity shortage). For predictive costing, the appropriate resource capacity to be supplied should ideally match the resource capacity needed. Further, required resource capacity expense is unknown whereas the quantity and volume of the output demand is known—meaning it is routinely estimated. This is just the opposite of descriptive (historical) costing. Hence the business problem focus shifts 180 degrees from descriptive (historical) costing, where the resource expenses are exactly known but the output costs are not, to predictive costing, where the outputs (e.g., sales volume and mix) are estimable and you solve for the needed resource expenses.

A reason that predictive costing is a bit trickier than descriptive (historical) costing is because in addition to good causal tracing of expense and cost relationships required for descriptive costing, you must also consider how the future capacity would need to be adjusted to react to changes in the intensity, frequency, and quantity of volume of the future demands that drive the need (i.e., workload) for the work activities. And because resources come in discontinuous amounts (i.e., you cannot purchase one-third of a machine or hire two-thirds of an employee—it is all or nothing), then you have to consider whether each resource expense will behave as fixed, semifixed, semivariable, or linearly variable with incremental changes in the demand volume and mix.

For predictive (bottom-up) costing, activity-based resource planning is a technique that reverse-models the push ABM to solve for the future level of resources needed. This type of pull-ABM technique relies on consumption rates (e.g., gallons per minute, pounds per unit) calibrated from its companion push ABM system for prior periods. Of course, if management chooses in the cases where volume and/or mix demand declines to retain or not remove the calculated excess capacity, then higher potential profits will not be realized for that period. And, with the opposite situation, in the cases where demand increases, resulting in capacity shortages, if management chooses not to add resources, then declines in customer service levels (e.g., delays, shortages) will result and adversely affect future business. Activity-based resource expense planning also requires relatively more granularity and detail than its companion push ABM system because if the consumption rates calibrated in the historic, descriptive ABM are too lumpy, they reduce the accuracy of the derived future resource capacity expenses.

Did you notice in the last paragraph I referred to this "type" of pull ABM system? I did so because there are varying types of pull systems. And these are more mountain ranges that accountants have to evaluate when considering whether the incremental effort level is justified by greater incremental benefits. An appeal for pull ABM systems is they can dynamically generate cost and profit margin data in almost real time due to their being tightly integrated with transactional systems (e.g., enterprise resource planning data). However, you must be cautious of the promises and perils of real-time cost data. If misapplied, more permanent long-term damage may be be caused by poor decisions that are made based on recent cost anomalies.

PULL DESCRIPTIVE COSTING: TIME-BASED ACTIVITY-BASED COSTING

In environments where a substantial amount of the outputs and the work activities they consume is highly repetitive and management is less concerned about managing the indirect support expenses (e.g., a high-volume document processing center), then the consideration for measuring costs for unused capacity may increase. With conventional push ABC, all expenses, including nonvisible excess capacity (assuming the rate of workers producing outputs remains constant and they are not slowing down when inbound workload demand appears declining), are fully absorbed into the products, standard service lines, channels, and customers. This overstates the true cost of the output because unneeded capacity that the output did not cause is included in its cost. (However, if available or safety capacity for demand surges is reasonably estimable, then it can be traced and assigned to a business-sustaining cost object called unused capacity. This reduces any overstating of an output's cost). If senior management feels that small improvements in processing times and/or postperiod reactive adjustments to remove reported unused capacity will materially improve the enterprise profit performance, then it might investigate an ABM variant: time-based ABC. Time-based ABC addresses descriptive costing, but, like conventional push ABM, consumption rates calibrated in the descriptive costing can be applied for predictive costing (expense planning).

Time-based ABC recognizes that atomistically, time (e.g., the number of seconds or minutes to perform a task) is the lowest common denominator to measure diversity and variation differences in outputs. In all costing methods, you always must calculate for known information and unknown information. With time-based ABC, the standard time, typically measured in minutes and possibly seconds, for all the various work tasks that combine into output (e.g., a call center customer order) are each individually measured. Frederick Taylor's "scientific revolution" for manufacturers in the early twentieth century was based on such measures.[1] Once all times are documented, then each period the quantity of all the various types of orders are tallied (typically from imported transaction data already captured in a production system) and multiplied by the standard minutes. Because the employee labor rates are known, this consumption-based pull (bottoms-up) method then calculates each work activity cost "at standard." That is, it presumes the work is exactly completed on average at the standard times to solve for the activity costs. Because the total payroll is also known for the same time period, the difference calculated between the sum total of all the processed outputs "at standard" and the total payroll (adjusted for coffee breaks, team meetings, etc.) will net to the idle capacity for that period. Senior management may then wish to adjust manpower based on the reported unused capacity, or estimate future workloads.

In contrast to time-based ABC, conventional ABM relies on time collection of the employees or equipment performing the work activities (or typically periodic surveys rather than administrative–labor-intensive time sheet collection). With conventional ABM, rather than the activity cost calculated as the unknown "at standard" derived from the output volume and activity time in time-based ABC, here the activity costs is calculated from the resources as "actual." Then, based on the quantity of the activity driver (e.g., the number of invoices processed), the cost of the period's invoice processing as well as the unit cost per each invoice is calculated.

What we have here with both methods is two knowns solving for the unknown, and each method starts with a different set of knowns. Conventional ABM's activity drivers are discrete measurable units, such as number of invoices processed, and in effect are a proxy equating to time-based ABC's time measures. You can think of it as what molecules are to atoms in physics. The language of conventional ABM's activity drivers is useful to some to more easily understand cost management. For example, if the activity driver for the activity cost "resolve disputed invoices" is the number of disputed invoices, then employee teams involved with that work (which in this case would also be attributed as a non–value-added cost) can easily relate to what governs the work activity; for example, the unit cost might be $45.32 per disputed invoice. Cost reduction can be realized both by reducing the quantity or frequency of the driver and by more efficiently performing the work (e.g., target to get to $35.00 per disputed invoice). With time-based ABC, the initial metric might be 4 minutes and 35 seconds, which would equate to the $45.32.

Time-based pull ABM tends to focus on the primary cost centers that are product and customer facing and less on support cost centers, where time-based standards may be trickier to collect.

PULL DESCRIPTIVE AND PREDICTIVE COSTING: RESOURCE CONSUMPTION ACCOUNTING

In Germany in the mid-twentieth century, standard cost accounting that calculates both product costs and cost variances was expanded in robustness. Consider it a very elegant standard cost system that is true to cause-and-effect modeling. It is called Grenzplankostenrechnung (GPK), and recently articles have appeared in the North American media referring to the GPK method as resource consumption accounting (RCA).

RCA employs time-based cost drivers, so when combined with its additional features, RCA can be thought of as having the advantages of time-based ABC . . . and then some.

All ABM methods recognize that capacity can exist only as a resource (e.g., an employee or an asset) and not as an activity cost or output cost. But RCA takes this a step further by acknowledging that when tracing the relationships for how resource expenses are transformed into calculated costs, resources always consume other resources. That is, the resource expenses are the source through which RCA calculations are derived. In contrast to conventional push descriptive ABM where resources are converted to activity costs and then some support activity costs are causally traced as inputs into other support activity costs (ultimately causally traced to the product-making and service-delivering activities), RCA consumption modeling must always thread its cost assignments back through resource expenses. This requirement is needed because the purpose of RCA is not only to measure the same output costs (e.g., product costs) as the descriptive costing methods, conventional push ABM and time-based pull ABC, but also to provide operational feedback to the producing departments about their performance. It accomplishes the latter purpose by also providing what accountants will recognize as flex budgeting. Let us discuss both purposes.

- **RCA for operational control.** What does this mean? In contrast to static budgeting and standard cost variance analysis between the plan authorized (e.g., budget) and actual costs, flex budgeting considers how deviations in volume from the plan, whether comparatively higher or lower, would have resulted in proportionately higher or lower volume-sensitive expenses. As a result, the plan or budget is retroactively revised for the past period. The resources expenses that are not sensitive to volume, traditionally classified as fixed expenses, obviously remain unrevised. So, in a sense, RCA is performing pull (bottom-up) predictive costing, but for a past period. Again, this purpose for RCA is for operational feedback for cost managers to analyze how well they managed their resources and isolate potentially "avoidable" costs. This method also highlights unused capacity. The wrinkle that adds extra effort for RCA is that expenses for each cost center must be segregated as to whether its behavior is fixed or proportional (traditionally called variable) with changes in volume of the activity driver. The downside of this design is that the costing is more complex, particularly when expenses of support cost centers supporting other support cost centers are included.

- **RCA for output costing.** The accuracy of output costs and marginal cost analysis with RCA will be superior than conventional push and time-driven pull ABM. This should be expected because RCA is meticulous in treating proportional cost behavior and thus is capacity aware. Conventional push ABM users appear to tolerate less accuracy; they assume that operational managers use other means to balance future capacity to demand requirements (thus minimizing avoidable capacity costs) and that their cost assignment structure itself combined with the offsetting and dampening error effects of support activities cascading down the cost assignment network is good enough relative to the administrative effort to gain incrementally higher accuracy. Are they correct in those assumptions? As with any product or service, the marketplace will be the ultimate test for the adoption of RCA.

THROUGHPUT ACCOUNTING: CONSTRAINT-BASED COSTING FOR THEORY OF CONSTRAINTS

The theory of constraints (TOC) has an excellent approach to what are referred to as the logical thinking processes that aid in problem resolution. TOC views an organization as the integrated system that it truly is with interdependencies rather than as having individual parts. When viewed this way, for example, a physical capacity constraint such as a large heat treat oven in a manufacturer through which all parts must pass will result in different economic decisions than using conventional standard costing if that oven is full to capacity 24 hours per day, 7 days a week, for 365 days. TOC comes with problem analysis methods based on the impact of constraints and related constraint-based thinking.

A subset of TOC is assumptions about cost accounting. Because it focuses on capacity, TOC presumes that any calculated cost is meaningless and irrelevant. All costs are assumed to belong to the operating system, not to any parts that pass through it, except for the purchased price of the part from a supplier. Hence product costing, and any cost allocation, even if ABC-principled, is considered improper. In the special case of the heat treat oven, TOC considers only the highest profit margin layer, a part's selling price minus its purchased part prices. TOC costing, called throughput accounting, ranks all customer orders by this margin and would suggest running the most profitable orders first until the physical capacity constraint is fully exhausted for the time period. With this logic, the product mix run can produce greater short-term profits in total for the period than if products based on ABM margins had been run.

Unlike ABM pull predictive costing, throughput accounting is capacity-centric and typically presumes little or no adjustments to capacity in its decision analysis. (To TOC advocates, the change in operating expense is zero.) The premise is sort of: You own the capacity, which is like a sunk cost, so let us maximize what we can get out of it. Unused capacity costs in all the nonconstrained cost centers are not reported. (However, that unused capacity is relevant for scheduling purposes.) ABM practitioners understand that ABM data should not be used for short-term product mix optimization, which is a different problem to solve. In real life, however, physical constraints rarely exist, so TOC reverts to identifying market demand as the system's constraint. With the absence of the special case of rank-ordering orders, which rarely occurs, then TOC's throughput accounting becomes the same decision rule as conventional ABM marginal cost analysis: The incremental change in price should exceed the marginal change in cost for a profit positive decision.

Product manufacturing organizations are becoming a smaller sector in most nations as the rise in service industries, such as banks and telecommunications, displaces them. And even in manufacturers, typically the need to understand indirect factory product-making costs are not as big an issue as is understanding all nonproduct costs related to types of orders, channels, distribution, and customers. ABM-principled costing approaches apply to all of these nonproduct costs. Throughput accounting has chosen to state that any calculated cost is meaningless and irrelevant, which in part may explain why so few organizations that have looked at it actually adopt it.

THE BIG PICTURE OF MANAGERIAL ACCOUNTING

Cost accountants will debate and struggle with these various methods, but the critical issue is that most organizations continue to rely on the general ledger cost center expenses (i.e., inputs) as their primary source of financial intelligence. But these data are structurally deficient, except the primitive budget versus actual variance accounting police mentality. It is not until you transform those ledger expenses into their equivalent work activity costs (that belong to the processes) and further transform activity costs into outputs that you can draw insights. And typically accountants who do attempt to transform use broad-brushed averages rather than cause-and-effect relationships. It is no wonder that managers and employee teams typically do not trust their cost accounting data and continue to wait for the day when the hidden costs that comprise their outputs are visible and transparent and they can get insight into the activity cost drivers that cause their cost structure.

There is a shift under way from cost control to cost planning and shaping. It is a shift away from trying to react to cost data after the fact toward proactively adjusting capacity expenses in advance of need. Traditional cost control via "variances" between plan-authorized and actuals is declining because increasingly much of the organization's expense structure cannot be heavily or quickly influenced.

This book describes organizations that decided to get started rather than postpone the inevitable.

Gary Cokins

ENDNOTE

1. Frederick W. Taylor, *Principles of Scientific Management* (Easton, PA: Hive Publishing, 1985, originally 1911).

1

PERFORMANCE MANAGEMENT

GARY COKINS

Direction, traction, and speed. When you are driving a car or riding a bicycle, you *directly* control all three. You can turn the steering wheel or handle bars to change direction. You can downshift the gears to go up a steep hill to get more traction. You can step on the gas pedal or pump your legs harder to gain more speed.

However, senior executives who manage organizations do not have *direct* control of their organization's traction, direction, and speed to increase value from their organization. Why not? Because they can achieve improvements in these areas only through influencing people—namely, their employees. And employees can sometimes act like children: They don't always do what they're told, and sometimes their behavior is just the opposite!

Performance management is about giving managers and employee teams of all levels the capability to improve their organization's direction, traction, and speed—and most important, to move it in the *right* direction. That direction should be as clear and focused as a laser beam, pointing toward its defined strategy. The process of managing strategy begins with focus. You never have enough money or resources to chase every opportunity or market on the planet. You have to believe that you are continuously limited to scarce and precious resources and time, so focus is key and strategy yields focus.

There is evidence that it is a tough time to be a chief executive. Surveys by the Chicago-based employee recruiting firm Challenger, Gray & Christmas repeatedly reveal increasing rates of job turnover at the executive level compared to a decade ago.[1] In complex and overhead-intensive organizations where constant redirection to a changing landscape is essential, the main cause for executive job turnover is the failure to execute their strategy. There is a big difference between formulating a strategy and executing it. What is the answer for executives who need to expand their focus beyond cost control and toward economic value creation and other more strategic directives? How do they regain control of the direction, traction, and speed for their enterprise? Performance management

1

provides managers and employee teams at all levels with the capability to move directly toward their defined strategies like a laser beam.

WHAT IS PERFORMANCE MANAGEMENT?

Performance management (PM) is the framework for managing the execution of an organization's strategy. It is how plans are translated into results. Think of PM as an umbrella concept that integrates familiar business improvement methodologies with technology. In short, the methodologies no longer need to be applied in isolation—they can be orchestrated. The whole is greater than the sum of the parts. Each methodology can give good results, but when you integrate them, you get more. This makes PM a value multiplier.

All organizations have been doing performance management before it was labeled with this name. So the good news is that performance management is not a new buzzword and method that everyone has to learn. Rather, it is the assemblage of *existing* methodologies that most everyone is already familiar with, and most organizations have already begun the journey of implementing some of them. But as just mentioned, these methodologies typically are implemented in isolation from each other. It is as if the implementation project teams live in parallel universes. PM serves as a value multiplier by integrating the methodologies.

PM is sometimes confused with human resources and personnel systems, but it is much more encompassing. It comprises the methodologies, metrics, processes, software tools, and systems that manage the performance of an organization. PM is overarching, from the C-level executives cascading down through the organization and its processes. To sum up its benefit, it enhances broad cross-functional involvement in decision making and calculated risk taking by providing tremendously greater visibility with accurate, reliable, and relevant information—all aimed at executing an organization's strategy. But why is supporting strategy so key? Being operationally good is not enough. In the long run, good organizational effectiveness will never trump a mediocre or poor strategy.

There is no single PM methodology, because PM spans the complete management planning and control cycle. Performance management is not a process with recipe steps or an information system that you purchase on a disc. It is the integration of typically disconnected decision making. Think of PM as a broad, end-to-end union of solutions incorporating three major functions: collecting data, transforming and modeling the data into information, and Web-reporting it to users. Many of PM's component methodologies have existed for decades, while others have become popular recently, such as the balanced scorecard. Some of PM's components, such as activity-based management (ABM) described in this book, are partially or crudely implemented in many organizations, and PM refines them so that they work in better harmony with its other components. Early adopters have deployed parts of PM, but few have deployed its full vision. In the first few decades of the twenty-first century, the surviving organizations will have completed the full vision.

Many organizations seem to jump from improvement program to program, hoping that each one might provide that big, elusive competitive edge. Most managers, however, would acknowledge that pulling one lever for improvement rarely results in a substantial change—particularly a long-term, sustained change. The key to improving is integrating and balancing multiple improvement methodologies. You cannot simply implement one improvement program and exclude the other programs and initiatives. It would be nice to have a management cockpit with one dial and a simple steering mechanism, but managing an organization, a process, or a function is not that easy.

CONFUSION AND AMBIGUITY WITH PERFORMANCE MANAGEMENT

There is confusion about terminology. For example, there are several variants of PM including business performance management (BPM), enterprise performance management (EPM), and corporate performance management (CPM). Consider them all to mean the same thing. But a larger problem is that PM is typically defined too narrowly as being only about better strategy, budgeting, planning, and finance with an emphasis on measurement. It is much more.

As mentioned, PM tightly integrates the business improvement and analytic methodologies executives, managers, and employee teams are already familiar with. These include strategy mapping, balanced scorecards, managerial accounting (including activity-based management), budgeting and forecasting, and resource capacity requirements. These methodologies fuel other core solutions such as customer relationship management (CRM), supply chain management (SCM), risk management, and human capital management (HCM) systems, as well as Six Sigma. It is quite a stew, but they all blend together.

The executive team should always begin with a vision statement—and preferably not those hollow words framed in the organization's lobby or laminated on small cards for employee purses and wallets. The vision statement answers the question "Where do we want to go?" PM relies on the strategy map and its companion scorecard to answer in a mechanical way "How will we get there?" The remainder of the PM components answer "What will power us there?"

But PM also addresses trade-off decisions that will always be present because conflicts are natural conditions of any organization. For example, there will always be tension between competing customer service levels, process efficiencies, and budget or profit constraints. Managers and employee teams are constantly faced with conflicting objectives and no way to resolve them, so they tend to focus their energies on their close-in situation and their personal concerns for how they might be affected. An organization also constantly faces risk, threats, and opportunities. Problems surface when risks are not anticipated or there is minimal risk mitigation and when good opportunities are missed. PM addresses all of these issues by escalating the visibility of actual and potential quantified outputs and outcomes—in other words, results. PM provides explicit linkage between strategic, operational, and financial objectives and provides predictive what-if scenario testing of the enterprise-wide impact of decisions.

In the end, organizations need top-down guidance with bottom-up execution. PM does this by converting plans into results. PM integrates operational and financial information into a single decision-support and planning framework. Simply put, PM helps an organization to understand how it works as a whole.

Performance Management for the Public Sector

Performance management (PM) is not just an integrated set of decision support tools but is also a discipline intended to maintain a view of the larger picture and to understand how an organization is working as a whole. PM applies to managing any organization, whether a business, a hospital, a university, a government agency, or a military body—any entity that has employees and partners with a purpose, profit-driven or not. In short, PM is universally applicable.

In the not-for-profit and public sector, including government agencies at all levels and the military, there appears to be a convergence toward many of the management practices of the commercial sector. One obvious difference, however, is the relevance of "making a profit." That does not mean public sector agencies are given license not to use resources effectively or, in some cases, charge fees to users to achieve a full cost recovery (i.e., a zero profit) as funding. Accountability increasingly appears as a mandate for public sector organizations. If you do a word search on the words "performance-based" and "government" on the Internet, you may be surprised by the large number of references.

Although PM often refers to for-profit concepts, such as measuring and managing customer value and product profits, the majority of PM principles can also apply to public sector organizations.

ALIGNING EMPLOYEE BEHAVIOR WITH STRATEGY

"Alignment" is a key word frequently mentioned in PM. Alignment boils down to the classic maxim, "First do the right things, and then do the right things well." That is, being effective is more important than being efficient. Organizations that are very, very good at doing things that are not important will never be market leaders. The concept of work alignment to the strategy, mission, and vision deals with focus and pursuing the most important priorities. The economics then fall into place.

How well the executive management communicates its strategy to managers and employees, if at all, remains a challenge. Exhibit 1.1 illustrates this. Most employees and managers, if asked to describe their organization's strategy, cannot adequately articulate it. Many employees are without a clue as to what their organization's strategy is. They sometimes operate as helpless reactors to day-to-day problems.

If asked to briefly articulate their executive team's strategy, how many employees could do it? Probably very few—maybe none. The consequence of this is critical. If employee teams and managers do not understand their executive team's strategy, how do we expect them to understand that what they do each week and

Exhibit 1.1 The Communication Challenge
Source: Gary Cokins, *Performance Management: Finding the Missing Pieces (To Close the Intelligence Gap)* (Hoboken, NJ: John Wiley & Sons, Inc., 2004). Reprinted with permission of John Wiley & Sons, Inc.

"Many leaders have personal visions that never get translated into shared visions that galvanize an organization. What is lacking is a discipline for translating individual vision into shared vision."

—Peter Senge, *The Fifth Discipline.*

month contributes to realizing that strategy? In short, there is a communication gap between senior management's mission or vision and employees' daily decisions and actions. An integrated suite of methodologies and tools—the PM solutions suite—provides the mechanism to bridge the business intelligence gap between the chief executive's vision and employees' actions.

PM can close this communication gap. Methodologies with supporting tools such as *strategy mapping* and PM *scorecards* aid in making strategy everyone's job. PM allows executives to translate their personal visions into collective visions that galvanize managers and employee teams to move in a value-creating direction. The traditional taskmaster/commander style of executives who attempt to control employees through rigid management systems is not a formula for superior performance. PM fosters a work environment in which managers and employees are genuinely engaged and behave as if they were the business owners. Destructive beliefs and unwritten rules that are commonly known in an organization's culture (i.e., "Always pad your first budget submission") are displaced by guiding principles.

BUSINESS INTELLIGENCE GAP

The gap between the executive team's strategy and employee operations is more than a communication gap. It is an intelligence gap as well. Most organizations are deluged with data, and the amount keeps growing. Estimates are that amount of information doubles every 1,100 days.[2] Yet the amount of time available to deal with information remains constant at 1,440 minutes per day. What complicates matters is the challenge of determining the important and relevant data to focus on versus data that are simply nice to know. Additional challenges involve collecting and moving data, transforming it from a raw reported state into meaningful information that can be leveraged, and having accurate, clean, and nonredundant data, or worse yet inconsistent data. To resolve these problems, PM is based on a common enterprise information platform (EIP) that provides a one-version-of-the-truth database rather than disparate inconsistent data that annoy both employees and customers.

But those are problems that advanced information technologies, such as data warehousing, can overcome. Even organizations that are enlightened enough to recognize the potential value of their business intelligence and assets often have difficulty in actually realizing that value as *economic value*. Their data are often disconnected, inconsistent, and inaccessible, resulting from too many nonintegrated single-point solutions. They have valuable, untapped data hidden in the reams of transactional data they collect daily. Unlocking the intelligence trapped in mountains of data has been, until recently, a relatively difficult task to accomplish effectively. Typically you find different departmental data warehouses built on different platforms using combinations of tools, some nonstandard, some with expired maintenance support, and some prebuilt in a tool purchased from a vendor no longer in business. This results in unintended barriers blocking systems from cleanly communicating among themselves. All organizations are reaching a point where it is important for computers to talk to other computers.

Fortunately, innovation in data storage technology is now significantly outpacing progress in computer processing power, heralding a new era where creating vast pools of digital data is becoming the preferred solution. Information technologies—namely data warehousing; data mining, with its powerful extraction, transform, and load (ETL) features; and business analytics (e.g., statistics, forecasting, and optimization)—all produce decision-relevant information from diverse data source platforms transparently. That is, these technologies convert raw data into intelligence—the power to know. As a result, these superior tools now offer a complete suite of analytic applications and data models that enable organizations to tap into the virtual treasure trove of information they already possess and enable effective performance management on a huge scale.

Most companies are still unable to get the business intelligence they need; and the intelligence they do get is not delivered quickly enough to be actionable. PM correlates disparate information in a meaningful way and allows drill-down queries directly on hidden problem areas. It helps assess which strategies are yielding desired results without the need to wade through a mountain of raw data. Executives and employee teams need to be alerted to problems before they become "unfavorable variances" reported in financial statements and requiring explanation. PM aids employees and managers to manage change *actively*—and in the right direction.

But make no mistake in interpretation; PM is much more social than technical. You are dealing with people who all have personal preferences, including appeal for the status quo as well as suspicion and skepticism of change. And elements of PM involve measurements and accountability, so you influence behavior because you typically "get what you measure." In summary, PM integrates operational and financial information into a single decision support and planning framework.

ACTIVITY-BASED MANAGEMENT: FACTS FOR JUDGMENT AND DISCOVERY

Methodologies like *activity-based management* (ABM) described in this book provide a reliable, fact-based financial view of the costs of work processes and their products, services, and customers (service recipients and citizens for public sector organizations). Having fact-based information is important. After all, in the absence of facts, anybody's opinion is a good one. And usually the biggest opinion wins—which may be your supervisor's opinion or your supervisor's boss's opinion. To the degree that they are making decisions based on intuition, gut feel, outdated beliefs, or misleading information, then your organization is at risk. A major benefit of PM is that when all people get the same facts, then they generally reach the same conclusions on how to act. Good managerial accounting is foundational for PM.

What makes today's PM systems so effective is that *work activities*—what people, equipment, and assets do—are foundational to PM reporting, analysis, and planning. Work activities pursue the actions and projects essential to meet the strategic objectives constructed in strategy maps and the outcomes measured in scorecards. Work activities are central to ABM systems used to measure output costs and customer profitability accurately as well as to assess future potential customer economic value. Knowing costs assists not only in judging results better but also in asking better questions. It is a great discovery tool.

ABM also aids in understanding the drivers of work activities and their consumption of resource capacity (e.g., expenses). With that knowledge, organizations can test and validate future outcomes given different events (including a varying mix and volume of product/service demand). This helps managers and employee teams understand capacity constraints and see that cost behavior is rarely linear but is a complex blend of step-fixed input expenses relative to changes in outputs. Workloads are predicted in resource capacity planning systems to select the best plans. PM combines strategy maps and its companion balanced scorecard with intelligent software systems that span the enterprise to provide immediate feedback, in terms of alerts and traffic-lighting signals to unplanned deviations from plans. PM provides managers and employee teams with the ability to act proactively, before events occur or proceed so far that they demand a reaction.

BALANCED SCORECARD: MYTH OR REALITY?

But cost management cannot be the focus. Cost management must operate as part of the more encompassing PM. And strategy is critical. Leadership's role is to determine strategic direction and motivate people to go in that direction. However, senior executives are challenged and usually frustrated with cascading their strategy down through their organization. Executives and management consultants have hailed the *balanced scorecard* as the new religion to resolve this frustration. It serves to communicate executive strategy to employees and also to help navigate direction by shaping the alignment of people with strategy. The balanced scorecard bridges the substantial gap between the raw data spewed out from business systems, such as enterprise resource planning systems (ERP), and the organization's strategy.

Strategy maps and *scorecards* are two more of the key components in the PM portfolio of methodologies. They enable leadership and motivate people by serving as a guide with signposts and guardrails. Despite much publicity about the balanced scorecard, the *strategy map* that should ideally precede the development of the scorecard is considered to be much more important. Strategy maps explain high-level causes and effects that facilitate making choices. With strategy maps and their resultant choices of strategic objectives and the action items to attain them, managers and employee teams easily see the priorities and adjust their plans accordingly. People don't have sufficient time to do everything everywhere, but some try to. Strategy maps and their companion scorecards rein in the use of people's time by bringing focus. Untested pet projects that do not contribute to the strategy are discarded or postponed.

Scorecards are derived from strategy maps, contrary to a misconception that scorecards are a stand-alone reporting system. Many organizations unwittingly err by beginning their reform of their performance measurement system by first defining their key performance indicators (KPIs) to monitor. They typically select the measures they already have as opposed to the measures they *should* have. The traditional measures they err in choosing are typically without depth. Users can view a result, but whether it is good or bad, they are unable to investigate the underlying cause. By starting with KPIs, they are skipping the critical initial steps. The executive team should first define the strategy map, then employee teams and managers should suggest the few manageable projects that can be accomplished or core processes that they must excel at. Once that is complete, then the employees and managers can properly determine the vital few, not trivial many, nonfinancial measures that indicate progress on those projects or core processes which in turn lead toward achieving the strategic objectives. These steps assure that the managers and employee teams understand the strategy—the major problem affecting failed strategy execution. If defining the KPIs is the initial step, then how does anyone know if those measures reflect the strategic intent of the executive team?

Once the appropriate KPIs are selected, then the scorecard provides ongoing feedback. Imagine if everyone in the organization, from the front-line workers to the executive team, could everyday answer this single question: "How am I doing on what is important?" The organization would remain focused. Note that there are two halves to that question. The first part answers the question: "Am I performing favorably or unfavorably to a target set for me?" But it is the second part that brings the power. By going through the discipline of first defining linked strategic objectives in the strategy map, identifying the few and manageable projects or core processes to excel at with KPIs derived from them, executives have preset and baked in the critical pursuits that reflect their strategic intent.

When all the employees are provided a line of sight from their measured performance up through their supervisors' and executives' measures, then everyone can also answer the question "How are *we* doing on what is important?" This aids in everyone's understanding of how one performance measure affects another. It also involves digging deeper to see causal relationships and manage work activities across the entire enterprise so that everyone is on the same page. If employees are given visibility to the feedback scores on KPIs across the organization, they can communicate with other functions without waiting for instructions to suggest problem resolutions. A scorecard is a powerful mechanism to constantly align the workforce with the strategy. It brings that needed direction, traction, and speed.

Scorecards solve the problem of excessive emphasis on financial results as the measure of success. Consider that telephone calls are still "dialed" even though there are hardly any dial phones left. A car's glove compartment rarely stores gloves. Eventually the motion picture "film" industry will rely on digital technology, not film. Similarly, "financial" results will likely be shared with more influential nonfinancial indicators, such as measures of customer service levels. Strategy maps assure that both financial and their causal nonfinancial measures are linked with if-then relationships—which is one reason you hear the term "*balanced* scorecard." Going forward, managers and employee teams will need to be much more empowered to make decisions, good ones, it is hoped, in rapidly reduced time frames. A strategy map and its companion scorecard, supported by business intelligence, improve decision making. Together, they describe an organization's strategic health and consequently its chances for increasing prosperity. The balanced scorecard expresses the strategy in measurable terms, communicating what must be done and how everyone is progressing.

Commercial software plays an important enabling role in PM by delivering an entire Web-based and closed-loop process from strategic planning to budgeting, forecasting, scorecarding, costing, financial consolidations, reporting, and analysis. Commercial software from leading vendors of statistics-supported analytics and business intelligence (BI), such as SAS (www.sas.com), provide powerful forecasting tools.

WHAT IS THE PURPOSE OF PERFORMANCE MANAGEMENT?

So, what is the purpose of PM? PM is the translation of plans into results—execution. It is the process of managing your strategy. Defining and adjusting the organization's strategy is of paramount importance and is senior management's number-one responsibility. For commercial companies, strategy can be reduced to three major choices:

1. What products or service lines should we offer or not offer?
2. What markets and types of customers should we serve or not serve?
3. How are we going to win?[3]

PM provides insights to improve all three choices by aiding managers to sense earlier and respond more quickly to uncertain changes. It does this by driving accountability for executing the organization's strategy to the lowest possible organization levels.

INCREASING FOCUS ON CUSTOMERS

It is a tough time for senior managers. Customers increasingly view products and service lines as commodities and place pressure on prices as a result. Business mergers, employee layoffs, and cutting costs are ongoing. And long gone are the days that private equity firms could squeeze out profits though balance sheet wizardry. Inevitably there is a limit on these approaches to impact profits, an impact that is forcing management to achieve real PM from the underlying business: Managers must come to grip with getting organic profit growth from existing customers and truly managing their resources, not just monitoring them. You can't simply create the scorecard's dashboard to look at the dials; you have to be constantly taking actions to *move* the dials.

If we had to point to one single reason for the interest in performance management, we believe it is the result of the shift in power from suppliers to customers and buyers due four key realizations:

1. It is more expensive to acquire new customers with marketing than to retain existing customers.
2. The source for competitive advantage is shifting—as products and service lines become commodities, thus neutralizing any competitive edge

from them, suppliers must shift to value-added services to differentiate themselves from their competitors.

3. Information technology (IT) automation allows microsegmenting customers to shift from mass selling to formulating unique marketing strategies and differentiated customer service treatment levels to each segment (and ultimately to individuals) based on their unique preferences.

4. The Internet is providing customers and buyers tremendous capabilities for price-comparative shopping and information about any supplier's products, service-line offerings, and deals.

These four factors are simultaneously forcing greater attention than in the past on understanding which of your existing customers are relatively more profitable and which might have future potential value. Collectively, these four factors are like a "perfect storm," bringing turbulence and wreaking havoc on the lives of marketing and salespeople. The marketing function needs to understand the characteristics and traits of their existing customers so that they target their marketing budget to acquire new customers with traits like the more valuable existing ones and not waste spending on acquiring less profitable (or unprofitable) customers. The salespeople must accept that their role is no longer about just increasing sales but rather increasing sales *profitably*.

Earlier it was mentioned that performance management is not a process or a system but rather the integration of multiple methodologies. Is there a way to visualize performance management as a framework?

PERFORMANCE MANAGEMENT FRAMEWORK FOR VALUE CREATION

One of the most ambiguous terms in discussions about business and government is *value*. Everybody wants value in return for whatever was exchanged to get value. We can have endless philosophical debates about the definition of value. The ancient Greek philosophers have already put a lot of time into that. The much more interesting question for the twenty-first century is "Whose value is more important?" There will always be three groups that believe they are entitled to value: customers/users, shareholders/stakeholders, and employees. Are they rivals? Is there an Adam Smith–like invisible hand controlling checks and balances to maintain an economic equilibrium so that each group gets its fair share? And, for example, after the expected cost savings from a project are realized in part or whole, how will the financial savings be divided among these groups?

Exhibit 1.2 illustrates the interplay among the three groups. Customers conclude that they received value if the benefits or pleasure they received from a product or service exceeds what they paid for it. At the opposite end of the exhibit are the owners, shareholders, and lenders. They also have entitlement to value. As risk-taking investors and lenders, if their investment return is less than the economic return that they could have received from equally or less risky investments, then they are disappointed; they would feel they got less value.

The weighting scale in Exhibit 1.2 indicates that there is a trade-off between customers and shareholders. Under certain conditions, increasing customer satisfaction can result in reducing shareholder wealth. For example, in a case where the enterprise adds product features, functions, and/or services but without a commensurate price increase or gain in market share and sales volume, then the customers gain value while the shareholders lose value.

Exhibit 1.2 also involves supplier-employees, which includes the executive management team. A perceived entitlement to employees is their job value. For many employees, this is their security and financial compensation. Heroes of the twentieth-century labor union movement, such as Walter Reuther of what is today's AFL/CIO labor union in the United States, confronted Henry Ford for "a fair day's

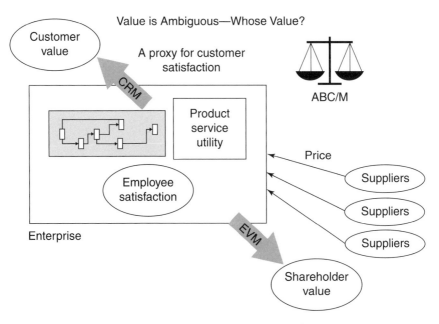

Exhibit 1.2 A Proxy for Customer Satisfaction

pay" for hourly workers. In today's more mobile knowledge worker labor pool, employees who are dissatisfied with their job value simply vote with their feet by switching to pursue a greater-value job with another employer. Or they become contractors and establish their own value with their own fees or billing rate.

PERFORMANCE MANAGEMENT OPERATING AS AN INTEGRATED SYSTEM

Exhibit 1.3 decomposes Exhibit 1.2. It illustrates the interdependent methodologies that comprise performance management for a commercial organization. Look at the boxes and ellipses and ask yourself which is the most important one. This is a trick question because the answer depends on who you are. If you are the chief executive or managing director, it must be the ellipse "Mission and Strategy" located in the upper left corner. That is the primary job of people with these titles: to define and constantly adjust their strategy as the environment changes. That is why they are paid high salaries and reside in large corner offices. However, after

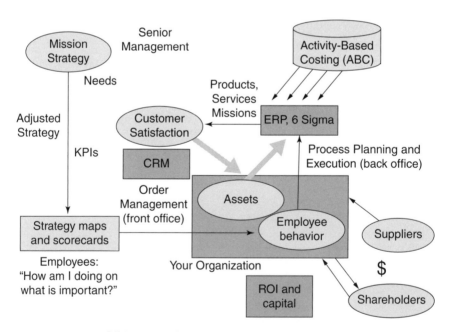

Exhibit 1.3 Performance Management Framework

the strategy definition is complete and maintained as current, then the core business processes take over, and there are competent process owners held accountable to manage each one.

Most readers will likely select "Customer Satisfaction" as the most important box or ellipse. This is a good choice because customer satisfaction encompasses four customer-facing trends, including increased focus on:

1. The need for higher customer retention. It is relatively more expensive to acquire a new customer than to retain an existing one.

2. Source of competitive advantage shift due to neutralized advantages from commodity-like products to value-adding service differentiation to customers and prospects.

3. Microsegmenting of customers to focus on their unique preferences rather than spray-and-pay mass selling.

4. The Internet's shift in power from suppliers to customers and buyers.

In Exhibit 1.3, the two ultimate megacore business processes, encompassing the specific ones that are possessed by any organization on the planet, are represented by the two solid inbound and outbound arrows. The two arrows are (1) take an order or assignment, and (2) fulfill an order or assignment. When stripped to its core, that is what *any* organization does. The two arrows are universal regardless of sector or industry—commercial business, governments, military, hospitals, churches. Can you name an organization that does not receive tasks and then attempt to execute them? Exhibit 1.3 reveals that the field of IT has named the support systems for these two mega processes as *front-office* and *back-office* systems. Other IT systems serve as components in managing the value chain. It is easy to conclude that a customer focus is critical.

The customer-facing front office systems are customer intelligence (CI) and customer relationship management (CRM) systems. This is also where sales and work order management systems reside. The back-office systems are where the order-fulfilling, process planning, and execution resides—the world of ERP and Six Sigma quality initiatives. The output from this execution box is the product or service or mission intended to meet customer needs. Imagine the three arrows continuously circulating the customer orders in the counterclockwise direction. To the degree that that the customer revenues (or fund transfers for public sector or not-for-profit organizations) exceed all of organization's expenses, including the cost of capital, then profit (and free cash flow) eventually accumulates into the shareholder's ellipse in the exhibit's lower right.

Now note that "needs" to satisfy customers is the major input to the senior management's "Mission and Strategy." As the executive team adjusts its strategy, it may abandon some KPIs (not that those KPIs are unimportant; now they are just less important), add new KPIs, or adjust the KPI weightings for various employee teams. As the feedback is received from the scorecards, all employees can answer that key question: "How am I doing on what is important?" With analysis for causality, corrective actions can then occur. And note that the output from scorecards does not stop at the organization's boundary; it penetrates all the way through to influence employee behavior. This penetration in turn leads to better execution.

AUTOMOBILE ANALOGY FOR PERFORMANCE MANAGEMENT

It was stated earlier that all organizations have been doing performance management well before it was labeled as such. It can be argued that on the date all organizations were first created, they immediately were managing (or attempting to manage) their enterprise performance by offering products or services and fulfilling sales orders. If you will, imagine an organization at start-up as a poorly maintained automobile. We would observe the consequences of unstable business methods: unbalanced wheels, severe shimmy in the steering wheel, poor timing of engine pistons, thick power steering fluid, and mucky oil in the crankcase. Take that mental picture and conclude that any physical system of moving parts with tremendous vibration and part wearing friction dissipates energy, wasting fuel and power. At an organizational level, the energy dissipation from vibration and friction translates into wasted expenses where the greater the waste, the lower the rate of shareholder wealth creation, and possibly destruction of shareholder wealth. In a different case, you may find a car that seems perfect to the customer in every way, but is not priced to make a profit—so shareholders are unhappy. In another, the focus may be on producing at the least cost to the point of undermining customer satisfaction.

Now imagine an automobile with its wheels finely balanced and well lubricated. The performance framework (i.e., the automobile) remains unchanged, but the shareholder wealth is created more rapidly because there is balance in quality, price, and value to all. No vibration or friction. That is how good performance management integrates the multiple methodologies of the PM portfolio of components and provides better decision analysis and decision making that aligns work behavior and priorities with the strategy. Strategic objectives are attained, and the consequence is relatively greater shareholder wealth creation.

The concept of value is embedded in Exhibit 1.3. The three groups entitled to value are defined in this way:

1. **Shareholder value.** This is measured by economic value management (EVM) methodologies, which detect whether the profit margin generated from satisfying existing and future customers is also sufficient to reward shareholders and lenders beyond risk-adjusted investment returns that those investors and lenders could achieve elsewhere, including financial returns from financial market instruments, such as U.S treasury bonds. With financial intelligence, accounting profits are not economic profits.

2. **Customer value.** The *front office's* customer intelligence and customer relationship management systems are intended to maximize communications, interactions, and sensitivity to each customer's unique needs. CI and CRM enable differentiated treatment levels, deals, and offers to more valuable customers.

3. **Supplier-employee value.** The *back office's* enterprise resource planning, advanced planning systems (APS), and process improvements ensure effective execution to *fulfill orders.* The PM strategy mapping and scorecard systems ensure that specific groups of people, equipment, and other assets are working on high priorities and performing in high alignment with senior management's strategies.

Activity-based costing (ABC) data, a key component in performance management, permeates every single element in this scenario to help balance these sometimes competing values. ABC itself is not an improvement program or execution system. ABC data serve as a discovery mechanism and an enabler for these systems to support better decision making. For example, ABC links customer value management (relying on customer intelligence [CI] and/or customer relationship management [CRM] systems) to shareholder value creation, which is heralded as essential for economic value management. The tug-of-war between CI/CRM and shareholder wealth creation is the trade-off of adding more value for customers at the risk of reducing wealth to shareholders. Ultimately, businesses will discover that customer value management is the *independent* variable in the equation to solve for the *dependent* variable for which the executive team is accountable to the governing board: shareholder wealth creation. Performance management provides the framework to model this.

How does this work? When combined with effective forecasting and risk management tools, ABM enables the only financial calculation engine that can quantitatively translate changes in customer value to measure the impact on share-holder value. We know all these components connect, but we struggle with how they do it. But research and work remains to be done, as described by this observation:

> "Customer value can be regarded as the key driver of shareholder value . . . [but] surprisingly, although being of obvious importance, literature taking a more comprehensive view of customer valuation has only re-cently been appearing. A composite picture of customers and investors is hardly found in business references."[4]

Is Exhibit 1.3 the best diagram to represent the broad, not narrow, picture of performance management? Probably not. But it is a start. Professional societies, such as the cost management organization CAM-I (www.cam-i.org), management consultants, and software vendors have their own diagrams. Perhaps a business magazine or Web portal can have a contest where diagrams are submitted and voted on by readers. But the key point is that performance management is not the narrow definition of "better strategy, budgeting, planning, and finance"; it is much broader.

PERFORMANCE MANAGEMENT: MAKING IT WORK

Rising specialization, complexity, and value-adding services cause the need for more, not less, PM. Despite the impact that technology and more flexible work practices and policies have on continuously changing organizational structures, without ongoing adaptation, the correct work at acceptable service levels will not get done. All employees must have some grasp of managing for results. Somehow their collective performance must be coordinated. A united and sustained perfor-mance is a challenging part of management. PM aids in accomplishing this goal.

WHERE DOES INFORMATION TECHNOLOGY FIT?

Where do software and data management fit in? Software is a set of tools that serves as an enabler to the PM solution suite of methodologies. However, in the big picture, PM software is necessary but not sufficient. Software does not replace the thinking needed for the strategy and planning that is involved in PM—but it can surely enable the thinking process. Software and technology are not at center stage for making PM work. However, software is no longer the impediment it was in the mid-1990s. Back then you could dream of what the tools can do today, but the technical barriers were show-stopping obstacles. That is no longer the situation.

Today advances in software and data management are well ahead of the abilities of most organizations to harness what can be done with these tools. Today the impediment is not technology but rather the organization's thinking—its ability to conceptualize how the interdependencies can be modeled, to configure software, and to incorporate the right assumptions and rule-based logic. Commercial software has made great leaps in the ease with which it can be implemented, maintained, and, most important, used. Casual users, not just trained technicians and statisticians, can readily use statistical and analytical software programs.

Information technology can substantially aid leaders in managing risk and being more decisive. However, a fool with a tool is still a fool. When world-class commercial software is used by people who understand business, commerce, and government, then watch for high performance. Such leaders will collectively aid their companies in achieving that elusive competitive advantage—or, if they are a public sector or not-for-profit organization, they will optimize their service levels with their finite resources.

Executives are recognizing that computers and technology are much more than just information management. The larger picture involves *knowledge management*. What good is capturing data if people cannot have access to it? What good is using data if you cannot use that data wisely? Information technologies enable performance management, but performance management is much more. It forms the foundation to escalate managing into a formal discipline.

Always remember that the main idea is not to examine business improvement methodologies in isolation but rather as an integrated solution set.

ENDNOTES

1. Alan Webber, "CEO Bashing Has Gone Too Far," *USA Today*, June 3, 2003.
2. Bill Jensen, *Simplicity* (New York, NY: Perseus Publishing, 2000), 11.
3. Alan Brache, *How Organizations Work* (Hoboken, NJ: John Wiley & Sons, Inc., 2002), 10.
4. J. Bayon, J. Gutsche, and T. Bauer, "Customer Equity Marketing," *European Management Journal* (June 2002, 20, 213–222).

2

LUBEOIL: SHAPING BUSINESS TODAY AND IN THE FUTURE

It is incredible that most organizations do not understand their fully absorbed costs and profits by customer. Most are stuck in the paradigm of products and gross margins. Overhead is not understood and neither are the true drivers of cost. Activities should be the focal point of business decisions. They drive costs and are consumed by the objects (products/services) that are offered to customers. Organizations which understand this and use it to their advantage will have tremendous advantage over those who do not . . . .

—Michael Porter, Harvard University

FOREWORD

Thomas M. Kangw

How do we measure performance? How do we know if we are succeeding today? How do we know if we will succeed tomorrow? What shall we measure?

Strategic and operational plans dictate the direction that organizations will take; meaningful performance management (PM) provides feedback about whether the strategic and operational plans are succeeding. The lack of meaningful PM can lead organizations to focus on activities that may not be aligned to intended business results. At the very minimum, this could result in a focus on non–value-added activities and suboptimized business results. If this situation persists over time, the consequences could be catastrophic: dysfunctional organizations that become less and less competitive over time. Performance measurement must be *meaningful, accurate, and aligned* to drive behavior that is aligned to an organization's objectives.

While an employee of Mobil Corporation, I was given the challenge of leading the global initiative to change the culture of performance management. Mobil, an oil and gas giant, had traditionally focused on volume-related metrics to measure performance. Because the perception of the business centered on dollars per barrel, everything was measured that way. What this led to was a culture of increasing volume at all costs without an accurate understanding of what it truly meant for the organization in terms of activities, costs, or profits. This volume-based mentality led to significant inaccuracies in product/service costing, often resulting in behavior that was contrary to real bottom-line impact.

INTRODUCTION

Like many lubrication companies in the mid-1990s, LubeOil Corp saw that the demand for finished lubrication products was forecasted to exceed 300 million barrels of product by the year 2005 (Exhibit 2.1). Believing that 60% of that demand would be in emerging markets, such as Africa and the Middle East, LubeOil wanted to understand what customers, products, and segments to focus on to capture as much of the market as possible to take over the number-one position in lubrication products worldwide. Understanding that it could no longer create business strategy based on historical sales volumes, LubeOil shifted focus to a small initiative getting little attention throughout the entire organization. That initiative was activity-based costing (ABC).

ORGANIZATIONAL ISSUES

Lubricants are one of the highest profit margin areas of LubeOil's downstream business. This product category includes items that are readily recognizable to retail consumers, such as its flagship passenger vehicle lubricant, and thousands of other industrial and commercial-grade lubricants. Uncharacteristically complex, the lubricant business is an exception to the conventional pattern of the few-products/high-volume oil industry. LubeOil is an integrated supplier of lubricants, meaning that it possesses the technology and infrastructure for producing lubricants from base components (i.e., crude oil and chemical additives) and delivering finished products to end-customers. There are over 30,000 lubricant stock-keeping units (SKUs) within LubeOil's network with multiple raw material supply, manufacturing, and distribution centers.

LubeOil operates lubricant businesses (called affiliates) in more than 60 countries with 40 manufacturing locations. Each country operates as an individual affiliate. These individual entities are loosely collected into regional groupings,

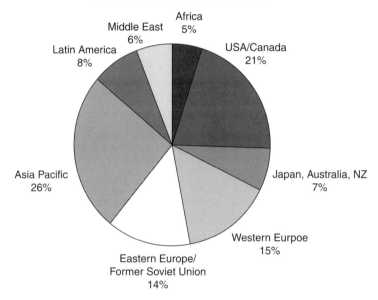

Emerging Markets Will Account for Approximately
60% of Global Demand by 2005 . . .

2005 Estimated Total World Demand

Total World Demand 275–300 Million Barrels

Exhibit 2.1 World Lube Demand 2005

which in turn sum to the global business. The principal business metrics are at the local affiliate level; profit and cost optimization occurs at this level.

The first ABC project at LubeOil and its results can be traced to the US Lubricants Division in 1994, when its general manager, recognizing that the U.S. business had thousands of SKUs and multiple manufacturing facilities, suspected that the high degree of complexity was adding cost to his business. He wanted to know the cost of the complexity—that is, the return for maintaining such a complex business.

A respected consulting firm was hired to help analyze the situation. Focusing at first on analyzing manufacturing complexity (the product dimension), the joint LubeOil and consulting team quickly realized that the current cost accounting system had no way of reflecting the cost of complexity, because it treated all products equally. Stated simply, manufacturing costs of $80 million were volumetrically applied to the 250 million gallons of lubricants that were manufactured. This method could not address cost to produce each product individually. At this point, the team suggested using ABC methodology to better reflect the real costs of producing the multiple product and package combinations within LubeOil's lubricant network.

ABC proved to be the perfect tool for identifying the cost of complexity in LubeOil's lubricant business. By using activity drivers instead of volume drivers, ABC could expose fundamental differences in the costs of producing thousands of product and package combinations.

In the past, when all costs applied to products based on volume, marketers added products with a high degree of manufacturing complexity to the product line by evaluating their economics on an incremental cost basis, believing that any new volume, regardless of production complexities, would decrease the unit cost. By applying costs using activity drivers instead, ABC exposed the weakness of the old school of thought.

The results were startling. They created a stir within the organization and were the start of a culture change. In surprisingly short order, the incremental volume/cost theory gave way to activity-based full cost theory. The view of manufacturing costs shifted from one pole to another within a matter of months.

Management liked what it saw and wanted to incorporate ABC into the everyday decision-making processes. At this point, managers took a risk. Without fully understanding the impact this new information would have on the decision makers in the business, they decided to incorporate ABC into the single profitability reporting tool used to manage the business. The tool contained the data used to evaluate all customer/product profitability. Every salesperson had access to it. The impact of ABC was to change the view of profitability of all products within the reporting tool. Reporting no longer reflected or rewarded indiscriminate volume growth. Enhanced with ABC, LubeOil now rewards profitable growth or divestment.

Management's risk paid off. In the years since adopting ABC into its profit reporting, every business indicator has become more positive: profits, return on capital employed (ROCE), manufacturing expense reduction. The only business indicator with a negative trend is volume, which decreased slightly during this period. Many years ago, this would have been anathema. LubeOil's principal metric had been volume growth for such a long time that even today some still have trouble comprehending the change, and some still manage the business primarily to optimize this metric. But an irrevocable culture change is under way. Profit focus and business simplicity are the themes, and the business results are their tangible manifestations. It would be incorrect to assume that ABC was the only factor contributing to the positive business results, however. A multitude of other initiatives along with ABC contributed significantly to the results: for example, the closing of multiple manufacturing facilities with excess capacity. The impact of ABC must not be underestimated either. In many instances, ABC served as a catalyst for decisions that would not have been made in prior years, including divesting of large-volume/unprofitable businesses, reducing product line complexity, focusing on target segments, and so on. This was the genesis of ABC at LubeOil.

CASE STUDY

Initial Efforts

In the mid-1990s, Chairman Lee Nevin announced a corporate-wide strategic goal to become number one (most profitable) in the sale of lubricants worldwide. To that end, a worldwide study was commissioned with the goal of achieving a 33% increase in after-tax profits by the year 2000. The study recommended three broad strategies: growth, cost reduction, and a stronger competitive position. These strategies, although not in themselves revolutionary, set the tone for LubeOil Corporation's lubricant business to begin developing tactical initiatives that would support these strategies. Growth and cost reduction were strategies that were very familiar to all of LubeOil's employees; the third strategy, strengthening competitive position, was not. To achieve this, they needed to leverage their company's global nature by identifying and sharing internal best practices used in the business around the world and creating a more efficient global manufacturing and marketing organization.

ABC was one of the key best practices identified by the study, based on the record of accomplishment set by the U.S. affiliate, which had already implemented ABC and increased profits through improved business decision making and a change in culture. The study also suggested that this best practice be shared throughout the company's entire lubricant network with the intent of producing beneficial results similar to those achieved in the U.S. business. Subsequently, a team was chartered to develop a global ABC model template and determine the best method to implement ABC throughout the multiple affiliates. Later that year, a team comprised of members from multiple global regions met in Europe to develop a global model template and develop an implementation plan with costs/benefits and a timeline.

The team also evaluated many ABM software products. They selected an off-the-shelf software package called Oros (today called SAS Activity-Based Management) by ABC Technologies (now SAS), for several reasons: their U.S. experience with the package; the recommendation of a respected consulting firm; and the features and performance characteristics of the software. Two initial pilot sites were chosen: LubeOil Korea and LubeOil Brazil.

Oros was selected due to several key features. It was important to choose an ABM package that would be suitable for a pilot project but also scale as the needs of the corporation changed. The most important capabilities in the software package were the way that it handled multiple dimensions of segmented cost objects, the ability to access legacy data on the back end, and the flexibility it had in meeting LubeOil's reporting needs.

Pilot Phase

Korea and Brazil were chosen because of the size of their businesses in terms of volume/revenue and complexity. Both affiliates were medium size with moderate business dimensional complexity (i.e., a manageable number of market segments, customers, and products). The original global ABC model template was divided into two parts: Sales and Marketing and Manufacturing. The two parts would be brought together into one model to enable dimensional analysis. Later, the template would be expanded to include shared services.

For the initial pilots, the decision was made to implement the manufacturing part only in Korea and Brazil. At that time, ABC was still perceived mainly as a product costing tool, and the implementation team concluded that driver quantities would be easier to obtain and validate (or defend) in manufacturing. The goal was to leverage the success of manufacturing ABC to promote the Sales and Marketing portion.

These pilots were conducted concurrently in late February 1997. Both were one month long and involved 15-hour days, conquering language barriers, flying tens of thousand of miles between São Paulo and Seoul, and both were hugely successful.

Korea proved to be the most dramatic example of ABC's success. The affiliate was wrestling with a decision to divest a large portion of its business because of its apparent lack of profit. The traditional cost accounting that applied all manufacturing costs to products volumetrically suggested that a designer lubricant comprising nearly 20% of the total affiliate volume was losing money. In lubricant manufacturing, however, there is tremendous variability in the effort, time, and capital required to manufacture equivalent volumes of various products. Activity-based analysis revealed that a specialty lubricant was among the simplest and least expensive to manufacture on a unit basis. The existing cost accounting overstated production costs for the designer lubricant by 300%. This was a real eye-opener as it corroborated the intuition that the designer lubricant business was profitable in Korea. The affiliate had grown in volume in the last few years, mostly in the designer product segment—production unit costs had decreased, and profits had increased nearly 100% over that period. ABC analysis helped explain these results.

What would have happened to cost/profit trends if the affiliate had grown in the most complex, expensive-to-manufacture products and segments? A similar relationship between manufacturing complexity and costs was seen in the Brazilian pilot.

Global Implementation Phase

Project Team

In creating the ABM team, LubeOil needed to include people with a variety of skills. For example, as well as a project lead, managers felt they would need an implementation specialist, a technical expert, and each region would need a part-time regional project lead.

- **Worldwide Project Lead (WW).** LubeOil headquarters employee responsible for all project deliverables, model design, benchmarking templates, and team design.
- **Regional Project Lead (RL).** Part-time LubeOil regional employee responsible for all the deployment and localization issues for the regional models.
- **Local Team (RL) (Lead and one or two Analysts).** LubeOil local employees responsible for getting data, assisting with the model build, and ongoing model maintenance.
- **Two Full-time Implementations Specialists (WW Contracted).** LubeOil concluded that the software vendor had the best resources for assisting in the model build at each site. Therefore, two implementation specialists from the software vendor were contracted on a full time basis to travel the globe and assist on the technical side of the model development.
- **One Full-time Implementation Specialist (WW Contracted).** After the pilot and first implementation, the team decided that it would also contract a senior technical support specialist from the software firm to exclusively handle all technical support calls from LubeOil.

Planning and Design

The pilot phase of the project helped shape the model design and also provided LubeOil with several key deliverables that were identified. Progress would be tracked to each one in four phases over two years (Exhibit 2.2).

The first and most important step was to roll out the ABM models and implement them at 38 lube manufacturing facilities around the globe. After LubeOil

	P&L Impact	Timeline
P1: Getting the Process Under Control (Building a Baseline of the Business)		Time "0"
a. Basic Training of local affiliate personnel in ABC Methodology, ABC/M Software	LOW	
b. Snapshot implementation of ABC (Products, Customers, Segments)	LOW	
c. Evaluation of Results	LOW	
d. Model Validation	LOW	
e. Define Interfaces to transactional systems (SAP, JDE, etc.)	LOW	
f. Define Standard Reports	LOW	
P2: Automation/Standardization/Access (Building a Reliable/Reproducible/Useful Model)	LOW	
a. Creating a repeatable model building process	LOW	
b. Building standard reports	LOW	
c. Ensuring standardization to global models	LOW	
d. Advanced training	LOW	
P3: Local Decision Making (Using ABC Information to Improve the Bottom Line)	HIGH	Year 1
a. Giving access to user base	HIGH	
b. Profit-focused marketing using ABC information (profitable segments, customers, products)	HIGH	
c. Cost reduction using activity information (valued added versus non–value-added activities)	HIGH	
P4: Network Decision Making (Using ABC Information to Improve the Bottom Line)	HIGH	
a. Regional/global network building and benchmarking/best practices sharing	HIGH	
b. Network sourcing of product based on ABC manufacturing costs—network optimization	HIGH	
c. Measurement/change of global segment strategy using ABC information	HIGH	Year 2

Exhibit 2.2 Phases of the LubeOil Global ABC Implementation

identified the regional leaders, an agreement was made that the model design template was sufficient to begin the rollout. Localization issues would be taken into consideration at each affiliate during the implementation. Two implementations would be done in parallel, and each would take three to four weeks at each local facility, depending on its size and complexity. The basic implementation process would follow a simple flow (see Exhibit 2.3): identify resources; complete the manufacturing activities first; follow with the sales and marketing activities; incorporate shared services if necessary (local issue); bring in the customers, products, and segments; and finish off with the assignment rules.

Resources, in all cases, were grouped into categories, and assignment rules would be created by the cost and profit centers in each category. Those categories were sales region, engineering, marketing, sales development, technical support, and customer service.

The manufacturing methodology (see Exhibit 2.4) differed from the sales methodology (see Exhibit 2.5) in most phases of the model. The resource module used both primary resources and secondary pools. Secondary resources were grouped into three types: plant management, administration, and planning. Secondary resources were also grouped into three cost pools: blending, filling, and warehousing. The processes in the activity module were split into three main areas: setup, machine, and warehouse occupancy. Those costs could then be easily

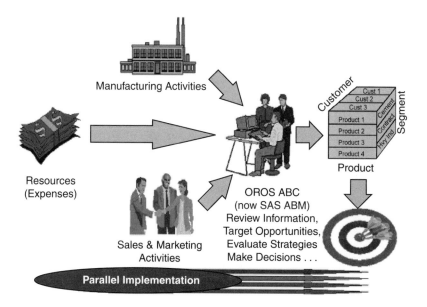

Exhibit 2.3 ABC Implementation Process: Three to Four Weeks

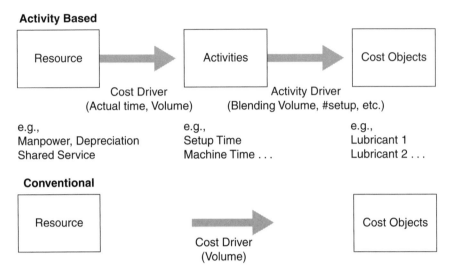

Exhibit 2.4 Manufacturing Methodology

assigned into product and product package combinations in the cost object module. The manufacturing section of the model lent itself to using drivers that were easily extracted from existing enterprise resource planning systems, such as SAP and JD Edwards.

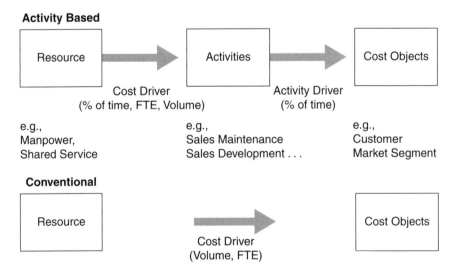

Exhibit 2.5 Sales and Marketing Methodology

By choosing a system like Oros, LubeOil had the flexibility to use these different modeling techniques. Some of these modeling techniques were resource to resource assignments and consumption-based assignments for the drivers that used setup and machine time and traditional ABM assignments for sales and marketing drivers like full-time equivalent (FTE) and number of sales calls. The shared services methodology (see Exhibit 2.6) was completely different, using many types of activity-to-activity assignments to represent departments that supported each other in a shared service environment.

The sales and marketing methodology (Exhibit 2.5) would not use primary and secondary resources; all resources would be grouped into seven distinct groups for assignment: sales region, engineering, marketing, sales development, technical support, customer service, and marketing. Unlike the manufacturing section of the model, the sales and marketing section would have six processes rather than three: sales maintenance, engineering calls, distributor calls, order taking, market research, and advertising. The cost objects that would receive these costs would be market segments and customers and some brand advertising costs.

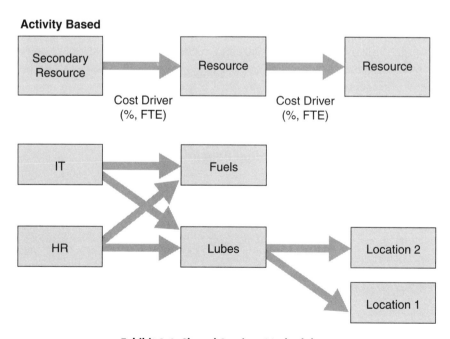

Exhibit 2.6 Shared Services Methodology

Shared services costs (Exhibit 2.6) were ultimately broken out into the type of business (resource pools) they supported, either fuels or lubes, and then finally into the locations that used them. Once those pools were assigned by percentage to the final location that used them, they could be assigned out based on either the manufacturing or the sales and marketing methodology. For all intents and purposes, the shared services section was simply an input into the other two main sections of the model.

Beyond the initial race to implement at all of the manufacturing facilities, six key deliverables were identified at a midimplementation planning summit in Brussels, Belgium, attended by all members of the worldwide team and regional leaders. Those items were:

1. Identify and implement ABM at ten key lube distributor sites.
2. Assess the applicability of implementing for LubeOil Fuels affiliates.
3. LubeOil's own chemical division was its biggest customer. Implementing at the chemical division could identify product pricing opportunities for the much-needed base stocks.
4. Develop a plan to incorporate ABC into other LubeOil downstream business units: chemicals, films, and so on.
5. Use ABC information to build a global lubes business/profit plan for 1999.
6. Build a global ABC benchmark template using ABC data; develop an ABC benchmarking database and deploy to an Internet portal to leverage benchmark information between affiliates; share ABC success stories—examples of ABC use to increase profits—between affiliates.

Initial Benefits

By the end of the fourth quarter of 1998, initial results were on track. By the year 2000, LubeOil attained its goal of becoming the number-one lube company in the world. In 1998, 34 of the 36 affiliates were completed, 2 fuels affiliates were completed, and the chemical division implementation was started. The ABM was later put on hold, due to a SAP R/3 rollout. In 1999, after the SAP rollout, the ABM project was re started and completed in the first quarter of the year 2000.

Using ABC information to build the 1999 and 2000 profit plan proved to be a success. By using ABC to validate their marketing plans and focus on unprofitable segments use, after-tax profits in 2000 soared (see Exhibit 2.7).

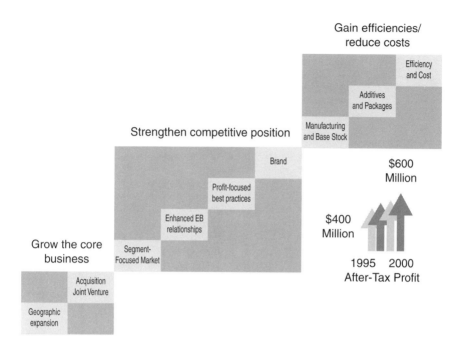

Exhibit 2.7 Lube Oil Profit Plan

Changing the paradigm from making decisions based on volume-related gross/variable margins to volume- and activity-related net margins would be the biggest culture change resulting from the ABM project. At the beginning of the implementation, all decisions were made at a gross and variable margin report. The reports (based on traditional volume-related allocations) lacked credibility. More than 50% of LubeOil's controllable expenses occurred at the net margin. The benchmark template (see Exhibit 2.8) using ABC data was determined to be a credible solution to this problem. Creating the models would be a critical step, but it was widely believed that unless the reports could be deployed to the decision makers, ABM at LubeOil would fizzle and die. The WW project lead decided that sharing this report through an Internet portal to all local affiliates and stakeholders was a perfect solution. Along with benchmarking best practices between local affiliates, the nature of the report allowed LubeOil management to use the benchmark template and additional benchmark data (see Exhibit 2.9) as a scorecard to manage affiliate performance.

BENCHMARK TEMPLATE #1
ABC Profit Value Chain
Affiliate: Various Global
Sort Criteria: Total Lube Business
Period: Full Year 1997 (2)

*All revenue/cost in USD/BBL

Affiliate	Volume (BBL)	Realization	Raw Material	Accounting Gross Margin	Lube Oil Blending Plant Cost	Distribution	Delivered Gross Margin	Sales and Marketing	Advertising	Net Margin
Local Affiliate 1	6,202,039	150.5	85.7	64.8	8.6	11.1	45.1	21.8	6.2	17.1
Local Affiliate 2	1,025,109	162.2	94.6	67.6	17.5	16.6	33.6	19.7	6.1	7.8
Local Affiliate 3	832,344	166.6	84.9	81.7	20.5	11.5	49.6	22.9	5.9	20.7
Local Affiliate 4	489,227	135.9	92.2	43.7	8.3	9.7	25.7	9.6	4.0	12.2
Local Affiliate 5	368,164	188.9	105.8	83.1	7.9	2.9	72.2	21.1	1.7	49.3
Local Affiliate 6	91,373	279.8	87.5	132.3	30.8	4.9	96.7	71.7	14.2	10.8
Affiliate Weighted Average		154.8	87.8	67.0	10.9	11.3	44.8	21.5	5.9	17.4
Regional Grouping	487,164	193.0	113.0	80.0	28.0	4.0	48.0	38.0	14.0	-4.0
VARIANCE TO AVG		38.2	-25.2	13.0	-17.1	7.3	3.2	-16.5	-8.1	-21.4

Exhibit 2.8 Global Benchmark Template (LubeOil Scorecard)

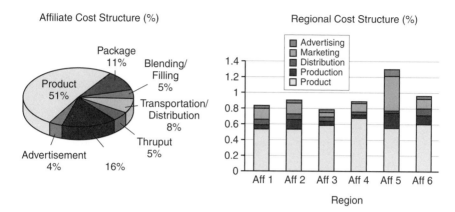

Exhibit 2.9 View of the Affiliates' Cost Structure Used to Illustrate LubeOil's ABC Global Benchmark Data

Lessons Learned: Initial Study

At the end of 2000, it had already been noted that ABC returns no bottom-line profits unless action is taken by management and line personnel. The ABM team learned a significant number of lessons, and it took actions against each one. The result was LubeOil's becoming the number-one lubricants company in the world.

The following are a list of the lessons learned by the ABM team:

- **Highlight and act on opportunities for cost reduction.** By highlighting best practices between global affiliates, deploying them on the benchmark template, and scoring and managing affiliates based on that data, more opportunities for cost reduction were found.

- **Categorize segment/customers/product combinations.** Deploying results in a segmented grid allowed management to develop action plans and strategies to facilitate more cost reduction, price increases, and outsource and divesting decisions to improve profitability.

- **Optimize logistics operations.** More efficient affiliates and plants were identified, which facilitated plant closures and transfer of production to efficient manufacturers. The most efficient distribution sources were also identified and used.

- **Link ABM to performance management.** Surfacing benchmark data as a scorecard made these changes possible. LubeOil was one of the earliest adopters of the balanced scorecard. In *Balanced Scorecard: Translating*

Strategy into Action, authors Robert S. Kaplan and David P. Norton state: "We are confident . . . that innovating companies . . . will expand the structure and use of the scorecard."[1] LubeOil, which was truly innovative with its early use of the scorecard, was able to reap more benefits than simply running an ABC project and hoping that it would receive cost savings on a silver platter.

- **Design a decision-making process.** Early on in the project, there was a general feeling that when the models were complete, there would be a pot of gold at the end of the rainbow. This is a common misperception. Once the model is complete, a strategy should be put in place to use the ABM data to make decisions. LubeOil designed a simple set of rules (see Exhibit 2.10) to follow once it found that it had better cost/profit information. Reviewing ABM data at each step of the process has rewarded LubeOil with substantial growth.

Next Steps: Initial Study

Ten "next steps" for the coming years follow.

1. Continue the validation of existing models.
2. Provide reports to regions.
3. Assess existing strategy in light of new information.
4. Access capability/fit within organization.
   - Management Information Services/Segmentation/ABC (redundancies and best sources)
5. Develop ownership and update process and procedures.
6. Develop training program for interested parties.
7. Give more access to stakeholders.
8. Assess and deploy resources to continue use of tool.
9. Develop future models.
10. Run an ABM strategy-building workshop.

It is always interesting to look back. At the end of 2000 there were a number of items identified as "next steps" considered to be critical for long-term success. As with every implementation of ABC, it is an iterative process, models will be continually validated and reporting will continue to be pushed out to the people who can make decisions.

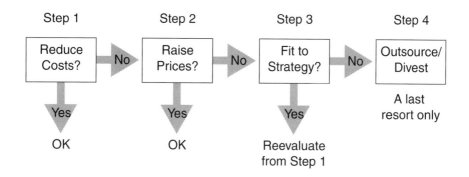

"This is a continual process."

Exhibit 2.10 Cost Reduction Process Rules

In the book *Performance Management: Finding the Missing Pieces (to Close the Intelligence Gap)*, Gary Cokins highlights how the key to using business intelligence is "Alignment."[2] Cokins mentions this concept frequently and illustrates how truly important it is to align employee behavior with a strategy. LubeOil's decision to take ABM benchmark data and link it to performance to change employee behavior is one of the keys to its early success. It is a challenge to get employees to make strategy part of their job. The early scorecards that LubeOil used were prime examples of how a "communication tool" can be used to shape an organization.

Current State: Today and Beyond

Mergers of large multinational oil companies began in the late 1990s, although consumer and environmental groups warned that the growing concentration of power and wealth of the oil industry is unsafe for the environment, communities, and consumers worldwide. California-based Chevron Corporation agreed to acquire Texaco for about $36 billion in stock, creating the world's fourth-largest oil company. The acquisition came at a time when crude oil prices hit their highest level in a decade, and oil company profits have skyrocketed. Later British Petroleum, Amoco, and ARCO received clearance from the U.S. Federal Trade Commission to combine their companies. The union will create a corporate group worth some $200 billion. To compete in this increasingly consolidated market, LubeOil also participated in a multibillion-dollar merger. ABM and these performance management tools and business reporting models helped shape the new organization.

Today LubeOil has ABM strategically embedded into its reporting process and is able to make many of its strategic decisions based in this information.

EXPERT WRAP-UP

Thomas M. Kang

As at Mobil, the key tools that LubeOil implemented to transform the culture of volume at all costs were balanced scorecard (BSC) and activity-based costing. These tools revolutionized performance management at LubeOil, and, I believe, the resulting change in culture and behavior had a profound impact on the bottom line. Activity-based costing allowed us to better understand our product and service offerings in terms of their consumption of activities and gave us good insight into what drives these activities and costs. In many instances, volume was clearly the wrong answer. At LubeOil, ABC proved to be a catalyst for real culture and behavior change and served as meaningful input for comprehensive performance measurement tools, such as the BSC. When used together, I believe that ABC and BSC clearly provide a system of performance measurement that is *meaningful, accurate, and aligned*.

Of course, all of this sounds good, but there is a major hurdle to implementing these performance management tools: existing organizational culture of performance management and a resistance to change. Without real commitment from senior management and a sustained focus on continuing to drive implementation of these tools, getting real results will be difficult. In embarking on any real culture change initiative, there are pitfalls to avoid and necessary components that you must have in order to have a good likelihood of success.

ENDNOTES

1. Robert S. Kaplan and David P. Norton, *The Balanced Scorecard: Translating Strategy into Action* (Boston: Harvard Business School Press, 1986), preface.
2. Gary Cokins, *Performance Management: Finding the Missing Pieces (to Close the Intelligence Gap)* (Hoboken, NJ: John Wiley & Sons, Inc., 2004), preface.

3

HOMEHEALTH: DELIVERING ACTIVITY-BASED COSTING

When a paradigm shifts everyone goes back to zero; your past success guarantees you nothing.

—Joel A. Barker, *Future Edge: Discovering New Paradigms in Success*

FOREWORD

John A. Miller

This case study is instructive in many ways and demonstrates the key principles of an effective activity-based costing (ABC) implementation. It is fair to say that HomeHealth was one of the pioneers in the history of ABC. This project was initiated in the mid-1990s, about the same time as the American Productivity & Quality Center (APQC) and CAM-I jointly launched a best practice study in the then emerging area of ABC.[1] At that time, it was estimated that only about 5,000 organizations had undertaken an ABC initiative. Most were manufacturing companies that were using the ABC cost tracing methods and techniques to determine their product cost more accurately. Only a handful of manufacturing and a few service organizations were going beyond product cost and using activity-based information to help them improve processes and business performance. HomeHealth was one of those service organizations that undertook ABC to help improve their business performance.

The best practice study, published in 1995, captured the combined knowledge and resources of the APQC and CAM-I, sponsorship by more that 60 leading companies, involvement by 6 subject matter authorities (including 2 from academia), 167 organizations willing to complete a detailed survey of ABC, and 15 best practice companies sharing their insights and knowledge. One of the key contributions of this study was the documentation of the ABM Value

Cycle, which specified applications of activity-based information in the areas of improvement initiatives, decision making, and performance measurements. The application at HomeHealth is in the area of improvement initiatives and could be classified as a process improvement application or a cost reduction application.

The main purpose of this section is to identify and document some of the best practices discussed in the survey (which still apply today) for ABC and to use the case study to demonstrate how they were used at HomeHealth. Best practices include:

- **Business reason for doing ABC.** At HomeHealth, the key business and challenges were to reduce cost, maintain quality, and improve access. The ABC model was positioned as a tool to meet these challenges.
- **Pilot test to confirm value and usefulness to the organization.** At HomeHealth, two pilot efforts were undertaken. Immediately after the first pilot, a second pilot was necessary to fully convince HomeHealth management of value, before commencing a full scale, agency-wide ABC system
- **Balanced project resources, timelines, and scope of work.** Any ABC project can be implemented, regardless of scope, provided the due date allows for sufficient time and resources to meet the requirements. What work has to be done and how long it will take is specific to the scope of the work. At HomeHealth, the scope of work (agency wide), timeline (19 months), and resources (5 to 7 cross-functional teams, including any consultants, dedicated 25 to 100% to the project) were balanced to achieve the project completion date.
- **Consistent application of ABC/M methodology.** Best practice companies consistently apply generally accepted activity-based costing/methodology (ABC/M methods), procedures, terms, and techniques and adapt them to their specific requirements. Examples include consistent use of the CAM-I Basic Model, the CAM-I Glossary of ABC/M terms and definitions, tested data collection methods and techniques, generic process classification framework, and general and industry specific activity dictionaries. At

HomeHealth, managers and employees were trained in the basic principles and methods of ABC, and consistently used the CAM-I Cross (basic model) within the organization. It is doubtful that any kind of activity dictionary existed for the healthcare industry at the time of this initiative, and HomeHealth would have had to develop its own from scratch.

- **Management commitment and priority.** Management commitment is defined as level of ABM sponsorship, breadth and scope of training, ABM project implementation resources, level of management involvement, and use of consultants or other outside resources when required. The HomeHealth ABC initiative had a high level of management commitment and priority. Sponsorship included director-level managers who sat on the ABC/M oversight committee, adequate resources in a three- to four-person full-time equivalent (FTE) implementation team, and outside support at project initiation and ongoing as required.

- **Ongoing, cost-efficient, and reliable ABM systems required.** Absent an ongoing system to report ABC information, the project effort is limited to a one-time study, for a specific period in time. Best practice companies place significant emphasis on installing the systems, procedures, and methods necessary to collect and report activity-based information on an ongoing basis. The systems, procedures, and methods that are installed are responsive to the needs of the users, easy to update and maintain, and reliable. Best practice companies have learned that the systems and software aspect of the ABM implementation cannot be ignored; in fact, it must be emphasized. ABM system design considerations include purpose and use, accuracy required, frequency of update, and relevance.

Overall, the HomeHealth ABC implementation would have qualified as a best practice in 1995. In these early days HomeHealth had a business reason for doing ABC, expected to see value, and required pilot tests to demonstrate that value. Management commitment and priority were demonstrated by the assignment of resources to the implementation and the willingness to provide outside support and training to the ongoing ABC system.

INTRODUCTION

Faced with rapidly changing customer requirements, a new governmental reimbursement methodology, and increased competition from national for-profit chains, home healthcare agencies are finding that their traditional methods for fiscal and operational decision making are no longer adequate. Activity-based costing/management (ABC/M) provides a more accurate way for a home healthcare agency to reduce costs while maintaining quality and improving customer access.

What is home healthcare? "Home care" is a generic term that encompasses a variety of health and social services. These services most commonly consist of nursing; physical, occupational, respiratory, and speech therapy; social service; dietitian; phlebotomy; and assistance with personal care and activities of daily living needs. Services are delivered at home to recovering, disabled, and chronically or terminally ill persons. Generally, home care is provided whenever a person prefers to stay at home but needs ongoing care that family and friends alone cannot provide easily or effectively.

ORGANIZATIONAL ISSUES

The HomeHealth (HH) Network is the not-for-profit home care agency of a large Presbyterian-Medical Center located in the Midwest and providing home health services to individuals in a major metropolitan area and five surrounding counties. Founded in 1975, the HomeHealth Network was the first hospital-based home care agency in its area. The network consists of an intermittent home health agency, which is Medicare certified and state licensed; a personal care service agency consisting of home health aides and homemakers; and an older adult program that provides services such as evaluation, community referrals, emergency alert, and programming to support healthy living. In addition, HomeHealth has seamless linkages with providers of infusion therapy pharmacy and supplies, medical equipment, home physicians, and hospice. Since its founding, HomeHealth has grown to the point where, at the time of the ABC project, it was visiting over 141,000 homes per year and taking in over $17.5 million of gross revenue annually. One dynamic that made evaluating the business unique was that 89% of the payers that HomeHealth dealt with were governmental.

CASE STUDY

Initial Efforts

During the 33 years since Medicare began paying for home health services, the business of home healthcare has become highly regulated but remains a "cottage industry." Although the professional care delivered to patients is consistent from one agency to another, there is wide variation in people and material resources, operational functions, and measurements and performance standards. Knee-jerk responses to regulatory oversight have resulted in the addition of positions, processes, forms, and activities in an attempt to "fix" the deficiency. This quick-fix mentality has led to a situation where structures are hierarchical and complex, processes are overly complicated and expensive, and outcomes are inconsistent and variable, and do not always serve the needs of customers. Today's challenge for home health agencies is to reduce their costs, maintain quality, and provide services that satisfy the needs and wants of customers. This task is formidable, as most home care agencies have no method for knowing what each process or activity costs and therefore no way to prioritize cost reductions or process improvements. Home care's traditional costing methods can provide information about cost per visit, aggregated cost (all disciplines), cost per discipline (e.g., cost of a nursing visit), or cost per episode (from admission to discharge). However, home care agencies need intelligence that is more specific to make appropriate operational and strategic decisions that will assure survival in our uncertain future. HomeHealth was presented three key challenges; an ABC/M project was proposed as a method to respond to those challenges.

Challenges

1. Reduce cost.
   - For reimbursement changes.
2. Maintain quality.
   - "Quality" as defined by our customers.
3. Improve access.
   - Provide services that focus on the needs and wants of our customers.

Responding to the Challenges

- Target high-cost processes for improvement.
- Identify what causes cost to vary.

- Eliminate what our customers do not want.
- Monitor and improve performance.
- Price services appropriately.
- Make the right program decisions.
- Provide better customer service.

Pilot Phase

HomeHealth initiated an ABC project, the initial goal of which was to determine if ABC could assist in identifying high-cost activities that would benefit from reengineering or process improvement. In the beginning the idea was to have one pilot project and then roll out ABC/M across the entire company.

Immediately following the first pilot and still needing to be convinced, the care delivery managers asked for an ABC analysis of the admission process. This question was posed: Does the cost of a nursing admission vary by type of service provided? The types of admissions examined were infusion/high-tech admissions, maternal/child health admissions, psychiatric admissions, admissions for physical therapy, and traditional admissions.

The result was two separate pilot projects focusing on two different goals.

Pilot Project 1

The first ABC project was limited to the referral intake process. Two questions were asked: (1) What is the cost of preauthorizing managed care referrals? (2) What is the cost of referral intake from various referral sources?

The staff was telling management that preauthorizing managed care referrals was cumbersome and time consuming. To control costs and assure that only authorized services are provided to enrollees, managed care companies (health maintenance organizations [HMOs] and preferred provider organizations [PPOs]) have required healthcare companies to call a case manager for approval before providing services. Home care agencies must receive approval to do an evaluation visit in the home and then report their findings before additional visits are approved. Without visit authorization, agencies risk denial of payment for services provided.

Using ABC, it was discovered that nearly 20% of all referrals required preauthorization, a statistic that was previously unknown. It also was found that preauthorization added nearly $36 to the cost of each referral. To place that finding in perspective, managed care companies have negotiated a rate of $55 to $60 per visit and approve an average of six to seven visits. It was also discovered that 10% of the average payment for a managed-care case was being used up by the cost of preauthorization.

Management also wanted to know about the variation in referral intake costs by referral source. It was found that costs varied widely. Commercial insurance referrals cost the most because they were required to negotiate rates on every case. The Physician-Hospital Organization (PHO) referral costs were the lowest because they were the only home care provider. Therefore, literally no time was spent in authorization. It was found that the activity of "accepting referrals" varied by source. Physician office referrals were the most expensive because the physician or his or her office staff was unfamiliar with the type of information needed; they required coaching or callbacks to complete the referral. Referrals received from hospital liaisons were the least expensive to accept because the work was being done outside of referral services. However, by looking at the cost of the referral intake "process," it was found that the total cost of referrals received from hospital liaisons was three times more expensive than the average referral cost. Liaison referrals were twice the total cost of referrals from physician offices. Faxed or phoned referrals from discharge planners cost the least, but the faxed referrals had downstream costs for data entry. Faxed referrals were hard to read and often necessitated a return phone call for clarification. These findings led to an analysis of the cost drivers of liaison activity and resulted in a redesign of liaisons' jobs and job activities. We also targeted the referral form used by discharge planners and jointly developed a form that would be legible after faxing.

Pilot Project 2

Interviews with nurses identified five common activities: (1) scheduling or planning the care; (2) traveling to the home; (3) making the home visit; (4) documenting the results of the visit; and (5) coordinating care with others involved or community resources. Management was able, for the first time, to identify the cost of each of these activities. It found that documenting the admission visit cost nearly as much as making the visit, something nurses had been telling management for years.

Cost of Direct Nursing Admission Activities

- Plan patient care $ 2.37 to $ 4.02
- Travel $8.04
- Make home visit $32.23 to $63.29
- Coordinate care $ 8.19 to $15.92
- Document care $12.41 to $29.29

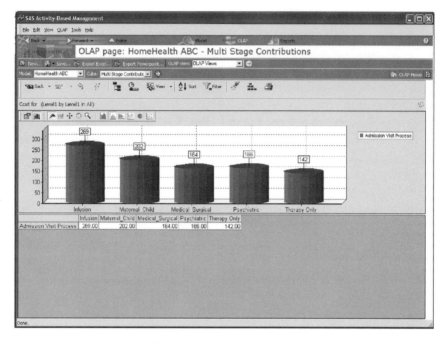

Exhibit 3.1 Example Activity Costs

The infusion/high-tech admission cost (see Exhibit 3.1) was the highest cost, followed by the maternal/child admission, the psychiatric admission, and traditional admission. The least costly was the admission for physical therapy. Further analysis provided information about the activities that added to the cost of each of these admissions. Each is being evaluated for the value it adds to the admission process.

Rollout Phase: Initiating an Agency-Wide Activity-Based Costing System

The pilot ABC projects demonstrated the value of ABC over the traditional cost reporting method. Management decided to implement ABC across all aspects of the organization. Representatives from each job class were asked to identify the five to six major activities they perform. Whenever possible, their responses were validated with existing data or verified by their supervisors. By adapting the CAM-I Process Classification Framework (see Exhibit 3.2) to typical home care

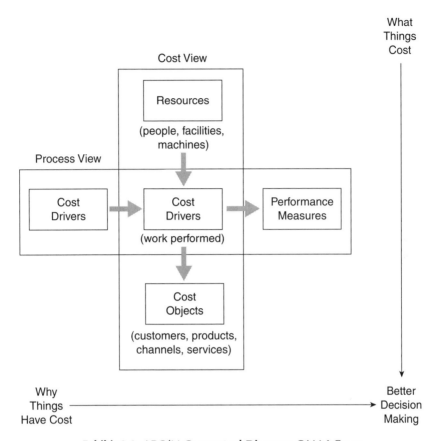

Exhibit 3.2 ABC/M Conceptual Diagram: CAM-I Cross
Source: Derived from the Consortium of Advanced Management-International (CAM-I).

functions, HomeHealth developed a dictionary that identifies and defines 11 processes and 84 activities.

Building the Model

Team and Team-Designed Project Timeline

In building an ABM project, it is common that the cross-functional team will consist of five to seven people dedicating between 25 and 100% of their time. Typically, the team will consist of internal people, external consultants, or both. This was no different at HomeHealth.

Project Team

- ABC/M Oversight Committee
  - Directors
  - Finance and Decision Support manager
  - Process improvement staff
- Model administrator
- Interview team (as needed)
- Consultant support (initiation and as needed)

At HomeHealth the project team had already been determined during the pilot phase. Team members were responsible to prepare an implementation plan, gather data, and input it into the commercial ABM software package that they had chosen just prior to the first pilot. HomeHealth selected the commercial package produced by ABC Technologies called Oros. SAS acquired ABC Technologies in 2002, and the package is now called SAS Activity-Based Management. Oros was chosen for many features but primarily for the ability to have a truly multidimensional cost object and handle any modeling methodology, whether a traditional ABC or a consumption-based approach such as activity-based planning and budgeting, resource capacity planning, or any other time- or event-triggered modeling style. (Exhibit 3.3 presents the project timeline.)

Planning and Design

The resource module serves as the starting point and is structured after the general ledger. Expenses from 12 cost centers in the ledger also serve as centers in the resource module. These centers represent each of the eight clinical specialties, medical supplies, and three administrative cost centers. Five other centers are included

ID	Task Name	Start	Finish	Duration	2000	2001
1	Orientation	1/3/2000	1/3/2000	0w	◆	
2	Completed Pilot #1	1/3/2000	3/31/2000	13w	X▬X	
3	Completed Pilot #2	4/3/2000	6/30/2000	13w	X▬X	
4	Completed All Interviews	6/31/2000	2/28/2001	34.8w	X▬▬▬X	
5	Completed Activity Dictionary	3/1/2001	5/31/2001	13.2w		X▬X
6	Resource and Activity Modules Complete	6/1/2001	7/31/2001	8.6w		X▬X
7	Begin Regular Module Updates	8/1/2001	8/1/2001	0w		◆

Exhibit 3.3 Project Timeline

in the module structure: (1) Wages, Salaries, and Benefits; (2) Hospital Overhead; (3) Clinical Expense Pool; (4) Administrative Expense Pool; and (5) Entered Benefits for employees paid by the visit. Wages, Salaries, and Benefits are listed by position, whether one person or multiple people hold a title. Their respective salaries and wages are then entered in the module. The expense accounts from the general ledger (GL) are entered as accounts under the centers in the resource module. This is done for all the centers that come from the GL. The Other Expenses (expenses other than Wages, Salaries, and Benefits) are assigned to one of the two expense pools. The clinical accounts are assigned to an account within the Clinical Expense Pool; likewise, administrative accounts were assigned to an account within the Administrative Cost Pool. The Hospital Overhead and Entered Benefits centers each contain one account. These amounts are calculated and entered.

The expense pool accounts are either assigned back to the Wages, Salaries, and Benefits or directly assigned to an activity. For example, the GL accounts for rent and electricity are assigned to one of the expense pools (depending on whether the expense is clinical or administrative in nature). The account within the expense pool is Facilities. Facilities are then assigned to the respective positions within the Wages, Salaries, and Benefits center. This is done strictly as a time-saving step when assigning resources to activities.

How did we know what activities were being performed? Interviews were done to determine the resource to activity assignments. During the interview phase, the team decided that it was important to keep it simple and set some ground rules to keep the results consistent.

- Consider time worked to be 100%.
- Consider four to six major activities, as identified by staff.
- Usually disregard activities under 5%.
- Identify purpose of activities, such as "meetings" and "paperwork."

The activity module is quite simple in structure. Every job title at HomeHealth is listed as a center in the module. Each center (job title) contains five or six accounts or activities attained from the employee interviews. There is one center in the activity module that is not a job title, Unassigned. This center contains hospital overhead and bad debt, which are expenses that could not be logically assigned to activities. See the interview example for the Special Services Supervisor (see Exhibit 3.4).

The next step for the activity module was to build the attribute structure (see Exhibit 3.5). This structure is identical to the activity dictionary. Every activity has

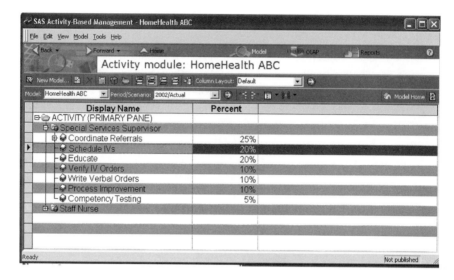

Exhibit 3.4 Activity Module

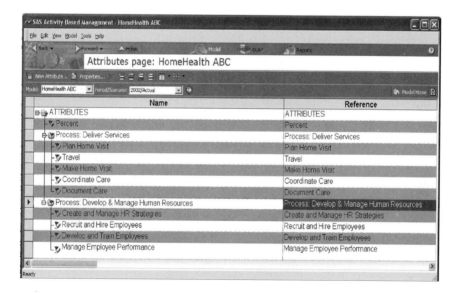

Exhibit 3.5 Attribute Structure

a place within the dictionary, and all major processes serve as centers within the structure. Each activity is then assigned to its respective dictionary item. This is very useful, because it is possible to look at the costs of total processes and then break down the process by activity to find the high-cost activities.

HomeHealth decided to use a multidimensional approach in creating the cost object module. The three dimensions chosen were Discipline, Visit Type, and Payer. A fourth dimension, Organizational Sustaining Costs, was added to catch those activities that could not logically be assigned to one of the other three dimensions. These activities are those of support people and administrative functions. The structure of the cost object module was carefully considered. HomeHealth's current billing and data system allows for sorting by a combination of only three fields. Therefore, the three listed dimensions were chosen. Other possible dimensions might be Referral Source, Diagnosis, and Supply Usage. A new billing system would allow HomeHealth to add dimensions as desired. Exhibit 3.6 depicts an example of the structure of a multidimensional cost object module.

Activities were then assigned to the appropriate dimension account. For instance, all physical therapy activities were assigned to the PT account under the discipline dimension. The sales table was created with estimated revenues. HomeHealth does not compile statistics on actual revenue by payer, but instead budgets the amount of reimbursement that each payer group will pay. Once visit volume is determined at the end of the quarter, the budgeted rate or percentage of charges is applied. Data are now available by payer, by visit type, by discipline, by sustaining costs (overhead for the most part), or any combination thereof. It is also possible to exclude a dimension in a view. It is useful to look at the cost per visit with or without the sustaining costs dimension, which is predominately indirect labor expenses and hospital overhead.

Some of the drivers HomeHealth uses may be unique to healthcare and even home care. Some of the drivers used to assign resources to activities are clinical mileage, budgeted clinical pagers and phones, interview ratios, FTEs weighted by interview ratios, square footage, vendor percent of visits, and direct assignment. Direct assignment was used for items such as overhead and other items assigned to the unassigned account in the activity module. Direct assignment was also used to assign accounts to the clinical or administrative expense pools. An effort was made not to use direct assignment for activities, because management wanted those costs to be spread by driver ratio.

Some of the same drivers were used to assign activities to the cost object accounts. Additional drivers are admissions by payer, patients served by payer, and

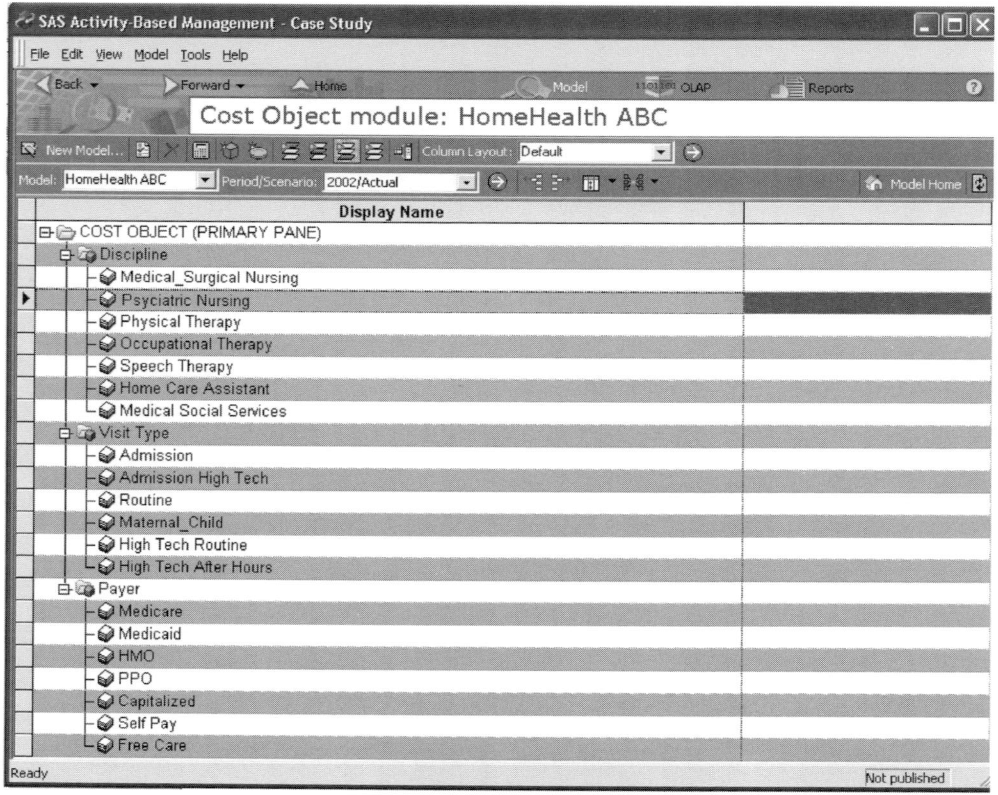

Exhibit 3.6 Multidimensional Cost Object

visits by payer. The driver used is determined by whether the activity is dependent on the volume of admissions, patients, or visits. For example, number of staff trained, used to assign activities associated with training staff on HomeHealth clinical documentation system. The final drivers called "Visits by discipline" and "Visits by type" were used. For additional accuracy, both drivers were used both with and without a weighting factor. The amount of time for each visit was the weighting factor used. The quantities for these drivers, as well as for the resource drivers, are available in our billing/data system, and many must be updated quarterly.

Initial Benefits

ABC reports are being used to review the cost of visit types by discipline by payer during budget review meetings. The more specific information that ABC provides changes the focus from the cost reporting view to an understanding of the true cost of providing services.

An example of the differences in the two views can be found in Exhibit 3.7.

The ABC model has been used to monitor possible changes and scenarios by creating "dummy models" to evaluate possible enhancements to the base model. These dummy models are created from the base model to run a much simpler cost object. This allows us to evaluate the possibility of adding new dimensions in the

Health Care Financial Accounting Formats			ABC Cost Object Module	
Cost per Visit	Comparison to Limits	DISCIPLINE	Cost per Visit	Unit Profit
$97.14	$1.35	Med/Surg. Nursing	$98.09	($3.61)
106.62	10.83	Psych Nursing	98.01	1.69
75.95	(27.64)	Physical Therapy	97.98	0.02
77.28	(26.32)	Occupational Therapy	89.71	7.39
86.06	(17.94)	Speech Therapy	105.41	(14.39)
107.96	(23.78)	Medical Social Worker	117.47	(30.22)
49.26	2.78	Home Care Assistant	74.15	25.78
94.29		OVERALL	95.35	

Exhibit 3.7 Comparison of Traditional Costing to ABC at HomeHealth

future. For example, one of the HomeHealth HMO contracts was renegotiated and resulted in a lower visit rate paid to HomeHealth. By adjusting the model to incorporate that adjustment, it was possible to see the impact the change would have on the profitability of the whole payer group.

Some other examples of how ABC/M will turn financial information into management information:

- Psychiatric nursing visits are three times more costly than medical-surgical visits.
- HMO visits cost 1.5 times more than Medicare visits.
- Admission process costs are $450 per client.
- Physical therapist travel is two times more expensive than registered nurse travel.
- Documentation costs $45 per visit.

HomeHealth also investigated the costs associated with providing medical supplies to patients. During the initial project the constraints of the current billing/data system would not allow expansion of the cost object, but once a new system was installed HomeHealth was ready (and did) make the necessary improvements to the base model.

Initial Lessons Learned

In *Activity-Based Cost Management: An Executives Guide*, Gary Cokins describes the organizational shock from ABC/M: "Ninety percent of ABC/M is organizational change management and behavior modifying, and 10 percent is the math . . . . This is a huge problem."[2]

HomeHealth found this to be true. Sometimes staff members react negatively to the term "activity-based costing." They fear that identifying the cost of their work may lead to unrealistic changes, added responsibility, or job reductions. They can become defensive and uncooperative with the process. The education of staff begins during the activity interview. In most cases staff members find that the interview process provides a voice for their complaints about rework and their aggravation with things that make their work harder to do. As ABC/M is used and the results are explained, staff concerns disappear, and they soon become believers in the method.

Some findings were that:

- Activity "costing" can elicit fear and defensiveness.
- Activity "management" may be more acceptable.
- Education begins with staff interviews.
- Sharing what makes work hard validates staff members' long-standing frustrations and involves them in the process.

HomeHealth overcame these "fears" by spending a large amount of time educating staff members about the value of ABC/M and it's uses. By focusing on quality improvement, and cost reduction, staff members began to see the value of ABC.

ABC/M was explained to staff members as leading to:

- Increased customer satisfaction:
  - Patient
  - Physician
  - Payer
- Improved clinical outcomes
- Reduced cost per visit/episode
- Better coordination/continuity
- Increased staff satisfaction

Other challenges that had to be addressed should have been planned for up front. In the book *Implementing Activity-Based Management in Daily Operations*, John Miller explains that "implementing a new ABM information system requires a considerable amount of effort and planning . . . overall requirements must be specified up front."[3]

Most of the goals for the ABC/M project at HomeHealth concerned how to keep the model updated. Five things that would have been nice to address up front would have been:

1. How often staff needs to be interviewed
2. Frequency of reports
3. When the assignment of resources needs to change
4. Revision of the activity dictionary
5. Model validation included after process improvement initiatives

Initial Next Steps

Integration of ABC/M throughout the organization has been ongoing. Managers are now receiving regular updates, and the cost-per-visit report is being used in the monthly Budget Work Team meetings along with more traditional operating and financial reports. The executive director serves as the driving force for Home-Health's ABC/M initiative. Various ABC data, such as attribute reports, reports on quarterly updates, and printouts of the model itself, are used to illustrate how an ABC approach can enhance management decision making, identify areas of high cost, and prioritize process improvement activities.

Going forward, the plan was to fully integrate ABC and ABM into existing processes: management decision making; process improvement; financial reporting; budgeting; strategic planning; job design, measurement, and evaluation; organizational evaluation; and marketing. One example of how ABC is being used to manage process improvement activities is the way projects are now prioritized. HomeHealth ranks processes of interest by total cost, potential for improvement, downstream cost driver, contribution to the organizational mission, interface with external customers, and readiness for change. Improvement projects are assigned priority based on their total score (see Exhibit 3.8). It was found, for instance, that their scheduling process is consuming 3.3% of the total expenditures more than the cost of billing and collecting for its services. HomeHealth has initiated a scheduling redesign project and will be looking at the cost of the process after it has been fully implemented.

Using ABM at HomeHealth to determine performance indicator (PI) priorities was simple but effective:

1. Identify processes for focus.
2. Rank order by decision factors.
   Total cost
   Potential for improvement
   Downstream cost driver
   Contribution to mission
   Interface with external customer
   Readiness for change
3. Prioritize.

Before ABC, the management team would focus on ways to reduce the cost of a visit that had been allocated overhead based on volume. With ABC, costs are

Process	COST	Consistent with Mission	Effect on External Customer	Readiness to Change	Downstream Cost Driver	Potential for Improvement	TOTAL SCORE	PRIORITY
• Referral Intake	3	5	5	4	5	3	25	#3
• Liaison Role	5	5	5	3	5	5	28	#2
• Schedule Patients	5	5	5	4	5	5	29	#1
• Billing	3	3	4	3	4	4	21	#4

1 = Very Low   2 = Low   3 = Moderate   4 = High   5 = Very High

Exhibit 3.8 ABM Process Improvement Decision Tree

57

now assigned to activities and processes based on resource use. Now management is able to direct its energies to reducing the true cost of producing each visit type for each customer. HomeHealth now has better information to manage, to negotiate, and to make decisions for the future.

Current State: Cost of Scheduling

Finding that scheduling was over 3% of the total dollars spent at HomeHealth was significant. As noted, the next step was to begin a scheduling project to reduce the cost of scheduling. Just documenting the scheduling process unveiled a scheduling nightmare (see Exhibit 3.9). More in-depth analysis uncovered that scheduling costs HomeHealth more than billing and collections. This fact became apparent after the scheduling costs were found and traced back to the time spent doing scheduling activities.

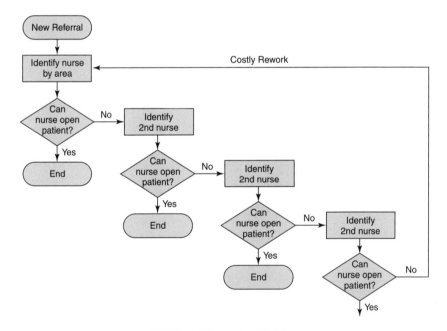

Exhibit 3.9 Scheduling Nightmare

Interview results revealed that time spent scheduling included:

- 39% team assistants with new admittances
- 24% team leaders' involvement
- 17% weekend scheduling
- 9% IV supervisor
- 9% team assistant with routine scheduling
- 2% supervisors

When ABM is applied to scheduling management, HomeHealth has the information to accomplish two very important goals:

1. Analyze and improve the process of scheduling by team assistants. Minimize the cost drivers.
2. Analyze the scheduling activities performed by the IV supervisor and team leader. Identify which activities are value added and which add no value to the customer. Eliminate or minimize non–value-added activities.

It also became apparent that reducing cost of documentation was important. After looking at five quarters of documentation and other activity costs, Home-Health can:

- Benchmark documentation cost with other ABC/M home care agencies.
- Evaluate the documentation process used by all disciplines.
- Observe (validate) documentation (psychiatric nurses and masters of social work). Use best-known methods.
- Determine cost by computerized versus traditional documentation. Track over time.

Next Steps/Future Plans: Today and Beyond

HomeHealth's short-term goal to understand and reduce the cost of scheduling and documentation is under way. One common misconception about doing an ABM project is that once the model is calculated you will start saving money immediately. This is not realistic; once an ABC/M model is complete, you will be armed with the information to do "good things," but the real work is just beginning.

The three areas that are important for HomeHealth in the future are strategic planning, budgeting, and job description and evaluation planning.

Robert S. Kaplan states in *The Strategy-Focused Organization* that it is important to align the organization to strategy. By tying compensation into strategic planning and incorporating worker incentives, HomeHealth will "have a powerful lever to gain the attention and commitment to our strategy."[4]

Budgeting is a key component of a performance management system. In *Performance Management*, Gary Cokins writes that traditional budgeting is an unreliable compass and that there is a better approach.[5] Now that we at HomeHealth can define our activity levels, our next logical step will be to incorporate it into our budgeting process.

Some examples of how HomeHealth intends to leverage the ABM model for strategic planning, budgeting, and worker compensation follow.

Strategic Planning

- Focus the strategic plan on areas that are most important to customers and/or high cost.
- Obtain organizational commitment to objectives and tactical plans.
- Identify responsible person(s)/team.
- Create an agreed-on timeline.

Budgeting/Job Description and Evaluation

- Define the activity level necessary to support the expected visit, episode, or patient volume.
- Adjust cost of activities inflation and improvement targets.
- Allow modeling based on activities necessary to provide different types of visits or episodes.

At HomeHealth, ABC/M has become an invaluable tool for all process managers. The project leaders say: "We are able to focus on the management of activities and results. We can drive rapid continuous improvements that result in lower costs and improved quality. We can standardize work and develop better measures. Through activity management, we can free up time for additional responsibility. And we can prevent the return to old and ineffective ways of doing things."

EXPERT WRAP-UP
John A. Miller

By today's standards, 19 months to build an ABC model that consisted of only 11 processes, 84 activities, 12 cost centers, and less than 24 cost objects would not be acceptable. It has been almost 10 years since this project was initiated at HomeHealth. Since then, the knowledge base of ABC application and use has grown by a factor of 10. Activity templates and examples are readily available, ABC software has improved significantly, methods for collecting data are faster, ABC/M best practice studies have been conducted, and the experiences of hundreds of ABC implementations have been documented. Undertaken today, an ABC project similar in size, scope, and resources, would be completed in 6 to 9 months.

Like many organizations in the late 1990s, HomeHealth purchased ABM software packages prior to attempting its first pilot. That is getting the cart before the horse, resulting in disappointing results when the ABM software tool did not deliver to the business expectations. More common today are "paper pilots" and the use of ABC design tools, risk assessments, change readiness assessments, and other ABC tools prior to making the software decision.

The way an organization codes and tracks its expenses (resources) greatly impacts the way the ABC model is built. Ten years ago GL systems often were not ABC friendly in the sense that some expenses were accumulated in a single GL account and department rather than distributing the costs as expense items to individual departments that used the resource. For example, some organizations accumulate all benefit costs in a single department, such as Human Resources. Other examples include utility costs, depreciation, and insurance, which are often captured in central cost departments. Assigning these types of GL expenses back to the correct departments before they go into the model greatly simplifies the tracing of resources to activities. Today this is no longer an issue; ABC software vendors have largely designed solutions to this problem and eliminated the off-model spreadsheets common to many ABC models in the past.

As this case illustrates, the variability in the cost for individual activities can be high. For example, the cost of the Make Home

Visit activity for Nursing Admission ranged from a low of $32.23 to a high of $63.29. Presumably these differences reflect differences in the way this activity is performed by individual nurses, or it might reflect differences in the type of home visits. Many ABC systems report the average cost of an activity and do not provide the granularity of information managers often require.

A significant amount of time (eight months) was devoted to the collection and documentation of information. Interviews formed the primary method of gathering activity information. Interviews can be conducted at a high level (e.g., department managers) or at a lower level (e.g., department employees). Other methods of information and data collection include questionnaires, analysis of historical records reports and documents, panels of experts, observation, and group-based techniques. Group-based collection techniques include RapidVision, FastTrack ABM, and Storyboarding; they significantly reduce the time and effort to collect ABC information. In many cases these advanced data collection techniques reduce the collection time from weeks to days.

The debate rages on as to whether ABC is a closed-loop system where all cost must be assigned to activities or cost objects. For HomeHealth, it was the one center in the activity module which included hospital overhead representing expenses that could not logically be assigned to activities. In the cost object module, the Organizational Sustaining Costs could not logically be assigned to cost objects. Today most ABC implementations attempt to include all resources in the cost of activities and objects, such as products and customers. If necessary, it is ok to use simple allocation methods.

It is fair to say that HomeHealth was innovative and far ahead of others in its ability to use an ABC model for what-if scenarios by creating "dummy models" that allowed the company to make changes to actual or budgeted data in order to understand the impact of changes. This capability has been available in most ABC systems only in the last couple of years.

ENDNOTES

1. CAM-I (www.cam-i.org) is an international consortium of manufacturing and service companies, government organizations, consultancies, and academic

and professional bodies that have elected to work cooperatively in a precom-petitive environment to solve management problems and critical business is-sues that are common to the group.

2. Gary Cokins, *Activity-Based Cost Magnagement: An Executive's Guide* (Hoboken, NJ: John Wiley & Sons, Inc., 2001), 3.

3. John Miller, *Implementing Activity-Based Management in Daily Operations* (New York: John Wiley & Sons, Inc., 1996), 36.

4. Robert S. Kaplan and David P. Norton, *The Strategy-Focused Organization* (Boston: Harvard Business School Press, 2001), 366–367.

5. Gary Cokins, *Performance Management: Finding the Missing Pieces (to Close the Intelligence Gap)* (Hoboken, NJ: John Wiley & Sons, Inc., 2004), 132.

4

SUPERDRAFT: ACTIVITY-BASED COSTING/MANAGEMENT AND CUSTOMER PROFITABILITY

Failure is not an option.

—Gene Krantz, former flight director for NASA

FOREWORD

Ashok Vadgama

In today's cost-cutting environment, companies have been successful in cost management and reducing costs by outsourcing, by using supply chain management to manage suppliers and customer, and by reducing the number of employees. This chapter focuses on the customer profitability area, an emerging area in today's marketplace. A lot of benchmarking efforts are under way for understanding the new product introduction costs and for establishing, by simulating and modeling, the impact of their market insertion.

CAM-I has launched a study on customer profitability.[1] Activity-based costing/management (ABC/M) becomes a foundation and an enabler to identify costs and understand the causal impact of the driver data. In this area, the value of data and information is essential. The impact of good information is explained in the book *Data . . . The DNA of Business Intelligence.*[2]

INTRODUCTION

SuperDraft (SD) Corporation, the world's leading check printer, is over 80 years old and generates over $2 billion in annual revenue. The quotation at the beginning of the chapter became a rallying cry as the company determined to build and deploy a sustainable ABC/M system in six months and during a simultaneous SAP implementation.

The urgency was born of competitive necessity. For SuperDraft, understanding customer profitability amid a maturing check market and an intensely competitive pricing environment was essential. At the same time, SuperDraft believed it could improve relationships with its customers by using ABC/M to identify costs along the supply chain and help customers reduce their costs and improve their profitability.

Heightening the urgency was the need to fund a growth strategy to ensure the check-printing company's long-term survival as the U.S. market begins to shift to a more electronically oriented payment system. Via ABC/M, SuperDraft sought to identify ways to maintain and enhance the precious fuel (i.e., profits from SuperDraft's core check business).

Realizing that SAP did not offer the needed ABC/M flexibility, SuperDraft decided to develop a "bolt-on" solution to SAP using leading commercial ABC/M software. The team set out to:

- Define profit by each of SuperDraft's more than 18,000 customers.
- Create a sustainable ABC/M system.
- Build and deploy an ABC/M system in six months.
- Deliver results of major impact, namely information that could strengthen sales strategy in an extremely competitive pricing environment and competitive banking industry.

Given the standards of quality set for the project and other significant changes under way at SuperDraft, including the SAP implementation and restructuring and downsizing, many of the potential partners invited to a special request-for-proposal (RFP) day deemed six months from start to finish impossible. Many also cited the big obstacle of gaining acceptance from senior and middle management and employees and transforming an eight-decade-old manufacturing culture in such a short time. The SuperDraft response was: "We can. We will. We have to." The company was proud to say "We did."

ORGANIZATIONAL ISSUES

Founded in the early 1900s, SuperDraft is the world's largest check printer. As a service to banks and their customers, it prints more than 100 million check orders a year. Although it has ventured into new payment-related areas, such as payment protection services and electronic funds transfer processing, the company still derives more than half of its annual revenues and net income from check-printing services provided to approximately 18,000 U.S. financial services companies (primarily commercial banks) and small-business customers.

Like other manufacturing companies trying to make the transition from the Industrial Age to the Information Age, SuperDraft has sometimes been a victim of its own success. SuperDraft's 80 years of prosperity gave the company no compelling reason to understand its costs in detail. The result was an unwieldy organization (people plus brick-and-mortar infrastructure) and a just-say-yes service philosophy in which the company provided what was essentially customization to each of its thousands of bank customers. In this environment, SuperDraft's cost to serve was close to its cost to produce. The cost system was much like a "Stage II System" as Robert S. Kaplan describes in his book, *Cost & Effect*.[3] Kaplan explains that this type of system satisfies regulatory requirements but "provides poor feedback for learning and improvement."

In the 1990s, things changed for SuperDraft as the company began to witness pressure on its check-printing revenues from the deregulation of the banking industry. At this time, the check market began to mature. The forecast was that it would begin a gradual decline after the year 2000 as other payment options—credit cards, debit cards, smart cards, and online payments—gained market share. This rapid growth of alternative payment methods and the fact that financial institutions were endorsing and funding new payment and business models caused a significant impact to SuperDraft's business (see Exhibit 4.1). As a result, banks continue to squeeze every opportunity for fee income from both their customers and their suppliers.

As pricing pressure and a maturing market began to erode SuperDraft's check-printing revenues, the company needed to reduce costs and increase productivity. It also had to reevaluate its high-touch, high-cost service philosophy and

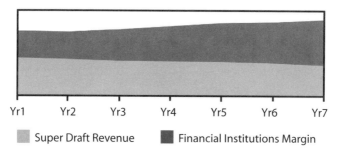

Yr1   Yr2   Yr3   Yr4   Yr5   Yr6   Yr7

Super Draft Revenue   Financial Institutions Margin

Exhibit 4.1 Financial Institutions Continue to Increase Check Order Revenue with Price Increases While Seeking Steeper Discounts

develop a more effective sales strategy in which successful bids would result in profitable business. Also mixed into the equation was that check printing remained—and would remain—a wonderful profit generator for SuperDraft, but it needed to be an even better profit generator to fuel the company's growth strategy and ensure its long-term survival.

New senior management came on board beginning in May 1995 (chief executive officer, executive vice president, and chief financial officer joined over three years in that order) to oversee building a "new" SuperDraft. The top areas of new management's focus were:

- Consolidating operations and infrastructure to improve efficiency and productivity and reduce costs
- Divesting nonstrategic businesses
- Implementing a value-added economic philosophy to calculate the return on any investment in the business and proceed only if the return meets approved targets
- Determining a growth strategy centered on information solutions that help banks and retailers increase their profits and lower their risks in a swiftly changing payment system
- Transforming the corporate culture into one of personal accountability

CASE STUDY

Initial Efforts

According to the Law of the Lid in the book *The 21 Irrefutable Laws of Leadership* "Leadership ability determines a person's level of effectiveness."[4] SuperDraft was lucky to have strong leadership. That leadership would not only determine the project's effectiveness but the organization's effectiveness. As SuperDraft moved to implement SAP, the ABC/M team, led by the director of Customer Profitability, set out with help from a respected consulting firm and on-site technical consulting from its ABC software vendor to build a flexible solution in its ABC package that would link with SAP.

The project scope was very broad: 18,000 customers, 8,700 employees, and hundreds of products and services representing more than $1 billion in annual revenues and $400 million in annual selling, general, and administrative costs.

Given that time was of the essence, a key point about the project staffing is that it was not a "finance" project, developed by and for the bean counters and delivered to the masses with a resounding: "Here. Implement. End of story." To avoid surprises, the project was set up to involve the right people from all levels. It was an inclusive effort, with cross-functional teams consisting of middle managers and others from across the process-driven organization who were challenged to understand the business, develop a better way of operating it, and address the urgent business need to define customer profitability.

Senior management buy-in was attained early in the project, and senior managers participated on the steering committee. Communication was consistent and two-way: bottom up and top down. Training, from ABC/M fundamentals to database modeling, was integrated into the various project phases so there would be no surprises once the system went live.

Project Team

The project team consisted of 40 people at four levels of engagement:

1. **Executive sponsor** (1 member). Provided focus, resources, monitored progress, and resolved high-level issues.
2. **Steering committee** (12 members). Approved the project approach, agreed on priorities, reviewed and approved interim findings, ensured senior management alignment, and approved deliverables.
3. **Project managers** (2 members). Developed methods and plan; were responsible for quality control, issues resolution, leadership, and training.
4. **Field teams** (25 members). Consisted of full and part-time team members responsible for executing the detailed work plan.

Project Description

The project progressed in five phases:

Phase 1: Establishing a Foundation

In Phase 1, SuperDraft identified and confirmed the business issues to be faced. There was a clearly understood base of knowledge and a common focus. During this phase, SuperDraft also created a project team and developed a detailed work plan.

In essence, this was a stage of definition. For example, SuperDraft adopted a supply chain view of its business—SuperDraft Paper Payments Systems—redefining it from a functional (vertical organization) to a process-driven framework (horizontal), which would lend itself to ABC/M (see Exhibit 4.2). As part of defining ABC/M, management determined how it could be linked to a new value-added philosophy or discipline that the company was adopting. Referred to as SuperDraft Value Added (SDVA), this theory is similar to the value-based management/value-added theory other companies have implemented. SuperDraft also defined ABC/M as the enabling system to help the company determine its return on investment (or SDVA) by a particular customer relationship.

In Phase 1, it was agreed that ABC/M was an analytical tool that would provide insight into value-added activities, non–value-added activities, performance improvement ideas, and customer profitability. There was also agreement on the major questions that the project needed to answer:

- Who are our most profitable customers?
- Which practices create win-win or profit-building situations for Super-Draft and its customers?
- What new practices should we adopt?

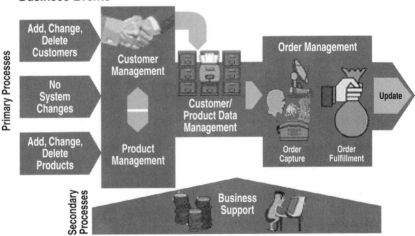

Exhibit 4.2 Process-Driven Framework

- What new products and services should we provide?
- How can we reengineer customer relationships to be more efficient while lowering costs?
- What is our cost to serve, and how does that cost affect customer profitability?

Phase 2: Activity Analysis

In Phase 2, all cost-driving activities and processes were in the SuperDraft Paper Payment Systems. The result was a dictionary of 150 activities. As SuperDraft looked at the business, it also identified process development ideas and opportunities to be explored.

Phase 3: Activity Costs Linked to Cost Objects

Calling a product or a customer a "cost object" may seem insensitive, but it is necessary in the world of ABC/M. In Phase 3, SuperDraft finalized all cost drivers, linked activity costs to cost objects, and raised awareness of key cost drivers through continued training. The result of this phase was ABC/M costs by customer.

Phase 4: Detailed Profitability Analysis

Phase 4 was when the revelations began to occur. With costs now linked to cost objects, SuperDraft validated revenue per cost object, then determined profitability. In this phase, management learned the profitability and SDVA for each of its 18,000 customers.

Phase 5: System Deployment

In Phase 5 (shown in Exhibit 4.3), all of the recommendations were finalized, the process improvements were ranking in order of impotance, and an architecture was developed for a self-sustaining ABC/M system that interfaced with SAP R/3.

Initial Benefits

The SuperDraft project team achieved the primary objectives of understanding profitability and SDVA by customer, identifying and making process improvements, and creating a sustainable ABC/M system (numbers refreshed monthly)

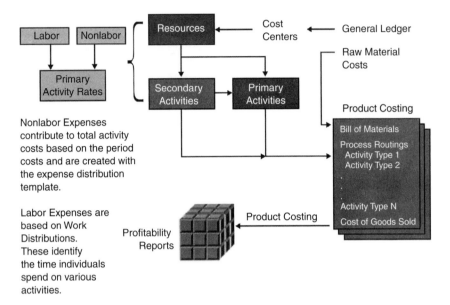

Exhibit 4.3 Final System Data Flow

that interfaces with SAP. The base for choosing a software package was its ability to interface with SAP. A package created by ABC Technologies was chosen to deliver seamless integration between SAP's R/3 and the Oros ABM (now SAS Activity-Based Management) software. SuperDraft was pleased when, in 2002, SAS acquired ABC Technologies. SAS ABM, the next release of the Oros Software, now has extended capabilities for leveraging not only SAP R/3 data but also SAP B/W data and a SAS ABM Adaptor for R/3 with a model-building wizard that can automatically load and build a model.

Sales Strategy/Customer Relationships

With a new understanding of customer profitability (see Exhibit 4.4) and cost drivers, SuperDraft is poised to identify win-win practices in its customer relationships. For instance, check orders submitted via paper order forms are labor intensive and costly compared to orders submitted via SuperDraft's electronic order channel.

ABC/M tells SuperDraft exactly what the cost differences are and enables it to present a supply chain approach to customers, positioning SuperDraft as a partner and establishing the sales personnel as profit-building consultants. This insight

Name	Bank				
Number	0000001				
Market Manager	John Doe				
Account Manager	Jane Doe				
		4Q 2004	% of Revenue	Market Average	National Average
Revenue		$ 7,000,000	100.0%	100.0%	100.0%
Cost of Sales		$ 3,320,000	47.4%	48.0%	47.2%
Gross Margin		$ 3,680,000	52.6%	52.0%	52.8%
Services Provided:					
Customer Management					
Demand Cultivation		514,000	7.3%	7.9%	7.1%
Customer Preparation		302,000	4.3%	4.9%	4.1%
Order Capture					
Order Capture—Teleservice Legacy		640,000	9.1%	9.7%	8.9%
Order Capture—Mail Legacy		540,000	7.7%	7.5%	8.0%
Order Capture—Electronic (ONE)		750,000	10.7%	10.1%	10.5%
Total Services Provided		2,746,000	39.2%	39.8%	39.0%
Net Profit		934,000	13.3%	12.1%	13.7%
Capital Charge		750,000	10.7%	11.3%	10.5%
Deluxe Value Added		$ 184,000	2.6%	0.8%	3.2%

Exhibit 4.4 Customer Activity-Based Profit and Loss Statement

has supported a strategy for migrating banks to the electronic ordering channel, as well as a streamlined paper order process to improve a bank's customer satisfaction levels and reduce SuperDraft's internal costs.

Understanding customer profitability allows SuperDraft greater advantage in bid situations and contract negotiations to make customer relationships more profitable. Business below certain price points may be declined if a customer is unwilling to collaborate with SuperDraft to remove cost along the supply chain. Moreover, SuperDraft considers its new understanding of customer profitability a best practice in its industry that enables the company to submit bids with the confidence that an ensuing contract will be profitable for SuperDraft and the customer.

Initial Lessons Learned

Undoubtedly, the most challenging aspect of this project was the time frame. Super-Draft had to build and install an ABC/M system, gain acceptance, and transform a culture, and do it all during a simultaneous SAP implementation. So how did it do it?

First, SuperDraft invited all potential consultants to a special RFP day to hear the same story from the same source. As SuperDraft communicated its objectives, schedule, and expectations, management emphasized that failure was not an option. "We can, we will, we have to" is what management told its prospective partners.

Several consulting firms declined right away, saying the project—given the quality standards—could not be done so quickly. The consultants who signed on did so with enthusiasm and a can-do winning attitude. The project got off to a great start with everyone aware of and ready to take on a major challenge.

Second, to gain acceptance and transform the just-say-yes service culture, SuperDraft built cross-functional teams, got the right senior managers on board early, and challenged all team members to market ABC/M as it would a product.

As a marketing effort, SuperDraft developed key messages and ready-to-use PC-based presentations that enabled each team member to be a true ambassador for ABC/M. These presentations featured videos of senior management and key leaders speaking about the necessity of ABC/M and urging all employees to support the ABC/M team. As the team members spread the news about ABC/M's ultimate benefits, management energized the employee group of almost 9,000.

As part of gaining acceptance, SuperDraft incorporated training at every possible step in the project to define and deliver the reasons for ABC/M. Both employees and senior managers were trained. Everyone understood ABC/M and participated in what was an inclusive effort.

Finally, to overcome the obstacle of a concurrent SAP implementation, theoretically two models had to be developed—one legacy and one anticipating the new SAP environment. ABC/M actually enhanced the SAP implementation by improving the accuracy of the activity costs and streamlining more than 500 cost-center feeds into SAP and enabling SAP to go live smoothly. The company has been asked many times: "What was the return on investment of your ABC project?" Although it is difficult to articulate in hard dollars, SuperDraft would reply: "What would it be worth to you if you could cut your SAP implementation time in half?"

Initial Next Steps

The main goal of the project was to understand the profitability of the SuperDraft customers. After the project was on track, SuperDraft realized that it would be advantageous to use ABC/M budgeting. Since wrap-up of the initial implementation, SuperDraft has begun to use activity-based budgeting as part of its annual operating plan process, including capital justification initiatives. It is also using ABC/M for forecasting purposes to provide additional information about financial results.

Beyond the budgeting aspect, the team identified that there could be a standardization of services. This new knowledge has aided in standardization services and elimination of those services that provide little or no value to their customers. This standardization removed a significant amount of overhead from SuperDraft's cost structures. Custom services are still offered, but at custom prices. Most important, results from recent customer satisfaction surveys show that service levels are improving. The SuperDraft goal is to provide consistent excellent customer service that customers want while making those services cost effective and efficient to meet shareholder approval.

Current State: Today

The current theme at SuperDraft is "Continuous Improvement and Performance Measurement." Its efforts in benchmarking and trending span internally to departments, locations, production sites. The information is used to justify new business cases and also contract negotiations. SuperDraft's process improvement efforts are supporting the identification of which process will be improved, what processes will be measured, and which key performance indicators (KPIs) can be surfaced in the future on a scorecard or balanced scorecard. One side benefit of the ABC project was channel costing. Understanding its costs of channels, products, and customers will influence the methods SuperDraft uses to acquire new companies and how it creates new marketing programs.

The ABC/M model is also used to evaluate these needs:

- Investment justification
- Make versus buy decisions
- New product and service evaluations
- New equipment evaluations

Next Steps/Future Plans: Today and Beyond

One of the four major deliverables that the ABC/M team set out to provide was results of major impact, namely information that could strengthen sales strategy in an extremely competitive pricing environment and competitive banking industry.

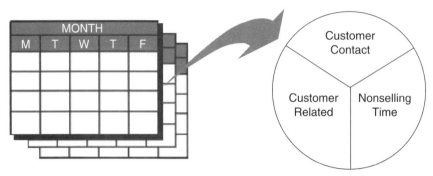

- Where are the opportunities to increase the number of selling hours?
- How can we better focus resources on the right customers?
- What's the financial benefit from decontaminating our sales jobs?
- How can we improve revenue productivity per hour of effort?

Exhibit 4.5 Implications for Sales Effectiveness

The implementation proved that there are often significant opportunities to increase "selling time." Based on recent surveys, less than 40% of a salesperson's time is actually spent on selling activities. SuperDraft is now looking at the implications for improving sales effectiveness (see Exhibit 4.5).

Eight sales management pillars depicted in Exhibit 4.6 encompass the disciplines SuperDraft must master to maximize its ability to grow profitably. Deci-

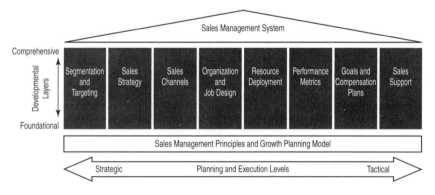

Exhibit 4.6 Sales Process

sions in each pillar may vary over time, to reflect changing business environments. SuperDraft must assess the alignment of each pillar continually to optimize the organization's effectiveness and growth capacity. In the future ABC/M will be used to enhance decisions in all of the pillars.

SUMMARY

There has been an educational/cultural transformation at SuperDraft. This is no small accomplishment. According to Mohan Nair, "Freeloaders resist change." In his book, *Activity-Based Information Systems: An Executive's Guide to Implementation*, Nair says that there are "[p]eople who enjoy the benefits of distorted information and tend not to want change."[5] At SuperDraft, the ABC/M project has blended well with the overall corporate goal of transforming the culture into one of personal accountability. Using formal and informal training, ABC/M is being incorporated into everyday thinking at SuperDraft.

Employees now clearly understand that time is money: What an employee does counts toward the company's costs, SDVA, and bottom line. "We can't charge for that" is a catch phrase understood to be part of an outdated just-say-yes service philosophy that SuperDraft can no longer afford, given market and industry conditions.

The results an ABC/M team can achieve with the proper focus, support, partners, and motivation in a short time frame is amazing. As with mission control bringing *Apollo 13* home safely, SuperDraft had no choice but to succeed. Having accomplished its objectives, the firm is now reaping the benefits that a sustainable ABC/M system can deliver to an organization and its customers.

EXPERT WRAP-UP

Ashok Vadgama

No software today can address all the issues. At companies I have worked for, we built a framework that encompassed use of software from many different vendors. The combination of these tools provided the necessary business intelligence.

The whole notion of change adaptation and learning is not easy to implement in a sustaining organization. Corporations tend to be complacent as their market value is increasing and lose their long-term vision, as occurred with SuperDraft. Bringing senior management on board early in the implementation is one of the best approaches used here. Doing this not only provided focus with organizational issues, but it also made implementation easier, as there was up-front senior management buy-in. "Transforming the corporate culture into one of personal accountability" is a great goal.

The logic of product numbering is also missing from the Super-Draft example, as are a good repository of product life cycle codes and an authorization approach to who makes updates and changes. Project scope of 18,000 customers, 8,700 employees, and hundreds of products and services representing $1 billion of products made project implementation more complex. The team took a good approach in identifying that this is not a "finance" project. At CAM-I, we understand that 80% of the data resides in operations. Our Target Costing and Cost Measurement projects have been successful because we understand this up front.

The whole notion of having a good cross-functional project team makes it easier to be successful in project implementation. If you have a good marketing plan, you do not have to sell frantically; likewise, a good project team makes the approach less cumbersome. The framework used in this example is good.

The five phases of approach is in line with the way most companies approach the CAM-I cross (see Exhibit 4.7) from the GL approach to output. Profitability analysis hence becomes one output termed "cost objects."

In an enterprise system implementation, it is recommended that two models be developed with a road map for integration. Doing this enables the company to identify the data and information thread from the perspective of what systems of record need to be retired, created, or collapsed.

Finally, coupled with strategic benchmarking, the theme of "Continuous Improvement and Performance Measurement" will be the differentiating factor for SuperDraft.

ENDNOTES

1. CAM-I (www.cam-i.org) is an international consortium of manufacturing and service companies, government organizations, consultancies, and academic and professional bodies that have elected to work cooperatively in a precom-

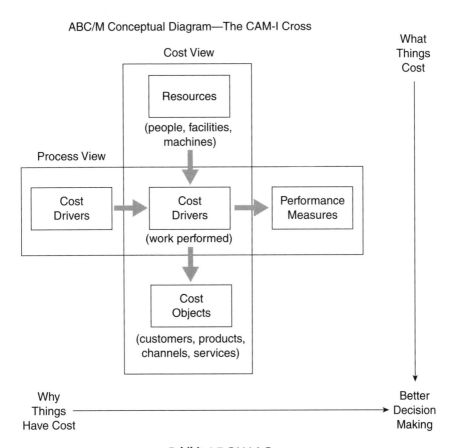

ABC/M Conceptual Diagram—The CAM-I Cross

Exhibit 4.7 CAM-I Cross

Source: Derived from the Consortium of Advanced Management—International (CAM-I).

petitive environment to solve management problems and critical business issues that are common to the group.

2. Ashok G. Vadgama and Wayne McCleve, *DATA . . . The DNA of Business Intelligence* (Martinsville, IN: Bookman Publishing, 2004)

3. Robert S. Kaplan and Robin Cooper, *Cost and Effect* (Boston, MA: Harvard Business School Press, 1998), 13–18.

4. John C. Maxwell, *The 21 Irrefutable Laws of Leadership* (Nashville, TN: Thomas Nelson Publishers, 1998), 1.

5. Mohan Nair, *Activity-Based Information Systems: An Executive's Guide to Implementation* (New York, NY: John Wiley & Sons, Inc., 1999), 142.

5

CANARUS ARMED FORCES: PERFORMANCE MANAGEMENT— THE NEW AMMUNITION

Creativity involves breaking out of established patterns in order to look at things in a different way.

—Edward de Bono

FOREWORD

Jonathan Hornby

At SAS we use a five-step information evolution model to describe how an organization consumes information. Consider the Canarusian Armed Forces, which are approaching level 3. The five levels are:

1. **Operate.** Individuals using technology/information in a silo of 1.
2. **Consolidate.** Teams sharing information among themselves, but still in a silo with little or no sharing across teams.
3. **Integrate.** Information shared across entire organization with complete transparency.
4. **Optimize.** Organization uses information to improve processes and activities to drive greater efficiency and effectiveness.
5. **Innovation.** Organization constantly innovates and through extensive use of analytics can predict what will succeed or fail with a high degree of confidence.

In this case study, you can see the evolution taking hold. At first, all organizations say they are different and need something specific to their cause. As information flows they realize that much is "common" and can be used across Canarus. The key is to translate information into terms individuals can understand. These terms can then be mapped through "families" to provide a powerful dictionary that allows management to roll up results consistently across the organization. Activity-based management (ABM) is a great way to create such focus: It talks about activities people do and measurements they understand. Mapping activities into families provides an excellent way to compare one group to another and identify patterns that can explain differences. Doing so also helps with ensuring alignment.

As the Canarusian Armed Forces get to level 3, they begin to see areas that can be improved—some may have already tackled it so "time to results" can be fast. With "transparency," they will be propelled to change the way they act—doing more for less and improving consistency and effectiveness. They have already identified the need to look beyond financials, incorporating a balanced scorecard—this is essential. There are many activities that influence the bottom line. Organizations need to understand the cause-and-effect nature of how business is conducted, from people to technology, process to outcome, and ultimately bottom line cost. In the expert wrap-up, I talk more about where the Canarusian Armed Forces should go next with more information on levels 4 and 5.

INTRODUCTION

Faced with important budgetary reductions, new government reporting regulations, the introduction of business planning, and an increased requirement to render managers and military leaders at all levels accountable, the land component of the Canarusian Armed Forces recognized its need for modern management tools. An integrated management environment (IME) proved to be the way of the future. The IME would be formed of many components including strategic direction, business planning, performance measurement, risk assessment, standards of service, and activity-based costing/management (ABC/M) that would ultimately provide an Executive Information System (EIS). The IME was designed to assist managers and leaders at all levels in fulfilling their role in accomplishing the Canarusian Armed Forces mission, which is to generate multipurpose combat-capable forces (see Exhibit 5.1).

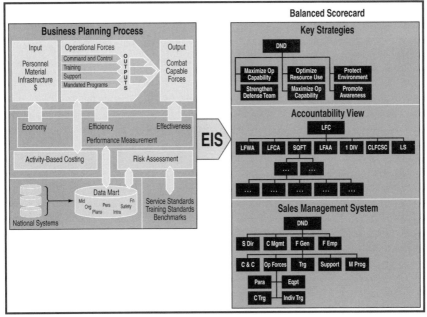

Oversight and Control Framework

Exhibit 5.1 Integrated Management Environment

ORGANIZATIONAL ISSUES

To understand the magnitude of the project, it is necessary to provide a quick overview of the organization. Located in the nation's capital, the Chief of Land Staff, who receives assistance from several directors, commands the Canarusian Armed Forces. The Armed Forces is then divided in four Geographical Area Headquarters (HQs) and one Canarusian Division Headquarters. Each Area HQ commands all the Armed Forces elements in its respective area and is made up of the Area Support Group including several support units, regular and reserve operational forces, and training centers. This represents about 40,000 people, civilian and military, dispersed from coast to coast. The five capacities into which the Armed Forces is divided are: Operational Forces (Regular and Reserve), Support, Training, Command and Control, and Mandated Programs.

Because the activities of all these capacities differ greatly, it was determined that a different model would be required for each of them (except for Mandated Programs, which would be shown as an activity under each model). The first capacity, the Operational Force, was split into two models to reflect the differences in the reserve and regular forces.

CASE STUDY

Initial Efforts

At the Canarus Department of National Defense (DND), activity-based costing (ABC) is highly favored as it is considered to be superior to traditional costing methodologies for generating accurate information for decision support and management control. Organizations putting in place an ABC capability are normally driven by two primary objectives:

1. To obtain more accurate data on product, process and service costs
2. To identify the relative costs of activities and the reason those activities are undertaken

DND, along with all other federal departments and agencies, is required to align with the federal government's planning, reporting, and accountability structure and put in place an accrual accounting capability. In order to meet these requirements, and because of a range of limitations of a 13-year-old system, it was recognized that the existing departmental financial information system was not up to the challenge.

Accordingly, a new financial and managerial accounting system, based upon R/3 software supplied by SAP, is being tailored to meet DND's needs, with two major components. A financial accounting capability with an external focus is the primary component; it will be put in place in order to capture transactions, provide expenditure reporting information, support departmental cash management, and provide a data source for the second component, the more internally focused departmental managerial accounting component. This second component is linked with the financial accounting side of the system, as it is a primary consumer of financial accounting information for decision support and ABC initiatives at the strategic and tactical levels.

Because it was already decided that the IME was to be the way of the future, DND had many significant challenges:

- Create ABC models to support business planning.
- Ensure the ABC models are fundamental part of the IME.
- Create a scorecard-driven system that could also be used for reengineering and continuous improvement.
- Tie the ABC models into the financial and managerial accounting system.

Pilot Phase

A pilot project was conducted in order to prove the IME concept. The pilot was conclusive, and the concept was fully endorsed by the Commander of the Armed Forces. Responsibility for the ABC/M component of the project was given to the Armed Forces Comptroller. Faced with this challenge, the Armed Forces Comptroller established this aim for the ABC/M component: to provide an integrated cost and performance management system to users of business planning at all levels, for all capacities, and for all Land Forces geographical areas, in order to meet the forecasting and reporting requirements of Strategic Operations and Resource Planning.

This meant that every component of the Armed Forces was going to be modeled and set up to use ABC. It also meant that the ABC tool had to be developed to assist managers and leaders at all levels of the organization. Another key aspect was that once implemented, the ABC tool would have to be sustained to provide continuous feedback to users. In addition, the system would have to be integrated to provide costing information not only for support activities but also for the Armed Forces core capability, the operational force. To achieve this goal, it was decided that the ABC/M information must be tied directly to a balanced scorecard.

This represented a major cultural shift for the Canarusian Armed Forces. Historically, the Armed Forces managed its budget allocation through baseline budgeting, focused on expenses and resources. The introduction of business planning shifted the focus from resource and expense management to results and activity management. However, the management system of that time was not tailored to provide activity information, making it very difficult for military leaders to prepare business plans. The pressing need for ABC was clearly recognized. The selection of the software tool was very important; it had to facilitate data gathering and data upload; most important, it had to be user friendly. Also, although the information that needed to be captured existed, most of it had never been systematically gathered in an electronic format. After careful evaluation, the Armed Forces selected ABC Technologies' (now part of SAS) Oros Software (now called SAS Activity-Based Management).

Implementation Phase

Project Team

An important part of this implementation was the cross-functional team assembled for the pilot, the implementation, and the long-term strategy. The team consisted of 11 individuals dedicating at least 25% of their time to ABM support teams. The inclusion of theses support teams was critical to ensure that all of the data integration was consistent.

The main ABM team (number of individuals in parenthesis) consisted of:

- Comptroller (1)
- Advisor (1)
- Project Director (1)
- Project Office (3)
- Area ABC Coordinators (4)
- IME Coordinator (1)

The support teams consisted of:

- Land and Staff Business Process Team
- Land and Staff Project Management Team
- Data Team
- Financial and Managerial Accounting System Team (SAP)

Project Timeline/Phases of Implementation

The financial and managerial accounting system ABC capability will be delivered in two phases. The Phase I ABC capability will be activated concurrently with the transition from using the current system to capture transactions to adoption of the new financial accounting system. This strategic-level ABC capability will be focused on satisfying the reporting requirement for Level 0 business plans. The more tactical level, Phase II ABC capability, was started up two years later with support for all levels of the business planning process. Exhibit 5.2 illustrates how the corporate ABC capability will fit within the financial reporting structure.

Planning and Design

After establishing the aim of the ABC project, groups of military experts for each of the capacities were formed. With the assistance of consultants, they developed

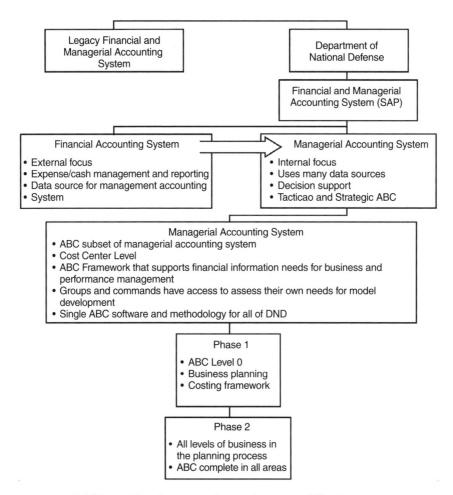

Exhibit 5.2 Planning, Reporting, and Accountability Structure

the ABC models for these capacities: Support, Operational Force Regular, Training, and Command and Control. Once satisfied with this first iteration of the models, the next step was to visit the different sites across Canarus to collect data from previous years. This step further validated the appropriateness of the models and all of the components, mainly the links and the drivers. Using a six-step implementation process over a nine-month period, data were collected and models were populated and documented for all Regular Force Brigade Units, two Area support groups plus one major Base, and one training center. A team of six consultants and three full-time staff members accomplished this.

Six-step implementation process included:

1. Develop universal model,
2. Populate one instance (pilot).
3. Validate and document model.
4. Implement remaining sites.
5. Show costing results.
6. Implement and sustain.

Support

As outlined in the description of the ABC/M team, DND hired four permanent ABC area coordinator positions responsible for all aspects of ABC. These items include but are not limited to training, trouble shooting, advice, input, and system design.

Initial Benefits

In his book *Activity-Based Cost Management: An Executives Guide*, Gary Cokins describes how difficult it is to relate the benefits of an ABM system as a return on investment (ROI). "Some organizations have strict rules for accepting proposals to invest and spend money on equipment and projects . . . . Organizations that are skeptical of ABC/M regularly ask, 'What is the ROI on ABC/M?' My blunt reply from what I have learned is that it is not possible to calculate ROI on ABC/M."[1]

With Conkins's comment in mind DND wanted to focus on its initial benefits in terms of the goals of the project, to create ABC models to support business planning and to generate multipurpose combat capable forces.

Initial Lessons Learned

The most important aspect of the Armed Forces's approach was to have standard models for each capacity. The activities had to be detailed enough so that they could serve the lowest levels of management, while also being broad enough in order to be identical and appropriate across Canarus for a given capacity. It was found that people working within a given work team had developed a strong sense of being unique; they had to be convinced to overcome this attitude. Education was the key, stressing the required shift in management behavior from resources, organizations, and expenses to activities and results. Once people understood that activities were what they should be managing, they also understood that the activities were the same across Canarus no matter who performed them. The importance of maintaining standard models across a given capacity had to be emphasized, and a universal ABC model for a capacity enabled an organization in one part of the country to benchmark itself against another elsewhere. In addition, it facilitated upstream roll-out of the results to assist in strategic decision making.

The second lesson learned was directly related to the implementation scope. After model development, the project tackled multiple organizations to capture data. Similar yet different comments and requests for changes from the various locations providing data were received. These comments often led to changes in the model and sometimes required the team to go back to a person who had already provided data. Changing the model during data collection greatly lengthened the process. Due to turnover in personnel or lack of records in the format now required, it was difficult to collect antiquated information. In an effort to cope with these issues, estimates and budget figures were collected, rather than the antiquated information. By proceeding in this fashion, the Second Area Support Group (75 processes and subprocesses, over 350 activities, supporting around 15,000 people) was implemented in two months as opposed to five months for the First Area. Once a site was actually faced with the effort of gathering data, the amount of scrutiny of the models and the level of interest in how the information would be used went up a great deal. The increased visibility allowed the Armed Forces to accomplish the goals of model validation and education of managers/ leaders.

From the beginning of the project, one of the most important success factors was the elaboration of a clear aim for the ABC implementation. Specifically, ABC had to assist in the formulation of the business plan; therefore, each model was structured to provide answers to business planning questions. DND found that models could provide information to meet some of these questions. Furthermore, proper analysis and interpretation would be required to support these secondary information needs.

Obtaining the buy-in of higher management was a daunting task, but essential in order to produce a good marketing strategy. Once unconditional support from higher levels was obtained, the next challenge was to convince lower-level managers of the value of the system. The lower echelons were important because they would provide the raw data for the models and ensure protection against corrupted data. Benefits and results of prior data collection efforts were identified, and all staff members understood the importance of their input to obtaining the results.

For the Armed Forces, a key issue was developing the data collection strategy from the start. Doing this involved deciding how data would be gathered and which tool is best suited to do this. Although having automated links to other systems may have been the ideal solution, interim mechanisms had to be found that would both meet validation objectives and still allow the system to be sustained after the consultants left the project.

SUMMARY

In short, the key lessons learned that should be applicable to any ABC implementation in a service or public organization are:

- Have a well-defined aim for implementing ABC.
- Have a good pilot to validate the model.
- An experienced and qualified implementation team is required.
- Employ proven conventions from the start.
- Show results early in the process.
- Use a well-thought-out data collection strategy and tool.
- Populate one site at a time instead of tackling many organizations concurrently.
- Ensure consultants have extensive knowledge of the software or make good use of your software provider expertise.

Initial Next Steps

Immediately after the first implementation with the Land and Staff went through a series of meetings to determine the direction of the ABC and performance management program. The result of those meetings was to outline six steps needed to ensure long-term success.

1. Implement a management-training package on all aspects of the new integrated management environment philosophy.
2. Continue integration with the IME and create a long-term sustainable structure.
3. Complete population of all sites. Model implementation continued and was expected to be completed for all Armed Forces entities on schedule within the year.

4. Review the data collection tool. The first results of data collection are now available to the originating entities and will be analyzed by all levels in order to further validate the models.

5. Consider implementation of full costing and reciprocal costing

6. Enhance costing information used for planning and budgeting by incorporating long term forecasts, evaluating resource capacity requirements and comparing actual and standard activity costs.

Current State: Today

DND is well on its way to accomplishing the goals and next steps outlined by the pilot project and first successful implementation.

In response to a need for a management training package, a three-day course was developed. Its aim was to provide a basic understanding of ABC principles, of how to develop an ABC model, of how to implement an ABC/M system, and of how to use such a system.

The course consists of these modules:

- The ABC Approach to Costing
- Link to Business Planning
- Implementation of an ABC system
- Development of an ABC Model
- Activity-Based Management and Performance Measurement

A second course designed to be more intense look at the issues surrounding BPM was also created. Over the course of a week, managers will become familiar with the business planning process and the content of a DND business plan and its supporting elements, with the goal of better enabling managers to meet future challenges in resource management. The course also provides an understanding of performance measurement and ABC/M.

The course consists of these modules:

- Business Planning
  - Business Planning Process
    - Strategic Planning (mission, vision, environmental analysis, goals)
    - Balanced Scorecard
    - Planning Structure Definition
    - Annual Objectives Setting and Activity Planning

- Activity-Based Costing
  - Resource Requirements
  - ABC Modeling
  - Activity-Based Management
- Performance Measurement
  - Performance Measurement Framework
  - Performance Measurement Model
  - Benchmarking
- Business Plan Publishing

There are also courses in business case analysis, interview workshops, leadership development, business planning/performance measurement, strategic planning, business process reengineering, and small-group facilitation.

Research in the book *The Strategy-Focused Organization* indicates that less than 5% of the typical workforce understands their organization's strategy.[2] DND is continuing to integrate the ABM data into the IME to create a long-term structure that can be sustained. By linking to the balanced scorecard in the IME, employees understand the key strategies and can have both accountability and a process view of the information.

According to Gary Cokins, "The increased flexibility from having immediate activity-to-activity assignments has met some resistance. Some people simply do not want to make the extra effort."[3] DND believed it would realize an increased accuracy of the system by accounting for shared services with activity-to-activity assignments. Currently all models are being redesigned to accommodate a shared service approach.

Next Steps/Future Plans: Today and Beyond

The Activity-Based Management Project was undertaken in fiscal year 2003–2004 to implement an integrated ABM approach in order to plan resource requirements, establish budgets, monitor the actual use of resources, and align workload requirements with available resources.

The challenge of using performance management to drive strategic change is forcing standard performance management tools to expand across the lines of traditional business intelligence. With the IME in place to provide a steady communication tool and the implementation of the activity-based planning and budgeting system, Superannuation, Pension Transition, and Client Services Sector DND believes it has a performance management system it can leverage for years to come.

EXPERT WRAP-UP

Jonathan Hornby

The Canarusian Armed Forces are approaching level 3. Everything looks rosy, the path seems clear. But are they wearing rose-tinted spectacles? There is a danger at level 4. With the clarity of information, there is a temptation to strip out cost and flexibility to deliver an optimal operating unit. But question "Optimal to what?" remains. Reality relates to what is optimal to the current situation. This means in the short term, you will see massive improvement, but as Murphy's Law kicks in, the Canarusian Armed Forces will recognize that they could have potentially:

• Stripped out too many people

• Not accounted for the unexpected within processes or activity

• Not left sufficient funding to deal with the unexpected

The unexpected could be both positive and negative. We all have stories about negative situations that arise: We go into firefighting mode; lose time, money, and confidence; and invariably make mistakes as we struggle to overcome the obstacles in our path. Unfortunately, if we have stripped ourselves to the minimum, we often do not even notice the positive opportunities that arise. In general business, that means we could lose competitive advantage. In the armed forces, it could ultimately lead to unnecessary loss of life through lack of investment at the right time.

At level 4 then, an organization must begin to exert more rigorous efforts at understanding and predicting risk. If it can do this, it can put mitigation strategies into place that can kick in immediately for fast and smooth remediation or exploitation. The challenge is to think beyond the obvious. Joel Barker, a prominent author and advisor on strategy, talks about "strategic implications."[4] Think of an outcome, then ask: "What are the implications?" Do this three layers deep—that is, think through the implications of your implications. Thinking through the future provides an opportunity to construct a great "preplan." Once the preplan is in place, the emphasis turns to monitoring and detecting outcomes, analyzing the data to better understand why events happened and what could happen next.

The knowledge gained at level 4 provides a solid platform for tackling innovation. Everyone has heard the phrase "innovate or die." The same holds true for the armed forces. They cannot go into battle and merely replay historic maneuvers; if they do, their enemy will know what to expect and adjust their strategy accordingly. At level 5, an organization has complete focus, alignment, and agility to act. It understands the probabilities of success and can move resources to meet demand ahead of time to ensure success at everything it does. Change becomes a way of life, and the organization adopts it daily.

Unfortunately, you cannot jump straight from level 1 to 5. You have to live each step and learn. Communication is the key—support from the top and clarity and alignment on what we must do and why. If we can understand this, level 5 can be a reality for all.

ENDNOTES

1. Gary Cokins, *Activity-Based Cost Management: An Executive's Guide* (Hoboken, NJ: John Wiley & Sons, Inc., 2001), 357–358.
2. Robert S. Kaplan and David P. Norton, *The Strategy-Focused Organization* (Boston: Harvard Business School Press, 2001), 215.
3. Cokins, *Activity-Based Cost Management: An Executive's Guide*, p. 54.
4. Joel A. Barker, *Future Edge: Discovering the New Paradigms of Success* (New York: William A. Morrow, 1992).

6

STANDARD LOAN: INTEREST IN ACTIVITY-BASED COSTING RATES HIGH

Drive thy business or it will drive thee.

—Benjamin Franklin

FOREWORD

John Antos

The most successful activity-based costing/management (ABC/M) implementations achieve a goal that all or most of senior management supports, especially the president. It has been 20 years since Jim Brimson started the CAM-I Cost Management section that created activity-based costing (ABC).[1] A great deal has been learned over those 20 years. We have all learned from our failures as well as our successes.

This case study exemplifies one of the more successful and sustaining ABC implementations. Some of the reasons for its sustainability are:

- This organization had senior management support from the top, including the chief financial officer, controller, treasurer, and president of operations. They were transitioning from a government-type organization to a private enterprise. They knew the cost management information would not serve them well in the more competitive publicly traded environment.

- The treasurer and a director invested time in learning about ABC/M by attending a two-day public ABM for Services seminar.

- They assigned a very competent team to work with an outside consultant. Some organizations select people who are available to serve on these types of projects. This organization selected a top-notch internal implementation team.

- They selected a pilot site where the manager was very open to better understanding her costs.
- They involved marketing, who would use this information for making decisions.
- They involved people from multiple locations to agree on common activities that could be used for benchmarking.
- They selected a tool called Oros (now SAS Activity-Based Management) to ensure that it would be easier to crunch the numbers.
- They invested in training for the ABC/Oros internal team so they would not be dependent on the ABC software vendor.
- The consultant transferred the information to the team so that after a couple of locations the team was able to finish building ABC models at the new locations.
- They issued ABC reports on a regular basis so all managers would realize that this information was here to stay and was going to be used by senior management.

INTRODUCTION

Standard Loan is the nation's leading provider of financial services for postsecondary education needs and the country's largest provider of funding for education loans. Standard Loan was chartered by Congress as a for-profit corporation in 1972 to provide a national secondary market for student loans. It is a stockholder-owned Fortune 100 Company with approximately $100 billion in assets. ABC was implemented at Standard Loan's six service centers throughout the country.

Standard Loan decided that the scope of the initial ABC implementation should be:

- Solving management problems and priorities
- Achieving common activity definitions across the organization to benchmark activities across locations
- Providing a better understanding of costs across multiple dimensions

ORGANIZATIONAL ISSUES

Senior management at Standard Loan felt the need to implement ABC with the initial focus on costing and pricing information. Further, management decided to pursue ABM's improvement components at some point in the future. Once senior management committed to the ABC pilot, the implementation went very quickly. Cost objects were determined and refined. The consultants then presented an overview of ABC to the top management at Standard Loan's Texas servicing center and shared their experiences with a variety of other organizations to obtain their buy-in. Finally, prior to the start of the ABC implementation, Senior Management sent a letter to the staff outlining their support and the importance of the project.

CASE STUDY

Initial Efforts/Pilot Phase

The initial pilot began at the Texas serving center, with the Director of Finance and Accounting managing the overall ABC project. The ABC team included three other Standard Loan employees and a world-leading consulting group. The goal was to transfer knowledge as quickly as possible from the consultants to Standard Loan.

The consultants initially facilitated two workshops for each of several departments. These workshops were attended by a cross-section of employees including directors, managers, supervisors, and line staff. In Workshop 1, a brief overview of ABC project was given to explain the need for better costing information. In addition, the activities were defined, activity dictionaries were created, and time survey templates as well as volume drivers were discussed.

As a rule, organizations will have more activities in their model when they focus on using activities for improvement. If the focus of the organization is better costing, it will tend to have fewer activities. In the case of Standard Loan, the goal was to accomplish both at the same time. The consultants encouraged the employees to define five to ten activities. Later, similar and/or small-dollar activities were summarized into cost pools in order to minimize the tracing of activities to cost objects. This approach of defining more activities to meet future performance improvement objectives helped obtain buy-in.

In Workshop 1, the consultants discussed various ways the departments could collect times for each activity. Some departments asked employees to think about their activities and make an educated guess on how much time they spent on each activity. This approach made the most sense for departments whose activities change throughout the year. For example, at calendar-year organizations, the annual close of accounting departments is in the first quarter; budgeting is in the fall; and special projects are in the summer. Doing a time study for two weeks would not provide much information. Other departments (e.g., phone centers) did a time study to track the frequency and time for different types of calls.

In Workshop 2, the consultants focused on output measure volumes, cost objects, and followed up on the completed activity dictionaries and time surveys. Activity volumes for 1996 were collected from various reports or were estimated based on current volume. The goal was to develop an approach for better costing rather than to obtain perfect numbers. If staff from various locations agreed that this approach made sense, systems would be set up in the future to collect the output volumes more accurately. Group members did not want to spend time trying to guess volumes only to find that they may want to collect different types of volumes in the future.

After the consultants facilitated early workshops, they observed the Standard Loan ABC team's workshops. The consultants shared their experiences with other organizations during these workshops and offered suggestions to Standard Loan facilitators after each workshop. Next, the Standard Loan ABC team facilitated workshops without the consultants for the remaining departments in the ABC pilot. Standard Loan determined that its initial cost objects were (see Exhibit 6.1):

For Servicing

- Loan programs (e.g., law, MBA, subsidized)
- Loan status (e.g., in school, current, delinquent)
- Loan source (i.e., originated, converted)

For Acquisition Methods

- Originations (e.g., application processing, disbursements)
- Conversions (e.g., note exam, load loan)

The initial model was built in Microsoft Excel until ABC software was selected. Standard Loan felt Oros would best meet its needs. With the help of the software vendor's client services, the Oros model's multidimensionality was expanded. When the ABM model was originally designed, no one realized how important it

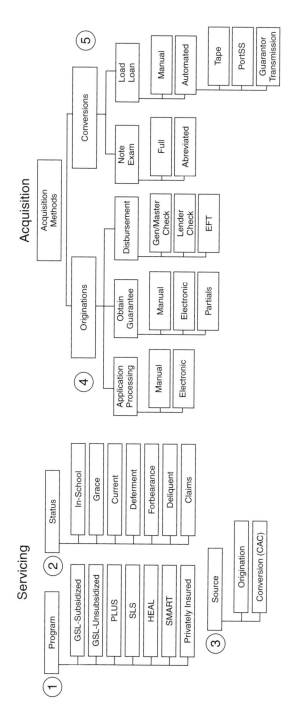

Exhibit 6.1 Activity-Based Costing Objects

99

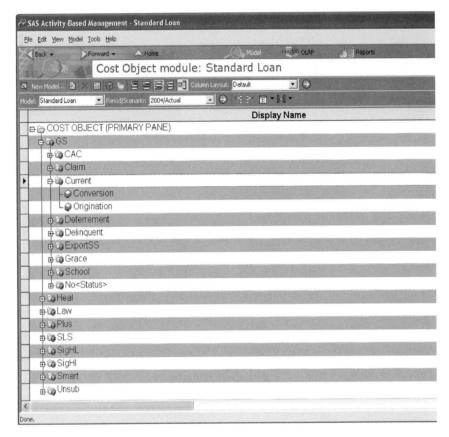

Exhibit 6.2 Model Base Dimensional Structure Program by Status by Source

would be to be able to analyze multiple dimensions (see Exhibit 6.2). Doing so turned out to be critical to achieve the Standard Loan objectives for costing loan programs, status, and source. This ability to slice, dice, and analyze these dimensions in any order proved the most valuable to the ABC Team (see Exhibit 6.3).

A presentation was made to top management and the chief financial officer. After giving positive feedback on the initial pilot, they approved completion of ABC at the Texas servicing center and rollout at all servicing centers on an accelerated schedule. The initial goal was to implement ABC at all six centers in time for the budget.

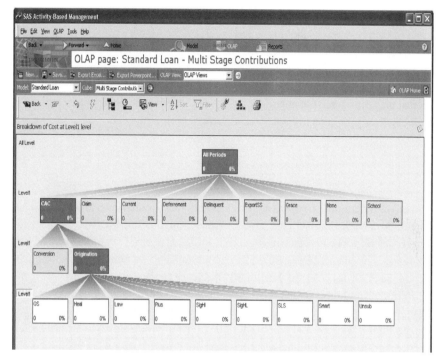

Exhibit 6.3 Dimensional Analysis Status by Source by Program

ABC Rollout Phase

The next step, before ABC rollout to all of Standard Loan's servicing centers, was to obtain consensus on activity definitions. Standard Loan has cross-functional teams that represent a single area (e.g., claims). These functional teams discussed the activity definitions compiled at Texas for their respective areas either during regularly scheduled meetings or by conference calls. As you might guess, some groups made only minor modifications to the definitions created at the Texas servicing center and quickly achieved agreement. Other groups made changes to activity definitions and were challenged when developing common definitions.

The focus of these discussions should always be on the activity and not on how a location performs the activity. If people are arguing that they perform the activity differently than another location, you may make the activity definition more broad. Defining the activity definitions at a higher level reduces the likelihood of people arguing about how they perform the activity.

The facilitators should stress that the focus of benchmarking is to learn from each other. The facilitators need to remind the managers that they are not competing with one another; instead, they are competing with other organizations. Senior management must also stress this sharing of information so the competition between locations does not interfere with the learning process.

Project Team

The cross-functional group sponsor was usually one of the center managers. That person became the contact person for obtaining agreement on activity definitions. The Texas pilot became the starting point for discussions. Deadlines were set for obtaining agreements. The goal was to maintain static definitions for a particular period, such as one year, to benchmark and learn from each other. However, the definitions would be dynamic overall. They would change as the processes changed. The dictionary was all-inclusive and included activities, tasks, customers, input, outputs, and output measures. The approach for ABC rollout to all of Standard Loan's servicing centers was refined based on the feedback received from the pilot groups. A presentation was made on ABC to all the directors, managers, and key supervisors in one center-wide meeting. Because the consultants had been transferring knowledge to the Standard Loan ABC team, some of these presentations were made by the Standard Loan team. The consultants worked with the team to provide a checklist for the facilitators. The consultants' expertise was utilized as needed.

Planning and Design

Some initial workshops were conducted by the consultant using a new format. After a couple of workshops at a center, the ABC team and the center staff facilitated the remaining workshops. Only one workshop per department was conducted. This reduction to only one workshop was made possible because the functional groups agreed on activities and activity definitions.

It was agreed up front that there would be two common activities for each department: manage department and train employees. This would give senior management and center management insights into the relationship between training and productivity as well as the amount of management and productivity. Some centers felt that more supervision created greater productivity, justifying the additional expense. ABC information would help them determine the cost benefit trade-offs for different levels of training and management.

During the ABC rollout for the other centers, data were collected on a quarterly basis instead of a full year. Performing time analysis for a shorter and more recent time period would improve the credibility of the numbers. This approach would better cost current processes.

The model was refined by Standard Loan's staff with review performed by the consultant. After the model was finalized, preliminary results were prepared. Key outputs were activity costs as well as expenses assigned to cost objects. Activity cost will mainly help to improve/manage the departments more efficiently and effectively than cost objects, which would be utilized for better costing/pricing.

Future models will incorporate subactivities into the ABC analysis. For example, the activity "process application" will be subdivided into "process manual application" and "process electronic application." This will give Standard Loan insights into how much it costs to process applications with different schools and/or financial institutions.

It is important to stress that sometimes an organization performs work in a certain way to satisfy customer demands. In some cases, an automated process actually may take longer than a manual process. It is important not to steer people to an answer while performing activity analysis, even if the answer is different from what senior management might expect. It is important to find out the truth and decide what you need to do differently.

Standard Loan created three servicing profit dimensions: program, status, and source for overlapping cost objects. In the profit dimension for loan programs, the highest level consists of the different types of loan programs offered—for instance, GSL (Stafford Subsidized), HEAL (physicians), Law (attorneys), and so on. The second level consists of loan status (e.g., claim, current, deferment). The third level consists of the loan source (i.e., a converted loan or an originated loan). "Source" is simply whether Standard Loan purchased the loan from someone else and converted it onto its system or whether it originates the loan on its system for another owner.

These different dimensions become very insightful for different types of questions. For example, with the profit dimension of program, Standard Loan can now determine the total cost and profitability of a particular type of loan program. If it is determined that a certain program is not profitable, Standard Loan's management can make appropriate decisions.

Standard Loan can also determine the cost of a loan in different status. Therefore, if the economy changes and more loans go into delinquent or claim status, the change in cost due to shifting of loans from current to delinquent or claim status can be determined. Note that details for each servicing center can also be obtained from the ABC model.

Profitability can be analyzed at the highest level and consists of all types of loans. The second level consists of the loan program, and the third level consists of the loan source. Standard Loan can look at the various loan statuses across the entire loan portfolio and determine if the entire portfolio is shifting loan status. It is critical to be able to drill down and analyze profit by loan program to determine if the shifting in loan status is a function of the loan program or a function of the entire portfolio. This information can be drilled down further to determine if the shift in status affects the loans purchased and converted onto the system or the ones originated by Standard Loan. For loan source profitability, the highest level consists of the different types of loan sources. The second level consists of the loan program, and the third level consists of the loan status. Standard Loan can look at its loan sources across the entire loan portfolio and determine the unit cost of loans that are originated versus loans that are converted. The information can be drilled down by loan program, by status of the entire portfolio, or by converted or originated loans. The profit dimensions can drill down further to determine if the shift in costs for converted costs versus originated costs is a function of changing status for a particular loan program. Remember that in a multidimensional environment, creating different reports and drill-downs to analyze profit takes only seconds to set up and calculate. The tough part is collecting the data to populate the different dimensions. For example, Standard Loan had to collect the number of converted loans that are HEAL loans and are in delinquent status. The next step would be to weigh that data when different programs take different amounts of time to perform an activity. Data collection for multidimensional models can be difficult and time consuming, as there usually is a need for sampling.

Initial Next Steps/Lessons Learned

Upon completion of the ABC, Standard Loan published a number of different lessons to the organization. Upon reviewing them, the team proposed seven enhancements to management. During future update cycles, these enhancements will be folded into the system.

1. Refine the ABC model to better segregate support cost.
2. Continue collecting quarterly data, which are critical because of the seasonality of the business.

3. Identify common data collection sources for each servicing center.

4. Explore activity-based budgeting for future budgets.

5. Move from activity-based costing to activity-based management.

6. Explore additional cost objects, such as base versus premium servicing, leader complexity, and guarantor complexity.

7. Roll out ABC for other functions.

Postimplementation Reporting Enhancements

After the initial six-month project, there was a push to transition to a monthly reporting structure and restructure the model. Finally, after the transition, the team would begin electronically distributing ABC reports to people who could use and make decisions with the data.

The original implementation included a general ledger that was downloaded and then re-imported with text files into the model. The time data were captured in Excel and formatted for import as well.

With enhancements that have come with newer versions of the software, general ledger (GL) and time data can be automatically imported directly into the ABM model.

After the first implementation of the ABM model, the cost flow (see Exhibit 6.4) and reporting output (see Exhibit 6.5) were relatively simple. Data were distributed via hard-copy reports.

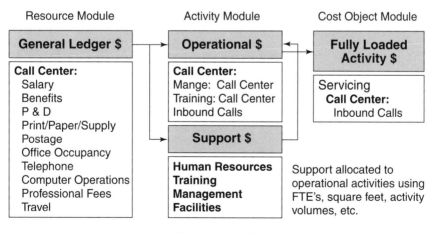

Exhibit 6.4 Cost Flow

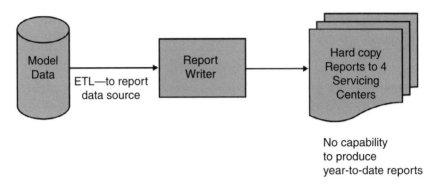

Exhibit 6.5 Old Reporting Process

The final reporting enhancements (see Exhibit 6.6) enable the ability to distribute electronic reports to the data consumers and give users access the report data via the Internet.

EXPERT WRAP-UP

John Antos

What made this implementation sustaining? Other companies have spent millions of dollars on an ABC system only to scrap it. What caused their failures? The introduction to this chapter mentioned some things this organization did to make the implementation a success. Here we list some of the things it did after the implementation.

- The marketing person used the ABC information to making marketing decisions. He knew this information was far more accurate and useful than the old way of doing things. He realized that the ABC information is not totally accurate, but it is much better than traditional costing.
- The president took the ABC numbers to his monthly review meetings. He did not require his managers to review the ABC information, but he did ask questions that would have been hard to answer unless the ABC information for that location was reviewed.

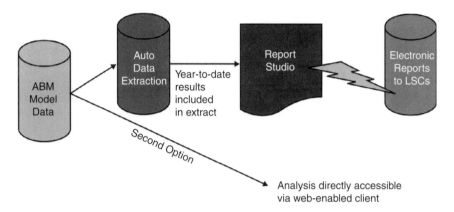

Exhibit 6.6 Enhanced Reporting

- ABC reporting transitioned from monthly to quarterly. This was a better balance of value for the time invested in collecting the data. Managers now had more time to improve the numbers rather than spending each month collecting the data.

- When the organization went private, it consolidated call centers from eight to four. The ABC numbers were used to show which call centers were the most productive and least costly to operate. These more productive call centers were chosen to remain open.

- When deciding where to move the activities from the closed call centers, the ABC data were again used. Those call centers that were most productive in certain activities received the workload from the closed call centers. Some activities were shifted in the remaining call centers that stayed open, so that activities were performed by the most productive call centers.

Even when the president, finance director, and director-level ABC Team person left the company, the ABC reporting continued. Many ABC projects have had similar challenges. As long as the champion remains with the company, the project continues. All too often, when that champion leaves, the ABC project stops.

One of the keys to a sustaining an ABC project is to have good ABC software that can:

- Minimize data collection so that much of the data are collected automatically from a variety of different systems (e.g., GL, human resources, operations, etc.).

- Provide OLAP (Online Analytical Processing). This is the ability for executives and managers to look at data from different points of view. An executive might want to see how the unit cost data are trending on average for all locations. A call center manager may want to see how the unit cost data are trending and how they compare to other locations.

- Marketing may want to look at parts of the data in order to make better marketing decisions.

- Those who acquire loan portfolios might want to understand the cost differences in processing loans in different stages of their life so they can more effectively buy a loan portfolio.

- Users of shared service data need to understand what they are paying for and how what they do affects cost.

- Providers of shared service data need to use ABC data to better explain to users why their costs are going up and what users are doing to increase cost.

- Executives need to understand the ABC trends so they can more accurately predict costs.

- Executives need to see the data in a form that will better enable them to set goals and strategies for their organization.

Sustainability of an ABC system and use of the ABC data by executives and managers for decision making and improving operations are true measures of successful ABC implementation.

ENDNOTE

1. CAM-I (www.cam-i.org) is an international consortium of manufacturing and service companies, government organizations, consultancies, and academic and professional bodies who have elected to work cooperatively in a precompetitive environment to solve management problems and critical business issues that are common to the group.

7

SIERRA TRUCKS: TRUCKING ALONG WITH ACTIVITY-BASED COSTING/MANAGEMENT

Success seems to be connected with action. Successful people keep moving. They make mistakes, but they don't quit.

—Conrad Hilton

Author's Note: Sierra Trucks from ABC to ABM to ABB

Activity-based costing (ABC) is not magic. It is just one of many information systems to help managers make better decisions and assist in controlling the processes to benefit the organization. Can ABC be the prime agitator in the process of moderating new demand?

ABC will have an impact on the organization; however, this impact will depend on understanding what ABC can do, and how it is used, and what the desired outcomes are. For instance, a basic ABC application is to determine the resource allocation, cost of activities, and the final cost of a product/service with a view of improving organizational performance and cost effectiveness. ABC is a management tool that will assist in enhancing the strategic direction of the organization by providing information on activities and their costs.

The next two cases provide an example of one organization's journey from the implementation of an ABC to an activity-based budgeting model that would support predictive day-to-day operational decisions or ad hoc requests effectively.

The ABC model allowed Sierra Trucks to:

- Better align financial information with management accountability.
- Improve product costing accuracy.
- Establish financial measures for management decision making.
- Directly link strategies to financial measures and operational performance metrics.
- Improve the accessibility of performance measurement information.

After the ABC model was analyzed, it was necessary to take the next step in forward planning—that is, budgeting.

This step followed the development of the activity-based budgeting (ABB) model for producing next year's budget for additional programs and space.

This method is a natural extension of ABC and is the reverse of the ABC model; that is, the budgeting process uses the south-to-north cost flow as opposed to the standard north-to-south flow in the ABC model.

Successful allocation of resources and cost effectiveness depend on the ability of the organization to become more efficient in terms of the activities that cause costs to be incurred—one of the most important benefits of ABC. ABC contributes to effective resource allocation to enhance the strategic direction/goals of the organization. The ability of the organization to improve resource allocation (in most cases budgetary constraints apply) and to reduce its costs, however, is affected by a time horizon also, as well as by knowledge of how costs will behave with respect to cost drivers selected. It is also important to be aware of the "unused capacities" in the organization and to establish a process that identifies these capacities and attempts to reduce idle capacity as much as possible, thus increasing productivity, streamlining activities, and contributing to the reduction of costs.

FOREWORD

Alan Stratton

When we are not feeling well, we go to see a medical professional. In our examination, we describe our various symptoms; the professional pokes, prods, conducts tests, and asks additional questions about the symptoms we are experiencing. Based on the symptoms and test results, the cause of the problem is identified and the appropriate treatment is applied.

Sierra Trucks is an excellent example of a company that was not feeling well. Most of its symptoms were expressed in cost measures. But rather than dismissing the symptoms as somebody else's responsibility, such as finance, everyone from Six Sigma Black Belts, to operations, and to finance got involved in assessing the symptoms, poking and prodding to test the symptoms, and conducting analyses to confirm the cause of the symptoms. Then, with a good understanding of the problem, they applied the appropriate treatment and the company subsequently returned to good health.

INTRODUCTION

The activity-based costing/management (ABC/M) initiative has been tremendously successful not just at the Truck Business Unit but throughout Sierra Trucks. According to Sierra Trucks chief executive Jason Franklin, "The ABC/M initiative provides concrete support to our corporate strategies and goals to create shareowner value. Without the comprehensive understanding of product and customer profitability gained through ABC/M, we could not make the informed, essential decisions necessary to achieve our strategies." There are three key areas where Sierra Trucks has focused its efforts and that have had the greatest impact: providing information for strategic decision making, motivating changes in behavior through the use of ABC/M information, and supporting operational excellence.

ORGANIZATIONAL ISSUES

Midwest-based Sierra Trucks Corporation is the leading North American producer of heavy- and medium-duty trucks and school buses. Posting sales and revenues in excess of $9 billion, Sierra Trucks maintains its position as the leader in the combined U.S. and Canadian retail markets, achieving a 28.9% market share for its largest truck brand.

The company is a world leader in the manufacture of midrange diesel engines. Sierra Trucks is also a private-label designer and manufacturer of diesel engines for full-size pickup truck and van markets, as well as selected industrial and off-highway markets.

Sierra Truck's Truck Business Unit had a very typical organizational structure—strong functional organizations loosely tied together by a weak matrix structure aligned along business lines. Silo-oriented thinking prevailed. Problems with this structure were readily apparent—there was little accountability for business-line management to control cost, profit, or product decisions. Sierra Trucks has been working hard to reduce operating expenses, simplify truck designs, and restructure manufacturing operations. The company also introduced a new truck strategy designed to increase profitability. To accomplish these ambitious goals, it needed to significantly improve its financial and performance information. The logical solution was ABC/M.

CASE STUDY

To lead the ABC/M effort, a team was formed consisting of professionals from other Fortune 500 companies with extensive ABC/M experience and finance professionals from Sierra Trucks. The ABC/M team developed a new financial management framework for the Truck Business Unit to support a move toward increased management accountability for business lines.

The objectives of the new framework were to:

- Implement the ABC/M solution.
- Better align financial information with management accountability.
- Improve product costing accuracy.
- Establish financial measures for management decision making.
- Directly link strategies to financial measures and operational performance metrics.
- Improve the accessibility of performance measurement information.

Under the new framework, costs are no longer viewed as simply "fixed" or "variable," and three types of activity behavior have been defined that are critical to performance measurement:

1. Transaction-related activities are all activities that vary with the number of units sold or manufactured. They are generally incremental with each unit sold or produced.

2. Business-line-specific activities are those activities that support a business line, or group of models, but are not related to production or sales volume.

3. Business-sustaining activities are those activities that support all models and business lines and do not vary with production or sales volume.

Based on a new understanding of cost and activity behavior, the firm has consolidated financial information into a new business-line income statement, which advances the use of financial measures in decision making. Each measure is clearly linked to specific business decisions.

Results of ABC/M

ABC/M has helped lead the way to new thinking within Sierra Trucks. The information provided through the initiative has been used to support a number of critical businesses decisions. Sierra Truck's Truck president cited the information provided by the new product income statement (see Exhibit 7.1) as the key enabler to a recent reorganization. The Truck Business Unit is now organized more tightly around business lines—each with its own income statement and true management accountability. The ABC/M data has played an important role in the negotiations with several large customers, providing a fact base to ensure understanding of what it will take to be profitable. ABC/M profitability information was instrumental in supporting the company's necessary but somewhat unpopular decision to exit a long-standing product market. ABC/M revealed the true economics of the business and allowed management to make a decision without doubting the financials. When confronted with unfavorable economics for a necessary product line, management used the ABC/M data to support the decision to enter into a joint venture—enabling Sierra Trucks to continue to meet customer needs, but at a profit.

Product Line P&L		Decision Applicability
Revenue (Material Cost) (Direct Labor) (Transaction Related Costs) Direct Margin	Direct Margin	Tactical measure used to support incremental sales decisions
(Business Line Specific Costs) Economic Margin	Economic Margin	Strategic measure used to support business-line investment decisions
(Truck Business Sustaining Costs) (Corporate Allocations) (Adjustment for Acct. Differences) (Business-Line Profitability	Business-Line PBT	Measure of total profit contribution of different businesses within truck division

Exhibit 7.1 New Activity-Based Income Statement

Partnering with ABC/M

The other major area of impact of ABC/M at Sierra Trucks is the delivery of process improvement and cost reduction information to manufacturing facilities and other organizations. ABC/M has been a catalyst for transforming the finance organization from back-office bean counters to business partners. This fact is demonstrated by the ABC/M team's partnership with Sierra Truck's Six Sigma Black Belt initiative. The two initiatives are perfectly matched—a group charged with undertaking cost and quality improvement projects and a team charged with providing fact-based financial information to support such improvements. Although Six Sigma provides a system for addressing problems and developing operational improvements, ABC/M provides a means to identify opportunities and track the progress of improvements (see Exhibit 7.2).

ABM Facilitates Analyses That Drive Operational Changes

- Cost of poor quality

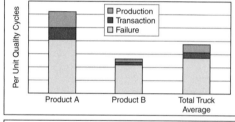

- Identification of core competencies

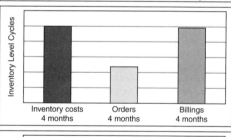

- Performance improvement support

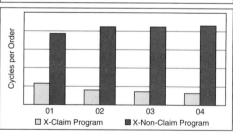

Exhibit 7.2 Opportunities for Improvement

EXPERT WRAP-UP

Alan Stratton

Many people think that they will run an ABC model, get results, and their work is done. Sierra Trucks has shown that the work actually begins when the first set of model results is complete.

Chapter 8 shows a progression of how a simple ABC cost management project can blossom into a full-fledged activity-based budgeting model. Today many organizations are seeing that the integration of their budget into their performance management systems will help their organizations drive change.

Using ABM metrics will help the organization understand costs, aid in budgeting and planning, and support an improvement process.

8

SIERRA TRUCKS: IMPLEMENTING REAL ACTIVITY-BASED BUDGETING

Evolution is a not a force but a process.

—John Morley

FOREWORD

Alan Stratton

In this case, Sierra Trucks decides to stop waiting until costs are spent before analyzing the impact of upcoming changes and possible scenarios. Sierra was well prepared for the change, as it had some excellent activity-based costing/management (ABC/M) modeling and decision impact experience. This prior experience proved valuable as Sierra turned its vision from the past to the future. Its past efforts and historical cost models served to calibrate and document its view to the future.

INTRODUCTION

Midwest-based Sierra Trucks Corporation is a leading producer of heavy- and medium-duty trucks and school buses and midrange diesel engines. Sierra began to investigate and apply activity-based costing/management (ABC/M) practices to provide management support and information systems. Its goals were to increase shareholder value, provide information to support strategic decision making, rationalize and motivate changes in corporate behavior, and lift operational excellence to a higher level.

Early in the project, the activity-based management (ABM) methodology had a firmly established record of success at Sierra. With a mature and reliable ABM process in place, Sierra was able to analyze where it had been effective. The operational managers were interested not in knowing what had already happened, but in knowing what would happen, and being able to plan and predict the impact of various product mix scenarios. Given a new product mix scenario, the system needed to predict both input and output quantities and costs for resources and activities. Then it needed to determine the feasibility of the scenario and optimize profitability by using resources effectively. This is not a new problem but an issue faced by every business.

Sierra hoped to find a new solution to this old problem based on new technology. As the discussions between ABC Technologies (now SAS) and Sierra progressed, it became clear that the solution was not in a new set of software functions or programming, but in a new way of thinking about how a business model could be designed and constructed. The technology was already there.

ORGANIZATIONAL ISSUES

Sierra's initial ABM objective was to achieve breakthrough results in cost improvement and strategic alignment. Its goals were to better align financial information with management accountability, improve product costing accuracy, establish financial measures for management decision making, directly link strategies to financial measures and operational performance metrics, and improve the accessibility of performance measurement information. Initial efforts were successful. Its sales, revenue, return on equity, and net income lifted, leading to the company receiving a major ABM award.

Key success factors for ABM at Sierra were the breadth and depth of corporation-wide ABC/M education, involvement, and information distribution. Managers on the floor as well as in the boardroom were involved in the ABM model development and validation process. The result of management involvement was well-understood ABC data that had a high level of credibility at all levels of the organization. Confidence in the ABM data allowed the organization to implement important decisions, such as product mix, based on the ABM data analysis.

The pace of change at Sierra was a significant factor. Rapid change is not easy to achieve in an organization with a long history. (Sierra traces its roots back nearly two centuries, to the start of the modern Industrial Age in the early 1800s.) Given Sierra's long-established corporate culture, the high rate of acceptance of ABM, and the implementation based on its insights were noteworthy.

Against this background, Sierra's management reviewed both the ABM effort and the larger set of management information issues that faced the organization. Sierra had for some time realized that there were two sets of customers for ABM data: strategic decision makers and operational decision makers.

The existing ABM implementation, based on historical data, supported the strategic decision-making process effectively. Because of the critical importance of some information that was not available to strategic planners without ABM, this aspect of ABM had been consciously emphasized in the initial stage of implementation.

Despite the operational content of the data, the existing ABM system did not support predictive day-to-day operational decisions or ad hoc requests effectively. Operational managers wishing to examine the future impact of certain kinds of business process changes did not find ABM support for these decisions, regardless of their deep understanding of the ABM data. The operational managers wanted to:

- View the impact of changes in the product mix on resources and activities.
- Forecast the potential impact of future growth and new products.
- Focus the annual budget cycle on activities and processes.
- Plan using a tool that considered capacity constraints by resource and activity.

Initially, the needs of the operational managers had taken a backseat relative to the strategic decision-making requirements. However, it was apparent that it was necessary to meet more of the operational needs while maintaining support for strategic decision making. For optimal performance, the organization needed to meet both sets of requirements effectively.

Sierra's ABM lead Kelly Hobart said, "If we didn't go through to the next step, we ran the risk of ABM losing steam because it wasn't meeting operational needs."

Sierra's executive staff and operational management in the plants began to pressure ABM management within Sierra to come up with a predictive activity-based budgeting (ABB) and planning solution.

The next case study describes the response to this pressure. Although corporate confidentiality and the constraints of space dictate that not every detail can be included, this case study attempts to capture and report the experience with candor and insight.

CASE STUDY

Initial Efforts

Predictive ABC (sometimes called activity-based budgeting or activity-based planning (ABP), often combined as ABB/P) has of late been receiving increasing attention and press from ABC thought leaders.

Sierra and ABC Technologies (now SAS) began to discuss a collaborative proof-of-concept effort. Sierra sought a strong technology partner to help define, investigate, and overcome problems involved in revising its existing, successful ABM models to add the capability of ABB/P. With an already deep understanding of ABM concepts and terminology, Sierra was looking for a partner that could readily grasp its situation and issues and was willing to participate actively. (See Exhibit 8.1.)

TIMELINE

Reflecting Sierra's need for this type of data, Sierra's executive staff set the target deadline for completing an ABB proof of concept barely six months after the initial conversations about the project.

PROJECT PLAN

An aggressive schedule was needed to meet the deadlines established by Sierra's executives. During an eight-week period, these actions needed to be accomplished:

- Define issue(s).
- Demonstrate proof of concept (including outlining a validation process).
- Implement at three sites. This implementation was a full-scale ABB modeling effort with the results being validated cross-departmentally throughout the organization. To meet the project timeline, the three sites were implemented concurrently.

KEY CONCEPTS AND METHODS

Approaches to Cost Management:
Assignment versus Consumption

In traditional activity-based costing, resource costs are known (usually from the corporate general ledger) and costs are assigned from resources, to activities, to products and services. Each cost is distributed based on its driver and the proportion of its driver quantity. All costs eventually flow into the final cost objects. This is referred to as assignment methodology or modeling, or more informally as the

	Early Stages ABC	Mature ABM	Advanced ABB
Organizational Information Requirements	• What activities does the organization perform? • What percentage of effort is spent on these activities? • What are the general ledger resources needed to perform these activities?	• What is the operational flow of the activities that the organization performs? • What are the inputs and outputs for each activity? • What process receives the activity? • What external forces decrease the throughput in the activity?	• What impact does the planned throughput of the activity outputs have on resource levels? • What are the resource and activity capacity requirements for the planned activities? • What process improvements can be implemented to achieve effective capacity usage?
Modeling Techniques	• Activity-based costing costs flow (are pushed) from resources to activities then to cost objects.	• Activity-based management. As in ABC, costs flow, but ABM puts significantly more emphasis on the causes of costs	• Activity-based budgeting. A two-step process. 　1. Cost objects place demands on activities and activities place demands on resources. 　2. Once quantities are determined, costs are calculated Emphasis on causes of costs and the impacts on the corporation. Also referred to as consumption methodology.
Technology	Oros (now SAS ABM)	Oros (now SAS ABM)	Oros (now SAS ABM)

Exhibit 8.1 ABC to ABB Evolution at Sierra Trucks

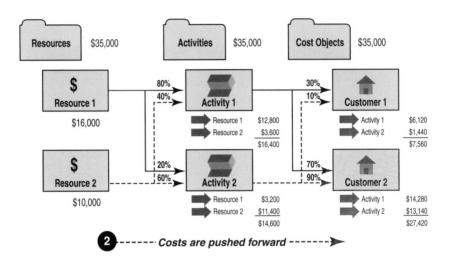

Exhibit 8.2   Traditional Activity-Based Costing Methodology

"push" approach of ABC/M (see Exhibit 8.2), because costs are "pushed" through the model to arrive at the destination, an activity-based cost for a set of products or services.

Another approach to cost management uses the outputs to drive the inputs (see Exhibit 8.3). In this approach, the required volume (outputs) of the cost objects determines the activity requirements; the activity requirements then determine the resource requirements (the inputs). Activity requirements, in the center of the model, are both outputs and inputs. This methodology, instead of pushing, pulls data through the model. The outputs, which are the products of customer demand, are the fully costed products. Some activity demands are driven by product volume; other activities are driven by process demands (as opposed to product demands).

This output-driven methodology is basically a two-step calculation process, which makes it more complex to both understand and implement than the push methodology. This approach assumes that it is known how much of an activity is required for an output of the cost object (its rate) and how much of a resource is required for an output of the activity. It is also necessary to know the capacity of the resource or the activity. These requirements dictate more detailed data collection and validation.

Assignment, or push, methodology currently is the predominant ABC modeling approach. This methodology is easier to implement and produces results that

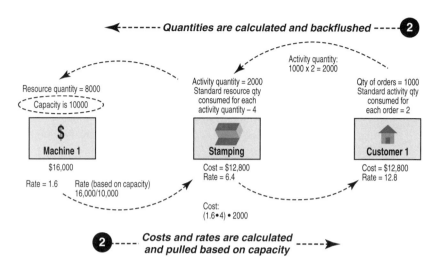

Exhibit 8.3 Activity-Based Budgeting Methodology

can be readily validated (because they tie back to data that are produced by the general ledger or other systems). The pull methodology also requires knowledge of the relationships between inputs and outputs (the rates of consumption), and this information typically is developed by creating an assignment model. Because the pull methodology predicts inputs (rather than matching data from other systems), it also produces data that are more difficult to validate.

The consumption methodology, which is the foundation for ABB, has these characteristics:

- Consumption methodology requires deeper understanding of cost behavior (causality) and more detail than the push approach. The data collection process is much more intensive. Sierra needed to collect internal customer data, measures, inputs, outputs, process flows, and capacities of activities (especially people, but also machinery).

- Data validation and calibration is critical. The data gathered should be rigorously reviewed and verified by both the ABM team and the process owners.

- In addition to validating the individual data elements, it is also necessary to validate the relationships between the elements. In standard ABC modeling, modelers can take comfort from the ties to existing, known, familiar data (e.g., from the general ledger). In ABB, these ties are no longer available, because these are what the model is designed to predict. This is one key reason that Sierra came to appreciate that it had done ABC first, then ABB. Sierra conducted exhaustive historical scenario testing to validate these linkages.

- Consumption methodology focuses on consumption of resources and activities and reveals unused capacity. The model captures only the quantities of activities and resources that are actually used, rather than pushing a generalized (full absorption) consumption across accounts (typical of the push method).

- Consumption methodology identifies bottlenecks (overload conditions) for resources and activities.

IMPLEMENTING THE SOLUTION

It became clear that the solution would be a change in the approach to modeling the organization, based more on consumption and less on cost assignment. Demand for cost objects (products and services) determines the actions or activities. Activities then consume resources to meet the demand.

Implementing such a model would require data from a traditional "push" ABM model. For the solution to be successful, it had to meet certain other criteria as well:

- The methodology had to be flexible enough to be adapted to more than one site.

- The results had to be validated cross-departmentally throughout the organization.

Sierra selected three sites that met these criteria:

- Their products were core to the truck business, and the problems and issues of these three were likely to be representative of the other business segments.

- They each had a mature ABM model (in place for more than two years) and staff members who were very familiar with the data. Executives of the organization felt reports of the data "told the right story."

To meet Sierra's project deadline, the three sites were implemented concurrently. The first step of the implementation was to assess the state of the current mature ABM model for each site and select an implementation approach. Three possible approaches were identified:

1. Convert the existing ABM model (assignment-based model, or push model) into an ABB model (a consumption-based model, or pull model).
2. Create a new model for ABB using some of the data already known, thanks to the ABM model.
3. Combine the two approaches.

At Sierra, each of the three sites selected for implementation used a different one of the possible approaches, for the following reasons:

- **SB Plant.** Convert an existing ABM model. This approach was selected because the ABM model for this site met current operational needs very well and was very clean (see Exhibit 8.4). It also helped that the structure of the cost object module was relatively simple and straightforward.

- Drivers in the model are clearly defined: Causality is clear.
- Driver names are meaningful and reflect the organization's business perspective, for example, "number of material shortages" instead of "direct assigned."
- All driver quantities are in number format; no evenly assigned or percentage drivers.
- A site-specific activity and driver dictionary has been developed.
- Each dictionary entry includes an example.
- The owner of each entry is specified.
- Many attributes have been defined.
- Typically, the data are organized to support "slicing and dicing" (looking at different aspects of the model).
- Feeds from other data sources have been automated as much as possible.
- Data cleanup issues have been resolved.
- Possible sources of error have been eliminated.

Exhibit 8.4 Hallmarks of a "Clean Model"

- **SA Plant.** Create a new model. This approach was selected because, although there was an existing ABM model, it did not meet all operational needs. Another factor was that there were some significant gaps in causality (relationships within the model). SA Plant's evolution and use of ABM by operational managers required the modeling of support (reciprocal) relationships between activities crossing functional boundaries.

- **CA Plant.** Combine both methods. This approach was selected because, although the ABM model was sufficient as far as it went, it would have to be extended to collect the additional level of detail needed to support ABB analysis.

In all three locations, it quickly became apparent that the in-depth understanding of consumption modeling, specifically the use of Bills of Cost, by Sierra's personnel was an important factor for success. Sierra had dedicated people who were well briefed and comfortable with the application of Bills of Costs prior to implementation. Without this in-depth understanding, building the consumption models would have been much more difficult and time consuming, because of the learning curve that would have been involved.

APPROACH 1: CONVERTING AN ACTIVITY-BASED MANAGEMENT MODEL INTO A MODEL FOR ACTIVITY-BASED BUDGETING

Converting an ABM model into a model for ABB was the most technically challenging approach. It required systematically examining the fundamental elements of the existing ABM model and converting them to reflect cost consumption rather than cost assignment. It was technically challenging because of the necessary level of in-depth knowledge of the existing model, in addition to a solid understanding of consumption modeling. The complexity of the network of relationships among resources, activities, and cost objects in the model meant that many existing relationships had to be examined.

Costs were loaded in the resource module in an availability section. This resource availability section is fed from an external units table. Each available resource is split between a fixed portion and a variable portion. The external rates for the fixed values are loaded as totals. The external rates for the variable values are loaded as cost-per-unit of demand (hours, full-time equivalents [FTEs], kilowatts). Then the availability section is used as the cost basis for each unit demanded in the resource requirement section. This cost per unit available is mated to the resource requirements, using the bill of costs. The demand triggered by the

Data element	Value
Activity name	
Activity reference number	
Activity account cost	
Activity driver name	
Activity driver quantities	
Data contact	
Data source	
Auto or manual data feed	
Data reliability	
Input measure	
Output measure	
Activity behavior	
Current PLP roll-up	
Activity cost	
Activity cost per	

Exhibit 8.5 Data Collection Template

cost objects causes the cost to flow from the resource module through the activities to the cost objects. (See Exhibit 8.5.)

For an ABC-to-ABB conversion, required information includes:

- An existing ABC model completely reconciled and validated
- The number of people in each department, by labor class
- Hours-to-FTE conversion rate for each department, for each resource account
- Fixed and variable percentages for each resource account
- Resource pool attribute mapping for each account

Using the ABB model, required information for analysis and what-if modeling includes:

- Forecast of the volume of finished items
- A set of external unit rates
- New hours-to-FTE conversion rate

To create an ABB model from an ABC model, changes required in the resource module are:

- Define the external units.
- Build the resource structure for each department twice: once to represent "required" and once for "available."
- Define the resource structure for the available section. The resource structure is the basis for all of the cost flow in the model. All of the costs are loaded as external units on bills of costs in the available section. The total of the available section should tie to general ledger expenses.
- In the resource structure in the required section, define the resource accounts based on the resource account in the existing ABC model. These resource accounts will be used as internal cost elements on bills in the activity module.

For building resource accounts the requirements include:

- Define a unit of measure defined (hours, pieces) for each account. This unit of measure is defined as the driver currently used inthe ABC model.
- To be able to plan effectively, convert the number of FTEs into a number of hours demanded by the activities. Therefore, you must convert all FTE drivers to number of hours per FTE. The measure name relates to the FTE hours.
- Load two attributes loaded into the model for each of the accounts:
  - A numeric attribute noting the number of hours per FTE
  - A calculated attribute noting how many FTEs would be required:

  Number of Required FTEs = Output Quantity / Number of FTEs Attribute

- Add the Bill of Cost structure. The Bill of Cost for the required section has two elements from the available section: fixed and variable. The fixed item is loaded with a Bill of Cost quantity of 1 and a Bill of Costs quantity type of "total." The variable item is loaded with a bill of cost quantity of 1 FTE / 462 or 520 (hours of work per quarter) with a quantity type of "unit."
- For the utilities (gas, water, and electricity), load the variable item with a Bill of Cost quantity of 1, with a quantity type of "unit." The variable item varies based on demand pull (gas, water, and electricity consumption), but it does not vary based on headcount or FTE hours.
- Review all existing assignments for viability as Bill of Costs consumption.

APPROACH 2: CREATING A NEW MODEL
FOR ACTIVITY-BASED BUDGETING

Although there was a mature ABM model in use at the SB assembly plant of Sierra Trucks, the team determined that the best approach to ABB was to build a new model rather than convert the existing model.

Two factors were critical to successfully building the ABB model at this plant:

1. Again, in-depth understanding of the use of Bills of Cost for consumption modeling by the Sierra personnel.

2. An innovative approach to validation while the model was under construction. Before an approach was implemented in the main ABB model for the plant, a small and simplified model was created and tested to determine that the modeling technique being applied would have the proper behavior when implemented in the real model. Trial modeling ensures that the approach being taken meets the client's objective before an ABB consumption approach is implemented full-scale. Building a sample environment allows you to see the result of certain actions in a controlled environment.

APPROACH 3: COMBINING BOTH APPROACHES

An ABM model existed at the SA Plant but it did not have sufficient detail in certain respects to provide the ABB data needed. In this case, the model was converted, although the operation was less complex than the full conversion performed at the SB Plant.

At this site, it was clear that both consumption and assignment techniques would be applied to handle specific modeling issues. Assignment-based techniques were used to ensure that some costs did not flex based on demand, but flowed based on a driver other than quantities and rate.

SPECIAL LOGISTICS FOR THREE SITES

Because all three implementations were being done in parallel, certain modeling problems arose at all three sites. When this happened, the teams conferred regarding possible solutions. After they jointly developed several possible solutions, each one of the sites would try implementing a different solution. Then they would compare results to determine the best solution (from the perspective of Sierra's plant controllers, who would be using data from all three locations).

ACTIVITY-BASED BUDGETING REPORTING

Having created an ABB model, the next step was to create the reports necessary to communicate the information to key stakeholders in the organization. Beyond the standard Oros reports, those specific to ABB are:

- Resource capacity utilization
- Activity capacity utilization
- Activity-level fixed and variable cost reports
- Performance variance reporting (volume, mix, and efficiency)

ACTIVITY-BASED BUDGETING VALIDATION

An important difference between an ABC or ABM model and an ABB model is in the way they are used. An ABC or ABM model is based on known costs and results. It allows users to accurately understand the organization's results for a given period. An assignment error in the model can cause misunderstanding only of what has already happened. An ABB model, by contrast, is used to predict the results of decisions; it looks forward, and it affects future results. It is not founded on known costs and results; it seeks to predict them. To the extent that managers rely on the ABB model in making important plans and decisions, they want to know that the model is valid.

At Sierra, the effort to validate the measures and rates used in the ABC model was very challenging. The critical role of the rates and measures in the model's calculations made validation imperative. Developing methods for determining that they were valid consumed many hours and required much thought.

Traditional systems will be operated at Sierra in parallel with the ABB models for a time, until the stakeholders have the same level of confidence in the ABB data as they have in the ABM data.

BENEFITS

ABB is not an immediate gratification effort; its payoff will maximize in the next year. However, short-term benefits were immediately realized, including:

- Improved operational reporting
- Enhanced understanding of cost and operational flow
- Better-costed operational metrics
- Ability to evaluate the impact of various volume and mix scenarios

Improved operational reporting was Sierra's biggest win. It fulfilled Sierra's goal of reporting relevant cost data to Operations, so Operations could begin to take accountability and responsibility for its data. Using ABB data, the root causes of activities are identified and continuous improvement programs can be put in place and tracked.

In the meantime, a significant benefit is the dramatic reduction in effort involved in evaluating the impact of various volume and mix scenarios. Sierra's traditional budgeting systems required extensive manual effort to respond to changes in industry forecasts; using the ABB models, such changes can be made and the impact can be recalculated much more quickly.

OTHER MODELING ISSUES FOR ABB

Sierra found a number of additional issues in creating an ABB model:

- The drivers flowing through the model must be reviewed. If drivers flowing through the model do not represent a volume number of units, number of moves, and so on, then they must be converted to volumes, if this is at all possible. Doing this will make the bill of cost conversion make more sense and the demand-consumption measures more meaningful. The specific areas of concern are these drivers: evenly assigned, percentages, and direct assigned.
- For accuracy, it is best to scale all direct-assigned drivers and all percentage drivers from 1 to 100, to improve the number of significant digits.

- For ease of understanding, you should change some percentage drivers to more appropriate ones that note the volume nature of the driver (number of cabs, number of wires).
- In an ABC model, many items can have user-entered output quantities. Most of these are purely for analysis purposes to create a unit cost for review. The only user-entered output quantities in the ABB model must be the final production items. All other output quantities must be removed, so that they do not affect the conversion of the assignments into bills of cost.
- All of the resource-to-resource assignments should be built with Bills of Costs and added to the resource-required items. Doing this will allow the demand-pull of the activities to create demand-pull of the resource-to-resource assignments as well.
- The resource structure in the required section should have the resource accounts defined, based on the resource account in the existing ABC model. These resource accounts will be used as internal cost elements on bills in the activity module.
- All of the existing assignments should be reviewed for viability as Bill of Costs consumption: resource-to-activity assignments, activity-to-cost-object assignments, and cost-object-to-cost-object assignments.
- The number of significant digits is critical when converting from assignment to consumption modeling. In an assignment flow, the driver quantities represent the total flow to the destination. For example, expressed as a driver, it might take 50 moves to create 1,000 of Part No. 123. In a Bill of Cost method, the flow is based on the quantity required to make 1 unit of the destination item. In the example, 50 moves to make 1,000 units translates to 0.05 moves/unit. As output quantity of the immediate destination increases relative to the driver, the converted Bill of Cost quantity decreases correspondingly. As output quantities grow to very large numbers, the converted Bill of Cost quantity required to make 1 unit becomes very small, requiring more digits to the right of the decimal point to avoid distortion by rounding. Therefore, you must set the model options to store 10 decimal places for the math to work correctly in the ABB model.

SUMMARY

A key question most organizations would ask before undertaking a commitment to ABB would be "Is the view worth the climb?" Sierra's record of success with

ABC gave it confidence that the ABB effort, while substantial, would provide the organization with sufficient value to make the climb worthwhile. The needs of Sierra's operational managers, in particular, were driving forces behind the organization's dedication to the effort. The partnership relationship between Sierra and ABC Technologies (now SAS) was also significant. It would be unusual for even a very strong climber to take on a new mountain without an equally strong partner. Because all the steps along the path for this journey were not known before the trek began, the relationship between the two organizations was key. Each party had to be certain that the other was committed to making the climb and would not falter or turn back when difficulties were encountered along the way. The caliber of the personnel involved in the effort and the rapport they developed were crucial. Having neared the top of the mountain (there are a few more steps to be taken to get to the absolute summit), the team is so far delighted with the panoramic view of options. Taking ABB from an appealing conceptual image to a real-world implementation was a major effort, but the view was definitely worth the climb.

EXPERT WRAP-UP

Alan Stratton

Although there are not yet any perfect tools to peer into the future, Sierra shows the value of applying activity-based concepts to future operations and future resulting costs. Sierra shows that there is additional effort required to look into the future, but the view is worth it.

9

WENDALS FOODS: MANAGING CUSTOMER PROFITABILITY WITH ACTIVITY-BASED COSTING INFORMATION

Profit in business comes from repeat customers.

—W. Edwards Deming

FOREWORD

Jeff Thomson

Intense competition is often an accelerator for innovation. In this case, Wendals Foods (a South African–based subsidiary of Aardvark Industries, Ltd.) turned its innovative spirit in serving customers *inside* to design and implement innovations in its business management processes. Wendals Foods was facing intense competition in the snack food industry from multinational companies returning to South Africa and from smaller, local niche competitors. It designed and installed an activity-based costing (ABC) process in conjunction with a customer profitability model, which enabled it to make more strategic decisions on pricing, margins (product, customer, distribution channel, and location) and resource allocation. Wendals describes its implementation approach in the next case, and provides practical lessons learned that are portable to organizations of various size and scope.

INTRODUCTION

In businesses whose strategic thrust is to be customer focused, the accounting function's cornerstone for adding value is providing customer profitability information determined on ABC principles. Customer profitability information helps to decide what to do, with what product, for which customer. It translates strategy into action by answering these types of questions:

- Do we push for volume or for margin with this customer?
- Is there scope to change the way we package, sell, deliver, and so on to improve this customer's profitability?
- Does the turnover justify the discount/promotion structure we give this customer?

Wendals Foods, a division of Best Brands Ltd., a subsidiary of Aardvark Industries Ltd., holds approximately 35% of the South African snack food market. Approximately 90 products are manufactured at two sites and are distributed to more than 24,000 outlets via close to 30 depots across 200 routes. This case describes what Wendals Foods did to provide customer profitability and process cost and performance information to better manage its business.

Best Brands is proudly South African. It encourages its staff to take the opportunity to make a difference for themselves and for the company by working together with honesty, integrity, and trust at all times and by embracing the challenges of change with a will-to-win-attitude.

Best Brands is passionate about excellence in satisfying its consumers and customers. Its business perpetually attempts to deliver number-one–rated service and constant innovation, which is strongly supported by good systems and leading conceptual approaches.

ORGANIZATIONAL ISSUES

The snack food industry is extremely competitive—to the extent that companies have not been able to recover from consumers inflationary cost increases. This position is not likely to change in the foreseeable future. Competition that has resulted in declining shelf space for Wendals Foods is coming from the return of multinational companies to South Africa and an increasing number of niche local competitors.

To be competitive in the marketplace, Wendals needs to know the source of its profits. The key issue for profitability management is the profitability of brands (products) and customers. Wendals' customers range from large hypermarkets to small corner cafés. Each individual customer affects the profitability of the brand and the market segment due to its purchasing habits, delivery location, and discount/rebate structures.

In this environment, managing all elements of customer profitability, not just product cost, is critical. Discounts and promotions represent a substantial part of the margin that must be managed, along with the cost of serving the customer, at the customer level. Most of the data needed to manage the elements of customer profitability is available, but spread across many systems and not readily accessible. Exhibit 9.1 illustrates how Wendals Foods will enable its management to drill

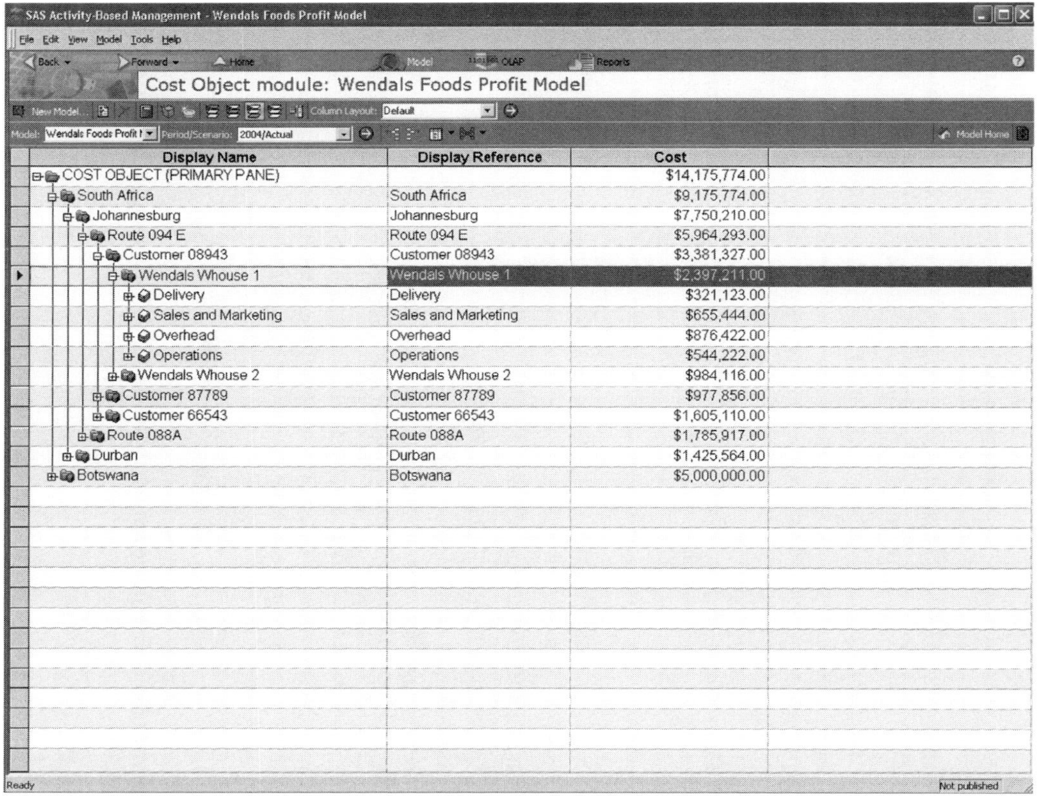

Exhibit 9.1 Wendals Foods "Drill Down"

SAS Activity-Based Management - Wendals Foods Profit Model

File Edit View Model Tools Help

Back ▾   Forward ▾   ⌂ Home   Model   OLAP   Reports

Cost Object module: Wendals Foods Profit Model

Model: Wendals Foods Profit ▾   Period/Scenario: 2004/Actual ▾   Column Layout: Default ▾

Model Home

Display Name	Display Reference	Cost
COST OBJECT (PRIMARY PANE)		$14,175,774.00
South Africa	South Africa	$9,175,774.00
Johannesburg	Johannesburg	$7,750,210.00
Route 094 E	Route 094 E	$5,964,293.00
Customer 08943	Customer 08943	$3,381,327.00
Wendals Whouse 1	Wendals Whouse 1	$2,397,211.00
Delivery	Delivery	$321,123.00
Sales and Marketing	Sales and Marketing	$655,444.00
Overhead	Overhead	$876,422.00
Operations	Operations	$544,222.00
Wendals Whouse 2	Wendals Whouse 2	$984,116.00
Customer 87789	Customer 87789	$977,856.00
Customer 66543	Customer 66543	$1,605,110.00
Route 088A	Route 088A	$1,785,917.00
Durban	Durban	$1,425,564.00
Botswana	Botswana	$5,000,000.00

Ready

Not published

137

down from a nationwide view of the business to the sales of a particular product at a specific outlet and then to query how those costs are built up.

CASE STUDY

Initial Efforts

Porter's value chain was used as the basis for defining Wendals' primary and support processes. Each process was then defined in greater detail by identifying up to ten activities. The processes that constitute the primary (product touching) processes are:

- **Inbound logistics.** The procurement and storage of raw and packaging materials
- **Operations.** The issue of materials into the factory, product manufacture, and packing and sealing of boxes
- **Marketing.** All advertising, marketing, and promotional activities
- **Outbound logistics.** Centralized warehousing, freight to depots, and depot warehousing
- **Sales and distribution.** Taking orders, delivery from depot to customer, invoicing, and collection of payments

Inbound logistics, operations, and marketing are product-related costs that vary primarily by the nature of the product and the pack size. Outbound logistics and sales and distribution are customer-related costs that may vary primarily by the location of the customer outlet and the nature of the sales and distribution process.

Project Stages

The project to develop customer and brand profitability was split into two phases: (1) a pilot project to prove the concept and develop an implementation plan and (2) the actual implementation.

Pilot Phase

A pilot ABC project initially was implemented to prove the value of the information and gain executive buy-in. A snapshot of six months of actual data was used to illustrate the information that could be produced by an ABC approach to customer profitability. Six steps were taken to implement the pilot:

1. Value chain processes were identified.

2. Key activities within each process of the chain were defined, including appropriate output measures and performance measures.

3. Five project teams comprised of different functional representatives were established to collect financial and nonfinancial data.

4. The data collected by each team was used in spreadsheets to illustrate and test basic ABC principles for each process. The results of each process were consolidated into a "snapshot" result for a sample of products and customers.

5. Mock-up customer and product profitability statements were developed.

6. The full-scale implementation approach and project plan were developed.

Pilot Project Output

The pilot project highlighted several issues for the business. Previously, a key measure was the "cost per case," where various summary costs were divided by the number of cases produced. The ABC model proved that this was a gross simplification of the business and was more likely to mislead than to provide insight. Because high labor and capital costs were incurred in establishing a three-shift manufacturing environment, nonworking time in operations had a significant effect on product cost.

The sample ABC customer profitability information clearly demonstrated that outlet profitability would allow Wendals to reengineer its trading relationships with its customers to manage profitability. However, because of the cyclical nature of the business, the snapshot data were not good enough to illustrate the dynamics of the customer relationship; monthly information was necessary. Summarizing activity-level ABC costs up to their processes also helped to identify the future directions for ABC development.

It was obvious that although the inbound logistics and the marketing processes managed large cash outflows, their process costs were insignificant relative to the potential costs if their activities were performed ineffectively. Consequently Wendals decided to focus its process management efforts on process effectiveness and control the costs using good old-fashioned budgets.

As far as the Operations process was concerned, the key issue was line utilization. The capacity for each machine in the line was determined, and the bottleneck machine that was the throughput constraint was identified. However, for the initial implementation, it was decided to split each production line only into processing and packaging because their different cost drivers (kilograms and packs per case, respectively) yielded good insights into cost behavior in the different parts of the manufacturing process. At a later stage the process costs would be broken down into greater detail for better management and improvement of the individual operations.

The outbound logistics ABC analysis led to a questioning of the extent to which cost savings would be achieved by moving to "roll-on, roll-off" technology. This process was simplified for the initial implementation by calculating an average cost to move a case to a depot. The ABC analysis of the sales and distribution process highlighted the cost differentials between "preselling" and "knock and drop" routes and the dynamics of route profitability. Wendals is in the process of implementing hand-held computer technology for route accounting. The detailed data recorded by route accounting provide the ideal input into a route ABC system. That data will allow Wendals to identify each call that is made, how long the call took, and the product quantity sold. A key factor influencing route profitability is the number of calls that do not yield reasonable sales levels. However, for the initial implementation, this process was simplified by averaging the route costs per client on the route.

The rationale behind simplifying the data in the ABC implementation is to ensure that a successful implementation can be made in a 3-month window. It is better to have information of reasonable quality quickly than to wait 18 months for perfection with a high risk of project failure. After the initial implementation, the model can be extended down into the detail in a controlled fashion—also in 3-month windows.

Focusing on key result areas using the information developed by the pilot has already identified an annual savings in excess of R6 million to the division—many times the total cost of the pilot project. The output from the pilot was sufficient for the executive to give the go-ahead to a full-production monthly customer profitability measurement and reporting system using process-level costs.

Implementation Phase

The objective of the implementation project was to deliver monthly, actual, process-based information that could be summarized into product and customer profitability. The information is used by:

- Sales management to improve the profitability of trading relationships with customers

- Marketing management to determine product pricing
- General management to improve overall profitability using an activity-based management (ABM) approach to monitor cost and performance

The full implementation enabled the reevaluation of outputs required from the system and the approach to be used. Due to the seasonal nature of the business, Wendals decided to calculate customer profitability on a monthly basis. Wendals determined that rather than developing a model at an activity level of detail, it would be quicker, more certain of success, and cheaper to develop the ABC model at the process level. A process could be broken down to the activity level of detail later, when the need arose. The spreadsheet software used for the pilot was not suitable for an ongoing production system. Oros (now SAS Activity-Based Management) software was purchased to handle the ABC calculations.

To achieve product, brand, market, and customer profitability, a two-stage approach was required:

1. Use the ABC system to cost the products (including marketing cost) up to the end of the Marketing process in the value chain, thus producing a cost per case of each product and pack size variant. In addition, use ABC to provide the outbound logistics and sales and distribution costs to get a case of product to the customer's outlet and to collect payment for the sale.

2. Use a data warehouse to combine the rates per unit of output measure for each process from the ABC system. Use the distribution and sales data from the operating systems to calculate the required profitability statements based on actual customer sales for the period. A custom database was designed and built to handle the calculations needed to produce customer profitability data. An Executive Information System (EIS) tool and Excel were used to display the information and provide "slice-and-dice" and "what-if" capabilities. (The top-level information model design for the data warehouse is shown in Exhibit 9.2.)

Implementation Steps

The five steps in the full project implementation were:

1. Identify the source of all the data required for the ABC/warehouse systems. Develop download formats and procedures to dump data monthly into a designated directory on the file server. A reliable, flexible, and

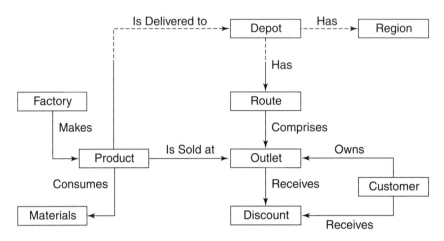

Exhibit 9.2 Wendals Information Model

automated tool set is required to handle the collection of data, the calculations, and the export of the data to the data warehouse.

2. Design the resource, activity, cost object structure in an ABC package to calculate product and customer costs. Develop the import file structures to be able to import financial and nonfinancial data.

3. Develop a data model and build a data warehouse to process the sales and ABC data. Two key features of the warehouse are: (1) the ability to reverse out erroneous data and reimport the correct data and (2) the ability to give each data set a name and to mix and match the data sets across the value chain. This gives the capability, for example, to assess the impact of a price increase for potatoes on June actual sales.

4. Design custom reports for users based on their requirements using an EIS tool or Excel. This step was crucial for gaining buyer buy-in; giving the managers the opportunity to specify exactly what they wanted ensured their commitment.

5. Provide "goal seek" and "what-if" capability for scenario planning. This gave the user the ability to flex the profitability calculations based on changes in volumes, costs, and pricing, for example: What if we decreased the price by 10% and got a 5% increase in volume across the board? How would this affect the brand profitability?

Initial Benefits/Outputs

In a typical profitability statement from the data warehouse, the source of the data is shown for each element. The EIS has a drill-down capability that provides the details behind each element on the statement (see Exhibit 9.3). The building block for this statement is the cost of manufacturing each product and the cost of getting it to the customer's outlet. The profitability can be viewed along any of the dimensions shown in Exhibit 9.3.

Initial Lessons Learned

Most times when people say they have implemented ABC, they are referring to a snapshot analysis. Although a snapshot ABC project has its challenges, these are minor in comparison to the effort required to install a monthly running ABC program. A key success factor is ensuring the company has at least one person dedicated to the project—ideally the person who will take ownership of the system when the consultants leave. The speed with which the implementation of a

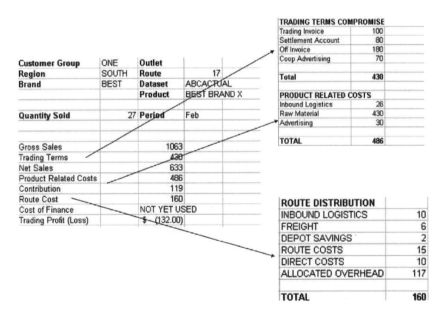

Exhibit 9.3 Wendals Outlet Profitability Statement Support Detail

monthly ABC system can be achieved is dependent on three issues: (1) easy availability of data, (2) quality of data, and (3) the extent to which history is required.

A system has to be established to obtain the required data (normally nonfinancial) quickly and easily. Although it may be feasible to gather and input the data manually for a short while, ABC is sustainable only if this aspect is automated. This automation normally takes the form of modifying month-end runs of operating systems to download the required data into the ABC computer.

A major issue may be the inconsistencies of data across systems or data that have not been maintained properly in one or more systems. Although these errors create frustration, normally they are easy to sort out, particularly as information technology in many companies moves to a data warehouse concept for management information systems.

The extent to which history is required is the most insidious problem. Although it appears easy to provide six or more months of history for trend purposes, the effort required to gather and reconcile six or more months of historical data is such that it takes months, if ever, to catch up. One recommendation is to pick a month that is two months into the future as the starting month, then use dummy runs to iron out any problems. If you are unable to complete the first month within the month, abandon it and use the next month as the start. Complaints about the lack of history are better than accusations of being out of date. Accurate and timely history soon builds.

Current State: Today

Many ABC implementations are designed simply to determine more accurate product costs. For this purpose snapshots are adequate; however, this limited use of ABC seldom provides value for money. Structuring the ABC project on a process basis and taking it to customer profitability enables decisions to be made that will pay back the project cost many times over each year.

Taking a process view of the activities provides strategic insight that is translated into bottom-line benefits. Wendals Foods already has used the pilot's process and sample customer profitability information to restructure sales routes, close depots, and modify customer discount structures.

The effort to build a customer profitability database is not warranted if the information provided to users comes from an out-of-date snapshot of the business. The data and the database structures have to be kept up to date to reflect current trading relationships if the customer profitability information is to provide value for money.

The value of information is not in the reporting, but in the decisions that follow. ABC customer profitability information backed by a process view of both the costs and performance of the business provides the greatest value for money of all accounting information. It enables informed decisions on what to do, with what product, for which customer, and it provides insight for the holistic management of cost and performance.

Next Steps/Future Plans: Today and Beyond

Best Brands has its sights set on great things. Although the company is focused on growth opportunities in local markets, it continues to further expand its business and introduce its brands into more international markets. With its consumer, customer, and shopper always first in mind, Best Brands will continue to offer affordable South African brands with great taste, consistent quality, and a focus on health and well-being to discerning consumers around the world.

Armed with solid information from the ABC project, Wendals recently acquired the Baker Street range of snacks, further strengthening its position as a major player in the South African snack market.

Wendals Foods can benefit its EIS system by taking advantage of the true dimensionality of the next version of its ABC system, which has built-in EIS and can provide the "slicing and dicing" without having to use another tool to provide its reporting.

Baker Street Snacks was founded in 1993, and the business was built on a passion to manufacture superior-quality, differentiated niche brands. This snack company led the market through innovation, creating new categories within the snack market. Today Baker Street Snacks dominates these categories with many popular brands.

The Baker Street Snacks products will continue to be a dominant player within the South African snack market, appealing to a broad range of consumers through innovation, pack design, and a discerning snacking.

EXPERT WRAP-UP

Jeff Thomson

Wendals Foods is to be commended for turning its passion for customer innovations inward to focus on improving key business processes, in this case the strategic costing process. Making the "best" choices around customers, products, distribution channels, and resources was critical for Wendals to improve its market position in an increasingly competitive market. It appears that its implementation was successful in terms of dollar savings and implementation of a new way of thinking as it relates to strategic cost management. There are suggestions and questions that should be considered, which may form the basis for some follow-up initiatives by Wendals Foods:

- In its full ABC implementation, "Wendals determined that rather than developing a model at an activity-based level of detail, it would be quicker, more certain of success, and cheaper to develop the ABC model at the process level. A process could be broken down to the activity level of detail later, when the need arose." This approach is not advisable. The heart of an activity-based approach is to focus on the few key activities that drive downstream process costs. Doing this allows for strategic and tactical choices around value-added versus non–value-added activities and the appropriate level of investment. There are simplifying approaches, such as using the "80/20" rule to determine the relatively few key activities per major process. Additionally, in recent years an approach called time-driven ABC has allowed some level of simplification for cumbersome, data-intensive ABC implementations.[1] Related to the preceding comment, a key consideration for any ABC implementation is how the activity/process model will be updated. How will financial data from the general ledger and nonfinancial data from various operations systems allow for a transparent, seamless, efficient, and controllable flow of data? To what extent is the process manual versus systematized? Standards and technologies available today make data integration much easier. As an example, the evolving XBRL standard (eXtensible Business Reporting Language) is an XML-based tagging process that is making the data integration process much more efficient. Additionally, the aforementioned time-driven ABC approach simplifies the data collection process using an 80/20 rule of capturing time spent on key activities and minimizes the burdensome employee time study or survey.
- Critical enablers for ABC success include an enabling technology and data-centric platform. Wendals Foods employed a data ware-

house approach, which is a positive step, but often the population of data into the data warehouse and the extraction process from the warehouse is inefficient and not fully controllable. That is why evolving "tagging" technologies and standards are so critical to the future of the information supply chain; they allow for more rapid and controllable data integration. In this case, Wendals had to tackle the issue of how to pull "customer ID" data and intelligence from multiple data stores in the corporation. In many enterprises, customers are identified differently because of subsidiary relationships and retail versus wholesale relationships. Wendals also makes mention of a custom database to perform the calculations for customer profitability. Be wary of customization and one-offs—get very friendly with your chief technology or information officer and drive an integrated, data-centric set of requirements.

- It is not clear how specifically Wendals defined "customer profitability" and the appropriate level of analysis for strategic decision making. These are important considerations before implementing ABC. For example, does contribution margin, gross margin, or gross income make sense? Can actionable ABC customer profitability analyses really take place at the individual customer level? Wendal's customers ranged from large hypermarkets to small corner cafés. Perhaps profitability would make sense for the top X revenue-generating hypermarkets, and another criteria could be used to segment the rest of the high-end and low-end bases (e.g., distribution channel, location).

- It is also not clear from the case what Wendal's assumptions were with respect to fixed and variable/proportional costs. This is another area that is at the heart of any strategic costing approach. Treating all costs as entirely fixed or entirely variable is not likely to be appropriate at the activity, resource, process, or product levels. The lack of a robust method for determining fixed versus variable costs could result in inappropriate marginal pricing and "smearing" of costs across product lines (resulting in inaccurate investment and resource allocation decisions). A new body of knowledge emerging over the past few years called Resource Consumption Accounting (RCA) provides approaches for determining fixed and proportional costs at the resource level (e.g., people and machines that drive activities).[2]

- In its pilot project, Wendals mentions that "because high labor and capital costs were incurred in establishing a three-shift manufacturing environment, nonworking time in operations had a significant effect on product cost." A close second to fixed/variable determination in strategic costing is the treatment of idle capacity. Many ABC implementations fail or provide inaccurate data because idle capacity is smeared across resources or products and not separately addressed as a strategic issue. The RCA approach addresses the issue of idle capacity, as mentioned.

- On a more tactical and analytical level, Wendals indicates that a real challenge exists in sourcing history to keep the ABC model refreshed. It notes that a key issue is how much historical data to utilize, balancing time, cost, and accuracy. One basic statistical approach would be to utilize rolling or moving averages (e.g., a three-month moving average of history sourced from the general ledger).

ENDNOTES

1. Robert S. Kaplan and Steven R. Anderson, "Time-Driven Activity Based Costing," *Harvard Business Review* 82, no. 11 (November 2004).
2. For more detail on RCA, visit the Institute of Management Accountants (IMA) Web site at www.imanet.org.

10

VERI GLASS: SEE CLEARLY WITH ACTIVITY-BASED COSTING?

Vision without action is merely a dream. Action without vision just passes the time. Vision with action can change the world.

—Joel Barker

FOREWORD

Don Bean

Much can be learned from the study of performance improvement initiatives. Sometimes, though, you can learn as much from what is not said as what is. Although it does not state it explicitly, this case illustrates the rarely understood symbiotic relationship between activity-based costing (ABC) and Business Intelligence (BI).

Business Intelligence can be loosely defined as a group of technologies that assist in the gathering, storing, and analysis of data that support better decision making. Business Intelligence, like ABC, is dependent on the skill of the implementer to make a logical, understandable, and useful data model on which to build the reports and analysis that managers rely on to make decisions. Without some forethought and planning, BI can easily become a way to give managers fast and efficient access to confusing and misleading information.

Veri Glass set out on its journey with the following goal: implement an information system that would "provide adequate and useful support for decision making." It is at this point in a BI project that the real trouble starts. But rather than leap into building an all-inclusive data warehouse and reporting infrastructure, Veri Glass did something very smart; it planned, it developed goals for the project, and it selected a methodology (ABC) for communicating information to its audience.

INTRODUCTION

Ninety years after its founding, Veri Group maintains its position as the largest glass manufacturer in Latin America. Its products are exported to more than 70 countries and consolidated sales have eclipsed U.S. $2.5 billion. Veri's mission reflects its commitment to become the most cost-effective manufacturer in the markets it serves.

Within the five business units of the Veri Group, Veri Glass focuses on the production, distribution, and sales of a wide variety of products, from natural glass to solar panels, as well as the manufacture of domes, windshields, and polyvinilic films.

Veri Glass manages five business areas—Glass and Crystal, Automotive Products for Original Equipment, Automotive Products for Spare Market, Vitro Flex, and Chemical M—integrated with seven production and two distribution companies that contribute almost one-third of the group's annual revenues. The organization is affected by volatile changes to the global requirements of the highly competitive building and automotive markets.

Owing to the dynamic relationships among its companies and the complexity of its processes, the need for a dependable, modern information system emerged, one that above all would provide adequate and useful support for decision making. Thus came about the idea of implementing a methodology that would provide Veri Glass with reliable data to analyze the efficiency of its internal and external processes and ultimately allow it to be more competitive.

The general director made the decision to start the strategic project IFMS (Integrated Financial Management System). IFMS would allow Veri Glass to evaluate and implement the cultural changes necessary for effective information management. And activity-based costing (ABC) fit like a glove.

The attempt to create a cost-, performance-, and process-monitoring system was not a new effort in Veri Glass. There had been previous isolated efforts to adopt a methodology of this type, but those efforts diminished over time as they were either inadequate or provided too limited a scope.

Since implementing IFMS, Veri Glass can assert unequivocally that, with ABC, its business unit has found a reliable tool to support the decision-making process and, with activity-based management (ABM), it has a methodology that generates progressive business solutions.

ORGANIZATIONAL ISSUES

Until the introduction of ABC, Veri Glass had measured cost information with a traditional and inflexible system based on an accounting perspective. Although these data balance perfectly and are useful for creating financial statements, they do not fully reflect what Veri Glass actually manufactures as an organization.

The creation of the IFMS was a response to the need for integrating the administrative, financial, and corporate systems to drive its enterprise goals more effectively. The objectives that it had for IFMS are summarized in three functions:

1. To change the paradigm in the culture of information management, in its control as well as in its application, in order to generate a common language for division wide understanding

2. To establish a communication platform for setting and monitoring financial objectives

3. To develop tools that support operational and strategic decision making, measure performance, and support forecasts

In order to achieve these objectives, Veri Glass defined a strategy that would generate value through all its business processes. Its goal was to develop an information system that integrated and provided relevant information company-wide, but it lacked the ad hoc reporting tools for this purpose. The solution was to create an up-front data warehouse.

Veri Glass defined the different requirements of the necessary applications for the construction of the data warehouse. With cost information needs in mind, its management met and compared the available alternatives in the market to choose the most appropriate option for what it was pursuing with IFMS in the ABC area. The task was to find an integrated information system that normalized its measurements and that could give meaning to the information. After evaluating several alternatives, it was decided to adopt the Oros ABM software now produced by SAS, called SAS Activity-Based Management. It was time for Veri Glass to assume the challenge of changing, division wide, how it makes its products, handles its materials, and measures its performance.

CASE STUDY

Breaking Paradigms for a New Culture: Education as Foundation

The IFMS project was presented to company personnel as a complete system, not merely a financial one. IFMS was customized for each department and for the division as a whole. The time had come to showcase ABC as the ideal tool to realize improved operations planning and control, as well as provide support to the continuous improvement process. On this basis project implementers proposed to introduce ABC as a routine way of working, in a culture of cost administration.

Obstacles are faced that must be anticipated and overcome in any implementation of this kind. In Veri Glass's case, there were two principal obstacles. The first was lack of trust by employees because previous attempts with other methodologies provided bad results. This situation provoked an understandable rejection at the beginning. The other significant barrier that had to be dealt with was that certain processes were not included in the system's information.

From the very first, Veri Glass planned to surmount these obstacles simultaneously. It met with the department heads of each functional area to create databases that would be compatible with all others in the organization. It captured the interest of the staff by using questions about expenses in terms of human assets, material, technology required, and supplies and services. The objective was to help them realize that the information with which they had been working gave them only a partial view of the business and that with ABC, things could be different.

Beforehand Veri Glass knew that even with a heightened theoretical awareness, only in practice could it obtain users' trust in this tool. At this point, the pilot tests needed to be so useful as to not only refine certain points but to create, within the organization, an environment of optimism and an acceptance of change.

As business operations were the core of its model, the people responsible for these processes learned to measure their performance and their weaknesses. They began to discover areas of opportunity that were invisible before the pilot tests because of unreliable information and limited perspective.

Once the awareness of the personnel was raised, Veri Glass began an educational process to generate understanding of the management and interpretation of the information. This standardization of thought regarding its processes has allowed an improved analysis of costs and cost objects.

Let's Work: Building a Linear Model

Beginning with the premise that all human activity is capable of being measured, the decision to implement a model based on activities led Veri Glass to identify the tasks, processes, services, and cost objects of value chains. From that perspective, Veri Glass analyzed various types of models, their scope and limitations, until it designed the one that best met its expectations.

There are two important sides to the model:

1. **Operational.** A model in which all the levels of the organization must be convinced that the ABC model is a cultural model, that is to say, a way of life
2. **Strategic.** A model in which ABC, as with other systems, is part of a continuous improvement process used to align all activities

The model had four development principles:

1. **Participation.** All the functional areas were involved in the model design, as their interaction is the foundation of the business.
2. **Autonomy.** Each department is responsible for the model's correct implementation and operation.
3. **Flexible.** The model can be reoriented or adjusted according to the improvement and opportunity initiatives of the market.
4. **Communicable.** The model provides that any level of the company can count on standardized quality information in a timely manner.

Veri Glass focused its ABC model differently from most other examples it knew about. Instead of going from strategic to operational, Veri Glass said: "If we can arrange the operational base with short-, medium-, and long-term objectives, then with ABC we will be able to align the processes to our business goals."

After analyzing the relationships among the activities and the processes that were understood, Veri Glass first had to model these simple relationships and later interrelate them in growing degrees of complexity. Each department inventoried activities that automatically linked to the operational chains.

With this approach, the construction of the model (see Exhibit 10.1) was very simple. With its ABM software, Veri Glass could transform its accounting data to fit the model through simple relationships using natural language. It did not have to restructure its cost centers because it already had them identified in what is called value chains.

As not all the activities are consumed by a product or a client, but some support an internal process, client supplier relationships were constructed at the interdepartmental level. Through those relationships, Veri Glass had, on one hand, an understanding of what a specific department actually costs in activity terms and, on the other hand, and understanding of what costs that department receives

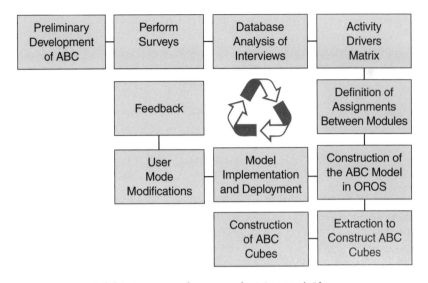

Exhibit 10.1 Development of ABC at Veri Glass

from other areas without mixing the information. With the application of this model management now has the scheme of each chain of value and Veri Glass can measure activities by unit, by segment, or by the whole division.

As examples, pilots are enough. The internal sales job takes a lot of time and work, but Veri Glass is convinced that the effort was well worth it. Although it was implementing the pilot tests in different areas, it was becoming more and more adept. The change from a skeptical organization to an organization whose staff not only believed in ABC but developed improvement initiatives based on ABC happened in a very short time.

Veri Glass established 11 pilot tests, with much good success. The goal for the pilot phase was that all the Mexican operations of the Veri Glass business unit would be using ABC and ABM.

During the installation of the pilot tests, performance measures revealed important areas of opportunity. With this knowledge, the members of the production and the support departments developed improvement initiatives naturally, which have favorably influenced yield, productivity, costs and inventory reduction, and efficiency and have, in general, resulted in better overall operations and administration.

The impact of the pilot tests has been very positive. When real results were generated, the improvement spirit became contagious among all personnel. The work centers have been pulling together and, as a result, have created teams that share the same business vision.

With the pilot tests, the implementation of a useful information tool allowed a practical application of the principles of IFMS information. This has not only simplified operational labor, but at the same time has demanded new work disciplines and ways of administration.

Changes Are Seen, Experienced, and Passed Along

With activity-based management, Veri Glass linked cost management with process assignments. The company can monitor them with the operational indicators from the production areas. This will allow Veri Glass, in the near future, to build a balanced scorecard to achieve continuous cost measurement.

By determining the cost factors and standardizing the systems that were scattered before, Veri Glass has been able to apply the criteria that allow it to monitor agreed-on performance measures, organizational objectives, and organizational goals. By bringing order to the process, Veri Glass is better able to manage the business.

In the ABM pilots, analysis of activities, cost assignments, and process views are now interrelated and generate added value to all the operations linked to these pilots. They also show the profitability of each client and products from various perspectives (see Exhibit 10.2). With ABC Veri Glass has identified product lines that are important value adders and those that were not considered useful because they were viewed from a distorted perspective.

With ABM, Veri Glass knows where it will have losses, and it can also identify why and how much they cost the firm. The company is structured with feedback channels on different levels, and the effects of continuous improvement of its systems and processes can be seen.

Currently it is working on the establishment of improvement initiatives in processes such as evaluation of scenarios, game plans, cycle times, definition of production measures, and minimizing reworks, useless pieces, or rejects. In addition, it is also working on the optimization of scarce resources, which impact cost reduction and reduction of working capital.

Veri Group has seen almost immediate results. Three months after implementing changes in the Veri Glass unit, production has increased by nearly 32,000 pieces. This additional production achieved a 1% improvement in the operational efficiency of this business segment.

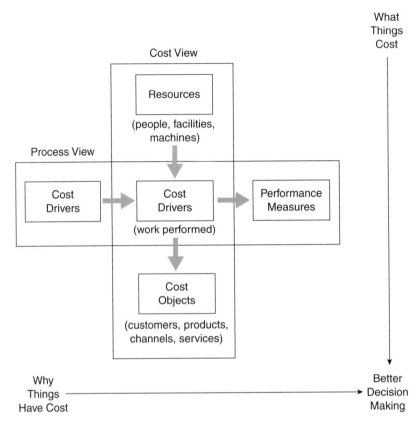

Exhibit 10.2 Veri Glass Activity-Based Management Model Using the CAM-I Cross
Derived from the Consortium of Advanced Management–International (CAM-I).

Veri Group is currently evaluating the suitability of employing outsourcing services. In summer 2005 it will start an ABC benchmarking project with companies of the same international character.

The Future Depends on the Color of Your Crystal Ball

The approach and management of information from Veri Glass processes will provide the business opportunities and competitive advantages of the future. The important thing in Veri Group's administration system is that all the Veri Glass levels—low, medium, and high—are now using IFMS to plan production, finance, sales, logistics, marketing, and cost strategies.

It is difficult to change a culture rapidly. A sense of urgency is important, but it is necessary to link this with a learning process to obtain commitment from the users. Beginning with a small group, Veri Group can grow with the number of applications and improvements that it can achieve.

The future of Veri Glass appears promising, now that the staff has confidence in the soundness and continuity of the information with ABC. The company is prepared to respond operationally and strategically to demands and changes in its environment.

EXPERT WRAP-UP

Don Bean

Like most companies using ABC, Veri Glass created a business model that explains how the business operates and is understood by all departments. In addition to calculating costs of each business process, the model is able to show the interrelationships between processes and departments as well as performance measures. The data from this model, and the newly created process terminology, became the communication standard for Veri Glass and the basis for the Business Intelligence/Data Warehouse project that ensued.

What Veri Glass achieved was made possible by implementing a Business Intelligence System, not just an ABC model. The system is made up of interrelated technologies, methodology, practices, methods, and audience that combine to form a whole that delivers on the definition and promise of Business Intelligence.

——————11——————

ABC AIRWAYS: IMPLEMENTATION LANDS MILLIONS IN PROCESS IMPROVEMENT SAVINGS

Kaizen: gradual unending improvement by doing little things better, by setting and achieving increasingly higher standards.

—Masaaki Imai

FOREWORD

Ed Blocher

This case is an excellent illustration of how activity-based costing/management (ABC/M) can provide new insights for strategic and operational decision making. In this case, as often in similar situations, the firm finds that questions about costs and a desire for a better understanding of costs within it lead management to ask other questions. The further questions usually concern critical business issues, such as changes in the firm's competitive environment and how the firm's strategy should be reconsidered in light of these changes. These questions can result in changes in marketing or operational strategies, as for the firm in this case. ABC/M provides the mechanism for answering these questions.

INTRODUCTION

ABC Airways is one of the world's leading air carriers and one of its largest. It is also one of the largest U.S. airlines and holds the dominant market position in the eastern United States. With about 42,000 employees, the company operates more than 2,000 mainline flights daily, serving more than 100 airports in the United States, Canada, Mexico, the Caribbean and Gulf of Mexico, Germany, Italy, France, and Spain.

The ABC Airways system also includes the Shuttle by ABC and ABC Express Airways, and the system as a whole operates more than 4,500 daily departures to more than 200 airports. The ABC Airways power plant department, or aircraft engine shop, at the Pittsburgh International Airport maintains and overhauls 350 jet engines powering 152 of ABC Airways' 380 aircraft. When an engine arrives at the ABC Airways Power Plant Department for maintenance, it can have as many as 11 separate modules that can be repaired or overhauled. In-house repair and overhaul capabilities focus on the seven model types of the Pratt & Whitney JT8 engine family. The engine shop operates 24 hours a day, 5 days a week.

There are about 500 employees in the engine shop. The workforce is divided into 24 separate, self-directed work teams. The majority of the power plant employees are represented by the International Association of Machinists (IAM). ABC Airways and the IAM have implemented a High Performance Work Organization initiative whereby they establish a collaborative work environment with common goals. Each work team develops its own charter and selects a team leader. Team members actively manage their work areas and identify opportunities for improvement.

UNDERSTANDING THE BUSINESS NEEDS

ABC Airways needed detailed cost information with particular focus on engine overhaul costs. The lack of detailed operational and financial information did not allow management to fully understand the costs associated with producing or overhauling an engine and, to a lesser extent, the costs of each of the modules making up an engine. This fact led management to ask other key questions, which would enable ABC Airways to determine the business solution needed to provide this information. Some of the key questions included:

- What are ABC Airways' critical business issues? (See Exhibit 11.1.)
- What industry trends are driving these issues?
- What is the strategy to meet the needs of the changing business environment?
- What operational and financial information would provide decision support to meet these business needs?
- What level of detail is needed to manage?
- What frequency of reporting is needed?

- Spending cash to buy new parts and overlooking opportunity to repair inventory
- Do not understand operating costs
- Lack of relevant operating metrics
- Need baseline to quantify improvements made by self-directed work teams

Exhibit 11.1 ABC Airways' Critical Business Issues

The answer to each of these questions would provide insight to the action needed to deliver the necessary information. ABC Airways determined that more detailed and insightful information was needed to manage the business, drive improvement, manage costs, and support third-party pricing. The business solution would have to support each of these needs.

BUSINESS SOLUTION

ABC/M was the business solution chosen for many reasons. ABC/M could not only help determine the true cost of engine maintenance, but could also provide operational and financial information to be used by the self-directed work teams to identify opportunities for improvement. ABC/M would also be the key enabler for ABC Airways to better understand:

- Repair in stock versus buy new—inventory decision making
- True cost of operations to support third-party pricing
- Operational metrics for improvement and benchmarking
- Impact of improvements made by self-directed work teams

An ABC team was formed at ABC Airways to implement ABC/M in the Power Plant Department. The team was composed of two full-time ABC Airways employees from the engine shop, an ABC Airways financial staff member, and two certified public accountants.

CASE STUDY

Project Approach

The project was divided into four main phases. The phases consisted of introduction to ABC, data collection and information gathering, model building, and data analysis and reporting.

Introduction to ABC Phase

To ensure a common starting point, several meetings were held with all employees to explain the ABC project, why it was being undertaken, and the insights it would provide. These initial meetings served to achieve employee buy-in and support. Subsequent meetings were held with team leaders and representative members of each of the 24 work teams who were most familiar with the engine shop processes and who could describe the objectives and the benefits of the initiative.

Data Collection and Information Gathering

One of the initial steps in the data collection phase was to understand the level of cost object detail to be costed. By understanding the level of detail to be costed, the team could gain insight into the types of activities and the level of detail to be collected and measured. Once the products to be costed were understood, the team began to gather specific cost pool information. The team determined it was necessary to collect and include the cost of rent, utilities, and benefits, which were paid by the corporate headquarters, in order to determine the true cost of the Power Plant Department. Costs were also collected for other areas, known as the periphery groups, that include warranty, stores, training, and purchasing. These are separate groups within ABC Airways that operate their own budgets and perform services not only for the Power Plant Department, but for other areas as well. These costs were also important to include in the analysis in order to understand the true cost of the Power Plant Department.

Next, activities were collected from each of the work teams, including core and noncore activities, such as tear-down, welding, waiting for tooling, and re-work. The diversity of the workforce and layout of work areas into teams made collecting the necessary operational and financial information challenging for the team. The final activity dictionary included 410 activities across the engine shop, including 47 non–value-added activities. Representatives from each of the 24 self-directed work teams were then interviewed to determine how their effort was distributed across their team-specific activities. The activities were captured on team-specific spreadsheets and populated by the representatives based on percentage of effort. In addition, the spreadsheet design captured any cost diversity between the different engine types, which illustrated if certain engine model types required more effort for a certain activity. To assist the employees in completing the effort spreadsheets, a time conversion table was developed to convert the actual time spent on activities into percentages. The periphery groups that performed services for the Power Plant Department were also included in this process in order to determine the number of employees dedicated to power plant tasks and the associated effort spent on those tasks. The team then attributed each of the activities as core, support, contractual, or irrelevant activities to understand how the power plant was investing its time and effort.

Across all four phases of the project, project management controls were used to assist in defining the scope of the tasks and progress being made in completing them. These controls were essential considering activity information was needed for 500 people working three shifts, with 12 separate classifications of employees, such as mechanics, welders, machinists, and inspectors—most with different labor rates.

Obtaining the final cost and headcount per process was complicated; teams of people were dedicated to many different processes. A headcount control sheet allowed the cost management team to identify the true headcount associated with each of the processes. Another project control included a progress chart. This chart detailed each task that needed to be accomplished for each of the 24 work teams. As the tasks were completed, the color-coded chart was updated. Using visual controls, any member could quickly see what remained to be accomplished as well as the scope of the remaining tasks.

Model Building

Using ABC Technologies' Oros (now SAS Activity-Based Management), the ABC Airways' ABC team constructed its entire model quickly and efficiently. The first module to be constructed was the cost object module based on the level of detail determined in the data collection phase. The cost object hierarchy would accommodate the variability in levels of service for each engine type. Each engine has different maintenance needs or service levels; the model allowed ABC Airways to determine the true costs for each type of engine by each service level. The activity module was built next. The activity dictionary, developed earlier in the data collection phase, was easily imported into the activity module from a spreadsheet format. Finally, the resource module was built. The resource hierarchy was also imported from a spreadsheet format based on the level of detail determined earlier in the project. Driver data were collected after each module structure or hierarchy was in place in the model. The cost management team built intuitive abbreviated names and initials into its model reference numbers to help it diagnose any problems it might have during model building. In doing so, the team could immediately determine where specific account dollar amounts were derived. The use of these intuitive reference numbers proved to be invaluable during error and warning diagnosis by enabling the team to quickly pinpoint the problem areas. Once the model was running, it provided true cost information previously unavailable within the power plant department (see Exhibits 11.2 and 11.3).

Data Analysis and Reporting

After the model was built and the ABC data were available, the data needed to be analyzed and reported. The team first conducted reasonableness checks to ensure the model was assigning costs appropriately. Next the team had to assimilate the data into a format that could be reported and easily understood by the engine shop employees. Report books were created for each of the 24 self-directed work teams

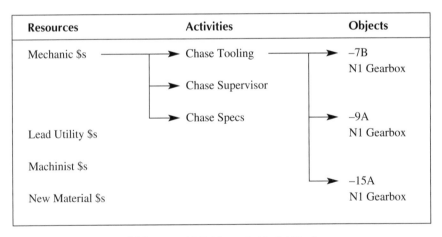

Exhibit 11.2 ABC Airway's Model Design

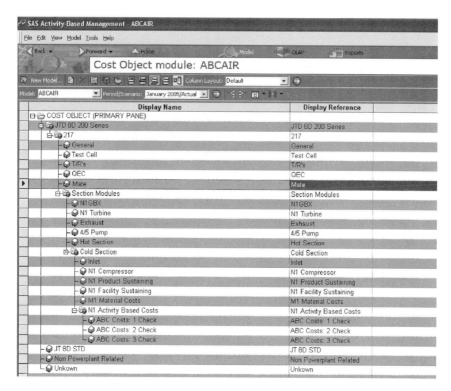

Exhibit 11.3 Cost Object Module in SAS Activity-Based Management

with their individual results as well as a view of the entire engine shop. These reports were well received by the teams and validated their contributions during the
data collection phases. Team leaders as well as all team members now had access
to operational and financial information that would enable them to drive improvement, measure results, and cultivate process ownership.

Project Results

The ABC model output provided ABC Airways with operational and financial
data to support strategic and operational decision making. The ABC information
identified process improvement savings opportunities for ABC Airways totaling
$4.3 million per year and 63 full-time equivalents (see Exhibit 11.4). The model
output provided numerous operational and financial metrics that were not previously available. The self-directed work teams could now see the activities' cost by

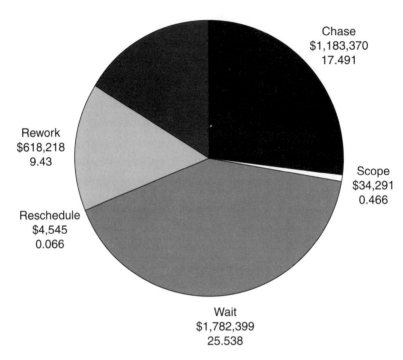

Dysfunctional Drill-Down by Costs & FTEs
Total Costs $4,343,786
Total FTEs 63

Chase
$1,183,370
17.491

Scope
$34,291
0.466

Wait
$1,782,399
25.538

Reschedule
$4,545
0.066

Rework
$618,218
9.43

Exhibit 11.4 Jet Shop Total Cost Report

labor classification and by shift. In addition, a rank-order analysis for the activity costs was conducted. This view provided insight into the most expensive non–value-added activities (see Exhibit 11.5) occurring in each work team. This information was immediately available to begin analysis for process improvement opportunities. For example, one work team found it spent about 80% of its effort, or $85,000 per year, reinspecting due to the use of an older piece of inspection equipment. The ABC information justified the purchase of the new piece of inspection equipment, which cost less than the $85,000 spent on reinspection each year.

The team, now equipped with operational and financial information, needed to capitalize on the identified opportunities in response to the business issues set

Dysfunctional	Support	Core	Contract
Chase	Meetings	Core	Lunch
Wait	Interface	Lead Mechanic	Vacation
Repair Related (Scope)	Training	Inspection	
Rescheduling Related	Customer Related	Unused Capacity	
Rework Related	Safety Related		
Resolving Problems	Housekeeping Related		

Exhibit 11.5 ABC Major Activities Broken Out by Activity Type

forth at the beginning of the project. The ABC model output could now be used to support the business through:

- Supporting repair versus buy inventory decisions
- Understanding the true cost of operations to support pricing
- Supporting benchmarking
- Providing a baseline for measuring improvements by the self-directed work teams

Although irrelevant activities were identified, the team would have to undertake root cause analysis to identify the causes for the effort. Upon identifying the true cause, the company and teams will be able to eliminate or reduce the impact of non–value-added activities. The ABC team now publishes a unit cost guide three times a year. This guide details per-unit costs for each of the seven engine types and their modules.

Next Steps

The Power Plant Department management made the decision to update the cost model on a trimester basis. Therefore, every four months, headcount for each of the teams and processes will be updated in the model. Plans also call for annual activity and effort updates via the effort grids, which will provide progress reports on process improvements made by the self-directed work teams in the engine shop. When the engine shop undertook this ABC project, a number of short-comings existed in its ability to provide necessary operational and financial data for the cost model. For example, although the company knew how many engines it produced, there was no accurate information on how many modules were produced. As a result, the team set up procedures to capture accurate production by engine and by module. The ABC team now publishes a monthly engine and module production summary for the Power Plant Department.

The team also found weakness in tracking for overtime costs. Many of these costs were grouped together, which did not allow a view of what team or discipline actually incurred the costs. The cost management team brought greater detail to these costs by using an overtime report, also published monthly.

The need for accurate and timely data to support the cost model will drive the team to continually validate data frequency, source, format, and capture methods. Communication of results is an ongoing effort. The team will need to communicate ABC results to the people who can and will implement change.

EXPERT WRAP-UP

Ed Blocher

This case explains the role of ABC/M in process improvement in the Power Plant Department at a major airline. This department is responsible for maintaining and overhauling the jet engines for 152 of the aircraft in the carrier's fleet. Driven by the need to better understand the costs within the department, management implemented an ABC/M project, using Oros. The ABC/M project led management to consider further questions dealing with critical business issues involving refining and execution of the firm's strategy. Most important, the ABC/M project identified process improvement opportunities that led to millions of dollars in savings. Other benefits included a better basis for strategic and operational decision making (including, e.g., decisions to repair or replace) and the development of better cost tracking systems, as the project identified weaknesses in accounting for certain costs.

POWER & LIGHT GETS A CHARGE OUT OF ACTIVITY-BASED COSTING/MANAGEMENT

Edison's greatest achievement came in 1879, when he invented the electric company. Edison's design was a brilliant adaptation of the simple electrical circuit: the electric company sends electricity through a wire to a customer, then immediately gets the electricity back through another wire, then (this is the brilliant part) sends it right back to the customer again. This means that an electric company can sell a customer the same batch of electricity thousands of times a day and never get caught . . . [T]he last year any new electricity was generated in the United States was 1937; the electric companies have been merely re-selling it ever since, which is why they have so much free time to apply for rate increases.

—Dave Barry

FOREWORD

Building an ABC/M model sounds like an easy way to cut costs: "Just build a model and then we can do it cheaper." However, simply building an ABC/M model is not the same as a managing an organizations performance. It does not abdicate your responsibilities your customers.

It has become a common development over the world—especially in the United States and Europe—to build ABC/M models and fail to maintain them over a long period of time. They key ingredients that are missing are the focus on the correct metrics to manage an organization, the alignment to an organization's strategy, and the agility that managers have to make key decisions.

Performance Management is the key to help us conduct business more intelligently. It does not provide all the answers. It should not be used in isolation, and it will not tell you why something happened. Nevertheless, once you know what has happened, it can point you in the right direction, so you can begin to find the answers you need.

Read this case critically, look for what is missing and think of ways to make sure that the information created in this ABC system can be used. After eleven cases, you should be in a position to review and understand the information gaps that can be created when an organization is not focused on its strategy. The key learning from this case lies in what is missing. Ask yourself, "How can I create focus, alignment and agility in my organization"?

INTRODUCTION

The Power & Light Company, like other electrical utility companies, is regulated by the Federal Energy Regulatory Commission. However, just as the telephone and gas utilities have been deregulated in the past, signs of deregulation in the power and light wholesale business have started to emerge. The balance of the industry will be changing in the next three to five years. Although Power & Light has always striven to control its costs for its ratepayers, the emergence of competition has reinforced its desire to be a low-cost provider.

Although three to five years may seem like a long time, it is not. In that time, the industry has to take a look at business, and more important its customers, in a whole new perspective. Electric companies could soon have house-to-house, company-to-company competition. This is where activity-based costing (ABC) and activity-based management (ABM) come into play.

In the past decade, the electric and other utility companies have been getting "charged up" over ABC and ABM. Power & Light formalized its interest in ABC/M and Economic Value Added (EVA®) by establishing a corporate goal to implement ABC, high-level ABM, and EVA. Further corporate goals have been established for the continued development of ABC and ABM results. These goals are focused on the training, reporting, and consulting of ABC, ABM, and their results.

MERRILL LYNCH AND CO.

According to a Merrill Lynch and Co. study, Merrill Lynch believes electric companies that implement ABM have a clear competitive advantage over other electric companies that have not, all other factors considered equal.[1] This study also indicated that the average electrical utility implementation (from the brainstorming process to full implementation and usage) is taking five to eight years.

Merrill Lynch, with the help of several other companies, has identified seven stages of implementation and their average implementation time:

1. Evaluation (4 to 6 months)
2. Definition (12 to 30 months)
3. System development (4 to 6 months)
4. Pilot (12 to 18 months)
5. Start-up (12 to 18 months)
6. Ramp-up (15 to 24 months)
7. Full use (Merrill Lynch's definition of "full use" is that the "utility's culture has changed" and that "management has the tools to rapidly adjust company efforts to meet corporate and strategic goals."

As a result of this study, Merrill Lynch believes that "ABM is one of the most important areas for improvement of management processes." Its research has provided the support and justification to tie stock prices with a risk adjustment related to the implementation of ABM.

POWER & LIGHT APPROACH

In the electric utility industry, change management is the key to success. The companies in the industry that have not started to prepare for the deregulated environment are already behind. At Power & Light, everyone—from the president to plant and department managers to clerks, operators, and linemen—has been informed and updated as progress continues.

The communication has traveled both up and down through the company. The bulk of the communication is directed through its steering committee. This is a cross-functional group, primarily managers, who are extremely knowledgeable about their department's activities. They understand not only the activities conducted within their own department, but interactions with other departments throughout the company. Steering committee members forward information collected and discussed up to the vice president and down through the organization.

The corporate implementation team is composed of two key members of the steering committee, an outside consultant, and an internal consultant. Two additional support teams are focusing specifically on the production and distribution areas of the company. These teams assist the implementation team by working on the detailed items and supporting these groups.

Power & Light's approach calls for an accelerated implementation of the process from conception through data gathering, model design, reporting, and training (both general and specific software training). Its schedule calls for ABC cost information and ABM performance measurements by the end of the year for comprehensive reporting.

Many companies may want to take a slow steady pace, going step by step. This, however, takes time, time Power & Light could not afford. For Power & Light, the opportunities of open competition demand a fast-paced approach. It took roughly nine months from the activity determination and definition step of its implementation before the company began to operate in a live mode of the ABC/M system.

Trying to fit its implementation into a step-by-step schedule was just not possible. It is not unusual for implementation simultaneously to be at two, three, or even four of the different stages just mentioned. Power & Light's split-team approach allowed it to be working on several different items at one time (e.g., model creation, report design and approval, and assignment methodology were all happening at the same time).

Everyone at Power & Light has been, and continues to be, very supportive of the project. Although some believe that ABC/M implementations are successful when management changes and decisions are being made with the information, Power & Light believes change is important from day one. That is one of the reasons why its project continues to be so successful. The other major reason is communication—with all levels and all areas of the company.

IMPLEMENTATION PHASES AND STATUS

Although Power & Light has a detailed implementation plan, the implementation of multiple steps at the same time adds complexity to the tracking progress. There are only three critical measuring steps, which are the same whether you are implementing ABC/M or any similar project. You have completed a major step when your company and its employees are:

- Talking the talk
- Walking the walk
- Running the race

If you were to ask management employees of Power & Light about its ABC/M implementation, in most cases they could tell you about the basics of ABC/M and the project itself. If you were to ask department managers questions about the implementation, you could have a good conversation about how they see the project helping them and the uses to which they plan to put the ABC information.

When individuals throughout the organization are talking about ABC/M, not only within their department but also with other departments, they are "talking the talk." Power & Light's implementation process entailed making presentations throughout the entire company. The initial presentation was provided to approximately 30 groups throughout the company, from the boardroom, to the mailroom, to individual plants and distribution centers. Presentations included the basics of ABC and ABM, its purpose at Power & Light, its involvement with the EVA implementation, and information relevant to specific areas of the company. Additional presentations are planned for those who were not involved in the first round.

The second level of presentations deal with the reporting available from the ABC/M system. Currently Power & Light has developed 17 different reports with plans to add additional reports later. These reports were developed with three different views in mind:

1. **Organizational view.** Reports designed for divisions and individual departments to view their individual costs as they are assigned to processes/activities. (This is similar to reports they currently receive except they are by process/activity.)

2. **Process view.** Reports designed for process owners that show all departments assigning costs to a given process/activity.

3. **Product/service view.** Reports designed for product owners that show all activity costs assigned to the various products and services available from the company by location and/or division.

Reports are presented year-to-date, monthly, or both. Many of the reports compare budget versus actual as well as provide performance measurements for comparison or trend analysis.

The reviewing of reports begins the "walking the walk" phase of the implementation. This phase is the reporting and "putting to use" phase of the implementation. Users of the information will review the information they are receiving to gain understanding. For Power & Light, this phase will begin in January with one full year's worth of both budgeted and actual historical costs by month. Reports will be e-mailed to executives, department managers, and process owners each month thereafter.

The second part of this phase will make reports available to all employees via a report warehouse on the network. By providing a system report warehouse, Power & Light will distribute the information faster and more efficiently.

Power & Light's OLAP (online analytical processing) report system gives users of information the greatest flexibility in obtaining the data they want to see. Power & Light has already had requests for report information in a graph chart format. Rather than creating "canned" reports, it wants to give users the flexibility to fit their own needs.

With the implementation of both the system report warehouse and the OLAP reporting system, Power & Light is charged up on ABC/M and ready to "run the race." At this point, individual groups will be running with their information. Internal consulting will be available for groups needing additional support or refinements of the model. Incorporating its ABC/M system with EVA and other projects and aspects of its change management approach, Power & Light will be running the race, if not leading the race.

EXPERT WRAP-UP

Power & Light is not unusual in its progress towards using their ABC/M data for key business decisions. Unfortunately, this case illustrates why many ABC/M implementations fail. The implementations focus heavily on the project management process, meeting modeling milestones and creating a crop of repots. A key to success is then to find what you need to measure, ensure it is in line with your company strategy, and make sure that the reports are relevant and are distributed to the people that an make decisions.

The strategy of Power & Light to be a low cost provider of energy requires them to measure and act on the costs of their products and services. Putting reports that give them a view into products and services is a good start. The question becomes, "Are they surfaces and distributed to people who can make decisions.

In the Foreword to this book, Gary Cokins describes how senior executives do not have control of the direct control of an organizations direction, traction, and speed. This case illustrates the need to give managers *all* of the capabilities to have the control they need.

Do not be fooled into the modeling trap. What is the modeling trap? It is many things but they all point to spending too much time building an ABC/M model and building reports, and not enough time communicating the organization's strategy and surfacing the reports to the people who can make decisions.

ENDNOTE

1. Merrill Lynch Study on Activity-Based Costing in the Energy Industry, October 1994, New York.

13

OBOK FOOD COMPANY: RIGHT INGREDIENTS COOK UP SAVINGS

You don't have to cook fancy or complicated masterpieces—just good food from fresh ingredients.

—Julia Child

FOREWORD

Songyu He

Facing increased competition, today's consumer packaged goods (CPG) companies constantly introduce new products, offer innovative services, and increase trade spending to drive demand of their customers. To ensure the success and positive return on investment (ROI) of these customer-driven programs, CPG manufacturers are challenged not only to manage the production and distribution processes cost effectively, but also to measure and understand the bottom-line contributions from each of their products and customers.

Companies historically used traditional costing systems to address the business needs for measuring the cost to produce and cost to serve. These systems arbitrarily allocated the indirect expenses to all products and/or customers, which could distort costs considerably and made it hard for manufacturers to pinpoint which products or customers were really making them money and why.

Activity-based costing systems like SAS Activity-Based Management, however, identify and calculate the costs of performing each activity first. The activity costs are then charged to the product, service, or the customer that causes the activity to be performed. Besides telling you which customers are profitable or unprofitable, the results also will yield insights about what drives the profitability and give you actionable intelligence.

175

Armed with the profitability insight, companies can optimize their resource utilization and increase profitability by focusing on more profitable products and customers while improving the unprofitable ones through repricing, changing customer behaviors, or improving internal manufacturing and service efficiencies.

INTRODUCTION

OBOK Food Company, established in South Korea in 1952, produces six types of soy sauce, seven types of bean paste, and five types of SSAM JANG, a specific type of bean paste. With a sales volume of $17,400,000, OBOK employs 160 workers.

The company initiated an activity-based costing (ABC) project to determine exactly how much its products cost and the profitability of each customer and to conduct a business process reengineering.

ORGANIZATIONAL ISSUES

OBOK Food Company decided to implement managerial accounting systems. It began by interviewing consulting firms and systems integration firms on what these resources could provide in terms of ABC systems and traditional accounting systems. Although several consulting firms could offer a traditional accounting system, KPMG presented an ABC system, explained the methodology, and discussed the benefits that an ABC system would provide to meet OBOK's purposes. After selecting ABC as a methodology, OBOK then began the selection process to choose the proper software. Ultimately, software from ABC Technologies was chosen.

In Korea, the sauce industry is fiercely competitive to the extent that it has not been possible to recover inflationary cost increases from consumers. Coupled with that is the increasing number of local competitors in niche markets as well as the rapid penetration of Japanese companies into the marketplace. This situation is not likely to change soon.

To remain competitive in the marketplace, OBOK needs to know the source of its profits, which depend on the strength of its products and on its customers. OBOK's customers range from large department stores to small shops throughout Korea. Each customer affects the profitability of the products and the market segment due to its:

- Purchasing habits
- Delivery location
- Discount/rebate structures

In this environment, managing all elements of customer profitability, not just product cost, is critical. Discounts and promotions represent a substantial part of the margin that must be managed, along with the cost of serving the customer, at the customer level.

CASE STUDY

Building the Model

The project to develop products and to determine customer profitability was split into two phases:

1. A pilot project to prove the concept and to develop an implementation plan
2. The actual implementation

Pilot ABC Project

An ABC pilot project was initially implemented to prove the value of the information and to gain the approval of the company's management. A snapshot of three months of actual data was used to illustrate the information that could be produced by an ABC approach to product and customer profitability. Then:

- Five project team members composed of different functional representatives were established to collect financial and nonfinancial data.
- Key activities within the company were defined, including appropriate output measures and performance measures.
- Cost drivers were defined for Calculate Product Cost and Customer Cost.
- Data collected by each team were used in spreadsheets to illustrate and test basic ABC principles for each process.
- The full-scale implementation approach and the project plan were developed.
- Findings and recommendations were presented to the president.

Pilot Project Output

Over two months, the implementation continued with the aid of ABC Technologies (now SAS), which assisted with model building and provided technical support:

- The source of all the data required for the ABC data systems was identified. Download formats and procedures to dump data monthly into a designated directory on the file server were then developed. Then an automated tool set was used to handle the collection of data, the calculations, and the export of the data to the data warehouse.

- The Resource-Activity-Cost Object structure was designed in Oros ABC-Plus to calculate product and customer costs.

- The import file structures to import financial and nonfinancial data were developed.

- A data model was developed and a data warehouse was built to process the sales and ABC data. Two key features of the warehouse were: (1) the ability to reverse out erroneous data and to reimport the correct data, and (2) the ability to give each data set a name and to mix and match the data sets across the value chain. This provided the ability to assess the impact of a price increase for raw materials on June actual sales.

- Custom reports using Oros were designed for the company's users based on their requirements and included reports such as Product Cost and Profitability, Customer Cost and Profitability, and Division by Division Activity Cost.

- Using a what-if scenario function, users were given the ability to manipulate the profitability calculations based on changes in volumes, costs, and pricing (e.g., What if we decreased the price by 10% and received a 5% increase in volume across the board? How would this affect brand profitability?).

CONCLUSIONS

What did the project tell OBOK? Profitable products were separated from non-profitable products in the final analysis. In addition, the ABC project told OBOK's management that the company's business approach should change from its current pattern because the profit structures were found to be very different based on:

- Customer needs and locations throughout Korea
- Service (achieving quick delivery and customer satisfaction)
- Market channel (large department stores, supermarkets, agents, retailers, etc.)

Finally, the ABC project revealed that the business process reengineering should be fulfilled to cut down the process costing and to improve the productivity within the current number of machines.

As a result of the study, OBOK is focusing on its profitable products and on its customers and is improving the cost of nonprofitable products in conjunction with the company's customers. In addition, OBOK is redesigning its manufacturing process along with its sales relations. With these efforts, and as a result of the study, OBOK expects to save US$300,000 per year.

What the Future Holds

Currently OBOK is planning to further develop the ABC system as a total activity-based management system consisting of activity-based budgeting, activity-based management, and a balanced scorecard.

EXPERT WRAP-UP

Songyu He

Managing an increasingly complex portfolio of products and customers is becoming an industry challenge. Looking deeper, OBOK's success clearly proves that the decision-making alignment between sales/marketing, operations, and finance holds the key to overcoming this challenge.

All too often an account manager will agree on a deal with a retail counterpart without an understanding of the impact on operations, production, and the supply chain. This could result in a customer being less profitable than originally thought due to higher-than-anticipated service demands that increase the cost to serve.

The ultimate goal for a CPG company should always be to balance and manage meeting customer demands with the optimal financial performance of the customers, or specifically the customer profitability contributions. When the sales, finance, and operations share the same view of cost and profitability, the alignment of decision making will happen naturally.

14

VETERANS BENEFITS: DISCOVERING THE COST OF DOING BUSINESS USING ACTIVITY-BASED COSTING

But the freedom that they fought for, and the country grand they wrought for, Is their monument to-day, and for aye.

—Thomas Dunn English

FOREWORD

In this case the name of the company was not masked and made anonymous. The case itself was originally authored by Richard Noorwood of the Veterans Benefit Administration (VBA). It was done in conjunction with ABC Technologies (now SAS) for their *As Easy as ABC* journal. The case illustrates a relatively small activity-based costing (ABC) project but has broader implications for cost management in the public sector.

Even today this case is relevant to cost and performance management due to the new guidelines for improving government performance. The Executive Office of the President and the Office of Management and Budget (OMB) published the President's Management Agenda in 2002.

The president sent what he called a "bold strategy for improving the management and performance of the federal government." The work that VBA has done already can be a beacon for others now struggling to meet the criteria outlined by the president.

Unlike the private sector, the public sector is not always motivated to review costs to shore up the profit line. The public sector, specifically in the Veterans Benefits Administration of the Department of Veterans Affairs, is motivated to meet requirements established by the executive and legislative branches of the government. Compliance with those requirements becomes the responsibility of the department through issuance of guidelines to its administrations. The Department of Veterans Affairs consists of three administrations: Veterans Benefits Administration, Veterans Health Administration (VHA), and the National Cemetery Administration (NCA).

INTRODUCTION

Historical Perspective

In the late 1990s, the Department of Veterans Affairs drafted and finalized general guidelines for establishing a full cost accounting. These guidelines were issued because of requirements in Financial Accounting Standards Advisory Board (FASAB) Statement No. 4, *Managerial Cost Accounting*, the Chief Financial Officer Act of 1990, Government Performance and Results Act, and recommendations from the National Performance Review.

The Office of the Chief Financial Officer (CFO) within VBA was tasked with developing a nationwide full-cost accounting system for VBA. The system would identify the true costs of providing a service or producing a product and would be based on sound cost accounting principles that would support VBA's performance-based strategic plans.

The CFO's office took an aggressive approach toward achieving this task as VBA was constantly bombarded with questions from its stakeholders about how it accounted for its costs. Some questions that begged to be answered were: "Do we really know what our employees are doing for us?" "Do we know how much time and resources it takes to provide a service?" "Do we know what it takes to generate an output or an end product?"

All of these questions pointed to the *one big question*, and that was: "Do we really know the cost of VBA doing business?" The answer was no. We did not have a system in place that could tell us how, why, where, and on what we were using the funds that had been entrusted to VBA as managers.

The VBA needed a system in place that would allow it to answer the one big question. A system had to allow VBA to develop full-cost accountability and allow its managers to better manage their resources. The decision as to how it would proceed, what it would use, and where would it use such a system was subject to much discussion. The system in place did not accurately reflect the cost of doing business. The solution was to develop a mechanism for capturing the cost of doing business in VBA.

From the beginning VBA knew that attempting to implement such a system would require culture change. Consequently, the CFO's office needed to think of itself as change masters/change agents. It also needed to think in terms of providing people with all of the tools necessary to implement change. It would not be an easy task because the environment in which VBA worked did not easily lend itself to change. Change had to be sold, taught, learned, and practiced; above all, it had to evolve.

After researching several costing methodologies, it was determined that the ABC methodology best suited VBA's way of doing business. Once that decision was made, some of the CFO's staff attended informational seminars and completed training on the use of ABC software applications. Other government organizations involved with costing were interviewed to get their perspective on implementing a costing system using ABC. Armed with this information, the CFO's staff was ready to proceed.

However, a critical step had to be accomplished before VBA could move ahead. It needed the support and commitment of management, not only from the CFO's office but VBA's executive management, program managers, and field site managers. Fortunately, VBA's CFO was an enthusiastic supporter from the outset, because he saw the value in using a tool like ABC to help better manage his resources. Soon he was able to garner the support of VBA's executive management. Their support made it easier to obtain the needed support at the program and field levels.

As VBA consulted with other federal entities involved with ABC, it noticed that they were using ABC only in "pockets" of their organizations. It was determined that VBA would implement its costing system enterprise-wide, rather than piecemeal, and that all costs would be allocated to the six lines of business. This would provide consistency in the production of cost data that would meet one of the requirements in the Chief Financial Officer Act of 1990 and promote the standardization of procedures and guidelines used to manage cost data.

ORGANIZATIONAL STRUCTURE

A quick look at the organizational structure of VBA will provide a picture of the complexities that must be solved to successfully build a cost accounting system using the activity-based costing methodology. VBA's mission is to "Provide benefits and services to veterans and their families in a responsive, timely, and compassionate manner in recognition of their service to our nation." Six lines of business (LOB) and several support staff offices are responsible for carrying out that mission. The six LOBs are:

1. Compensation
2. Pension
3. Education
4. Loan guaranty
5. Vocational rehabilitation and counseling
6. Insurance

There are 65 field sites and a central office that is staffed by approximately 11,000 full-time employees. Annually, approximately 700,000 compensation and pension claims are processed; 440,000 veterans are trained; 360,000 loans are guaranteed; 5,000 veterans are rehabilitated; and 470,000 insurance award actions are completed. VBA has a fiscal year budget of approximately $24 billion including $900 million for general operating expenses.

ABC PILOTS

One of the requirements in Joint Financial Management Improvement Program's Guidelines for Implementing a Cost Accounting System is the need to do pilots to validate the methodology that is going to be used to develop a costing system. Ultimately, the VBA began two ABC pilots. The first pilot, which was a four-week effort, validated the cost of the Education Line of Business at the St. Louis, Missouri, Regional Office. During this pilot these actions were accomplished: an activity dictionary was developed and measurable outputs were defined; costs were assigned to activities and their associated output measures; and unit costs were developed from the quantity of outputs associated with the activities. The director of the Regional Office became and still is one of the enthusiastic supporters of ABC because he realized the benefits that could be achieved as a result of implementing ABC. He even began implementing ABC in other LOBs at his regional office because he saw the value in giving his managers a tool to better manage available resources.

The second pilot determined the cost of managing the Insurance Line of Business, including associated support costs at the Philadelphia Regional Office and Insurance Center. This was a full-blown ABC pilot consisting of an 11-week effort that included a cross-functional process analysis of the insurance LOB and support areas. Four core processes were defined; 15 outputs were associated with these core processes; and approximately 60 activities were associated with the outputs. Cycle efficiency of each activity was calculated; and cost was assigned to the seven insurance funds within the LOB. Insurance program unit costs and improvement opportunities were identified. Because some activities were ranked as "less than contributing to providing a service or producing a product" and were identified as an opportunity for improvement, insurance managers implemented the recommendation almost immediately by reassigning three full-time employees to activities that contributed more toward producing a product. The use of ABC to allocate administrative costs to the Insurance LOB was validated by the Department of Veterans Affairs Inspector General.

Four additional ABC pilots were conducted, at the Debt Management Center, Hines Finance Center, Hines Benefits Delivery and Systems Development Center, and VBA Central Office. The pilots' results supported VBA's decision to continue its progress to implement a nationwide full-cost accounting system using ABC.

The Debt Management Center (DMC) that was VBA's centralized collection organization has now become a fully franchised entity and part of the department's Franchised Fund. In the future, the DMC will be using ABC in some form to determine its cost and pricing.

From the results of the pilots, VBA knew it could determine cost by activity, process, and output, and allocate that cost to the applicable lines of business. Additionally, it found the pilot participants at the field sites wanted to have the capability to continue to implement ABC at their individual sites.

The ABC pilot participants received a copy of the ABC Oros software including the enterprise-wide package and were provided technical training on the software. It was expected that these pilot participants would in effect become VBA's ABC subject matter experts.

IMPLEMENTATION PLAN/EFFORT

To ensure continuity of development and consistency of approach, a detailed implementation plan was developed that was used and continues to be used as a road map guiding VBA toward the full implementation of ABC.

Originally the CFO's office had determined that it would take at least a year and a half to build an ABC model that would capture VBA's cost enterprise-wide. However, the incoming VBA executive management had a different opinion and requested that a costing system using ABC be developed in half the time, with ABC supporting VBA's performance measure initiative with unit cost. Of course, that change threw a new wrinkle into the process. Management knew it would need to multiply the effort needed to sell the idea at the grassroots and the program level. Therefore, it was planned to implement ABC in two phases. Completion of Phase 1 would allow VBA to meet the new administration's goal to provide unit cost at the activity, process, line of business, regional office, and service delivery network level. Completion of Phase 2 would put VBA into a full costing environment. These were plans that could be achieved and allow VBA to meet the requirements of internal and external stakeholders.

PHASE 1

The objectives of Phase 1 were:

- Establish an ABC group consisting of an executive committee, steering committee, and a resident ABC team in the CFO's office responsible for overseeing implementation of ABC
- Provide education/ training
- Develop a nationwide activity dictionary
- Build a VBA corporate ABC model
- Develop a data collection instrument
- Distribute the activity dictionary and data collection instrument
- Populate the ABC model with cost and workload data
- Evaluate the data collection process
- Produce cost reports

Let us take a quick look at what was involved in accomplishing those objectives. The resident ABC team has the ultimate responsibility for implementing ABC in VBA enterprise-wide. Education was accomplished by way of weekly conference calls, monthly satellite broadcasts, and the Internet, where VBA has established an ABC Home Page.

An activity dictionary was developed that could be used nationwide. This was done to ensure consistency in the collection and allocation of cost data. The activity dictionary consisted of 159 activities, 17 processes, and 5 core processes.

The VBA corporate ABC model consisted of 65 individual models. Each model had costs allocated to each one of its cost centers from six general ledger accounts: Payroll, Nonpayroll, Federal Telecommunication System, Integrated Data Consolidated Unit, Rent, and Mail. Each model contained 2 to 13 cost centers, and each cost center consisted of 159 activities, 5 core process, 17 processes, and 13 outputs. The model allowed VBA to capture cost at these levels: corporate, service delivery network, regional office/site, LOB, core process, process, activity, and output. The data collection instrument (DCI) was used to collect data for labor only, showing percentage of time used to perform activities identified in the dictionary and to assign costs based on those percentages. These percentages became VBA's resource drivers. It received more than 400 DCIs from 65 sites. Considering that there were 159 activities for each DCI, a huge amount of data was being worked with.

An evaluation was completed to show where it would be necessary to improve the process for the next iteration of the DCI process. The questionnaire submitted to the participants concentrated on training, support, and future use of the DCI.

VBA Workload Measurement System data were used to drive activity costs to outputs. Working with the VBA Data Warehouse group, seven customized reports, including one for training, were developed, to report unit cost at the levels requested by VBA executive management. The seven reports have been provided to the regional offices for their review and comments. Feedback from the regional offices indicates that they want the capability to drill down from the summary costs shown on the reports. They could see that ABC was more than just accounting; they also saw it as a management tool.

ABC is not only about costs but about how we manage those costs. It is about defining relationships among resources, activities, and outputs. What was spent? How was it spent? What was produced? By defining those relationships and answering those questions, managers can move from ABC to ABM (activity-based management) because they now have information necessary to determine the costs of activities associated with delivering a service and the cost of the service itself.

PHASE 2

Moving to Phase 2 of implementing ABC in VBA brings with it a number of challenges. Changing its management philosophy will be of paramount importance. To move to the next level of "full implementation of ABC" will require use of ABM in its decision-making processes. Moving from a philosophy of managing resources (people) to managing those things (activities) that consume its resources will be VBA's greatest challenge as it moves toward completion of Phase 2.

A passage from John Miller's book, *Implementing Activity-Based Management in Daily Operations* reminds us emphatically that ABC can give the costs, but we need ABM to do something with those costs to realize the full benefits of ABC.[1]

VBA has established these objectives to complete Phase 2:

- Rerun the data collection process for analysis purposes only.
- Revise the activity dictionary.
- Revise the VBA corporate ABC model.
- Establish a Web-based training module.
- Develop a Web-based survey process.
- Automate the data collection process.
- Roll out ABC models to service delivery networks.
- Provide general and technical training.
- Continue the education process.

CONCLUSION

Completion of these objectives will put VBA in a full-costing environment with a fully functional integrated cost accounting system, which will be referred to as VBA's Cost Information Management System (CIMS) (see Exhibit 14.1). The

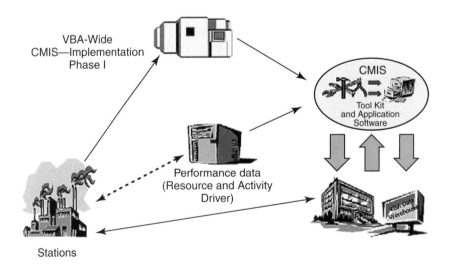

Exhibit 14.1 VBA's Cost Information Management System

system will provide consistent cost and workload data at regular intervals, as well as meet the cost accounting guidelines of the department and standards set by governing bodies inside and outside of government.

The value of ABC and ABM data is best summed by the National Performance Review: "Management is not about guessing, it is about knowing. Those in positions of responsibility must have the information they need to make good decisions. Good managers have the right information at their fingertips. Poor managers don't. Good information comes from good information systems."

EXPERT WRAP-UP

In his 2002 Management Agenda, President George W. Bush outlined 14 areas of improvement for improving government performance. In the fifth area of improvement, the president illustrated the importance of improvements in the management of human capital, competitive sourcing, and improved financial performance. Improvements in these areas will not matter if they are not linked to actual results. By creating an integrated cost information system, VBA can now use this information to satisfy the management agenda and can begin to follow on with a process for providing managers with timely and complete information to improve their results.

Performance measures, budgeting, and cost accounting vary from department to department and agency to agency. There are several ways to link budget information to performance measures and vice versa. Regardless, maximizing taxpayer dollars by resource allocation, program management, and accountability is the ultimate goal.

This case shows a good solid implementation of ABC/M. A sound philosophy of piloting, designing, and rolling out the ABC system was used. VBA now needs to leverage this information and become more mature in the delivery of results.

In response to the President's Management Agenda, SAS has created SAS® for Performance-Based Budgeting, a comprehensive solution that integrates costs, program performance criteria, and budget information, giving users a clear picture of their organization and helping them make forward-moving decisions with confidence.

SAS for Performance-Based Budgeting gives organizations the ability to integrate all phases of the performance budgeting process: formulating budgets, managing appropriations for execution, and reporting on results. Utilizing industry-leading capabilities in data warehousing, analytics, and business intelligence, this solution gives stakeholders intelligence that they can use throughout the performance-based budgeting process. SAS software is unmatched in its ability to access and integrate data from traditionally "siloed" budget, performance planning, and cost accounting systems, and to transform that information into insights that can drive confident decision making.

ENDNOTE

1. John Miller, *Implementing Activity-Based Management in Daily Operations* (New York: John Wiley & Sons, Inc., 1996), 193.

APPENDIX

MCI AND MICROCELL: TWO SUCCESS STORIES

In addition to the anonymous cases provided in this book, I am pleased to present some additional material regarding performance management.

This section contains two very important success stories written by SAS Institute Inc. Our customers MCI and Microcell have agreed to allow us to present these to you, and I hope you find them as exciting as we do.

While you read these cases, ask yourself, "What if I could meet all of my financial reporting requirements as well as understand my costs for over 15 million customers in 65 countries?"

An even more provocative question concerns profitability and customer lifetime value. The tools exist today to allow you to understand your customers' lifetime value, segment them into groups based on their profitability, and predict which customers you are likely to churn. What if those were your most profitable customers?

These two cases studies are very relevant to the current state of activity-based costing and performance management. Both retail and public sector industries are seeing an increased need to focus on cost management, because of increased competition, the president's management agenda, or simply tighter regulations.

PRESSING THE RIGHT BUTTONS: MCI RINGS UP SAVINGS TO IDENTIFY AND UNDERSTAND OPERATING COSTS

Until recently, the telecommunications industry was an expanding universe propelled by the big bang of deregulation. Now that the expansion has slowed, the competition has become as crowded as the night sky, and the market is saturated.

Telecoms like MCI know that the smart way to survive and thrive is by finding ways to cut costs while serving customers more efficiently. Using SAS® Activity-Based Management (ABM), MCI has mapped the complexities of its resources and assets to drive that effort.

Headquartered in Ashburn, Virginia, MCI reports revenue in excess of $20 billion annually, with more than 15 million customers in 65 countries and 48 U.S. states.

With SAS, MCI has a single solution that links operating expenses to individual products and by segment so that project managers first can understand the shared components of various costs and then improve how they communicate those costs with each other and throughout the company. "We were looking for ways to save millions of dollars," says John Nolan, vice president of planning and analysis for MCI. "SAS provides a way to identify and understand our costs so we can realize those savings."

Meeting Critical Deadlines

In the beginning, MCI sought an ABM solution to create a sales-channel segment profitability model. Yet the business analysis group quickly realized that, with SAS, MCI could meet the reporting requirements of the Securities and Exchange Commission (SEC) and Financial Accounting Standards (FAS 131), a set of accounting standards for public companies, as well as meet reporting needs necessary to emerge from bankruptcy.

"We crunched our original 13-week timeline for creating the model to meet a tough 8-week deadline to complete reports that displayed MCI's profitability across product and business lines," explains Chuck Utterback, director of financial systems. "The timing was critical because the reports were needed for an audit that was submitted to the courts as part of our efforts to emerge from bankruptcy, and the information was part of the required filings to the Securities and Exchange Commission."

Utterback and Leslie Mote, director of corporate business analysis, accomplished that early success thanks to their own ingenuity along with some late nights and weekends working alongside SAS technical consultants. Combining the SAS ABM solution with SAS technical expertise provided the one-two punch that knocked out the segment line profitability reporting with enough detail and intelligence to fully comply with FAS 131 and other SEC requirements while proving MCI's financial and corporate vitality, thus allowing the telecom to emerge from bankruptcy.

Making Smarter Decisions

In addition to using SAS to meet financial reporting requirements, MCI now has a solution for making strategic pricing decisions, driving effective network analysis, enhancing segment reporting, and creating data for sales leader compensation.

Before implementing SAS, the process of inventorying MCI's thousands of network platforms and IT systems—determining what each one does, who runs them, how they help business, and which products they support—was completely manual. The model created with SAS has helped MCI to catalog all that information and map the details to products, customer segments, and business processes.

"That's something everyone is excited about," Mote says. "Looking at the cost of a system and what it relates to helps you see the revenue you're generating from particular products or customers. I can see what I'm doing better."

Building a Legitimate Case

MCI chose SAS for its strong visual interface and high-performing calculation engine that offered structured, logical reporting and drill-down capabilities. Those characteristics helped ensure the accuracy of its FAS compliance despite an accelerated deadline. "Without SAS, we would have done spreadsheet summaries and would not have been able to reach the level of detail that we wanted," Mote says. "We were able to process more data and do it more accurately than we could have done without SAS."

SAS allowed Utterback and Mote to interview hundreds of groups of employees to gather and store cost information for granular scrutiny later.

Without SAS, details would have remained at a high level, which would have risked the possibility that one group's input would have skewed the final analysis. "SAS helped us build legitimacy into the process," Utterback says. "For us, the model we built with SAS is an open book for the MCI finance community, giving them a repeatable model that is transparent with all the different user communities. That went a long way in getting executive buy-in to make it succeed."

Improving Communications

MCI's SAS ABM efforts are also helping employees understand how their actions relate to one another and what those actions mean to profitability. Now conversations are taking place between sales leaders and engineers and between information technology leaders and support leaders. In turn, they are gaining a clearer picture of how each piece comes together to create a product offering and generate revenue.

"A lot of it was education," Utterback recalls. "SAS has really allowed us to broker our relationships."

The value is being able to identify cost streams across activities and knowing whether it is a shared cost or whether it is changing over time. Such knowledge gives managers a baseline for making cost-effective decisions. SAS allows MCI to be more efficient by making the ABM process four times faster while, at the same time, making it more effortless.

"Without SAS, we would need a group four times the size of what we have, and it would take four times as long simply to maintain the activity-based cost model and do only basic standard reports on a quarterly basis," Mote says. "Now our product leaders can look at engineering costs across a certain product, find out if it is cost effective and whether it could be done more cost-effectively. This information fosters significant cost savings across all of our product lines."

DIALING IN ON PROFITABILITY: MICROCELL CONNECTS WITH HIGH-MARGIN CUSTOMERS AND PRODUCTS

In an industry marked by intense competition and rapid expansion, Microcell has been at the forefront of the development of wireless telecommunications and fast mobile data connectivity in Canada. The only telecommunications operator in Canada devoted exclusively to wireless activities, the company has made wireless services an integral part of most Canadians' daily lives.

"As the market expanded, Microcell's business boomed. It took on a great variety of new customers," says Karim Salabi, Microcell's director of marketing, market, and customer management. "But we didn't know which customers were profitable or how best to serve their needs. And while we were gaining new customers, we were losing others as competition increased."

Needing a way to analyze and segment its customer base, the company turned to SAS.

Keeping the Right Callers on the Line

Founded in 1996, Microcell now has more than 1.2 million customers across Canada. With its wireless service, Fido®, it has led the way in providing state-of-the-art wireless products and services in the country. Microcell was the first Canadian carrier to deploy Global System for Mobile communications (GSM) technology, the most widely deployed wireless standard in the world. And Fido was the first wireless service provider in North America with a General Packet Radio Service (GPRS) data network, ensuring fast, always-on wireless connectivity to the Internet and corporate intranets.

Using SAS, Microcell measures the value and profitability of each customer to determine which departing customers it should try to retain. "Our short-term objective was to build a predictive model to show which customers were likely to churn," says Salabi. "We then built a customer lifetime value (LTV) model that would answer two questions: How do we evaluate our customers—have we made or lost money with them —and how do we retain customers at a cost we can accept?"

Salabi's database marketing team used SAS Enterprise Miner™ to develop an LTV model that divided customers into five segments based on profitability. The top three segments identified profitable customers; the bottom two contained customers who were not profitable and likely never would be.

Reevaluating High-Cost Customers

"Previously we assumed that customers who spent a lot on services in the first three or four months should be retained at any cost," Salabi explains. "But if these customers had a low LTV, then we weren't spending our budget wisely." They may be high users of the network, resulting in high network costs. They may contact the call center frequently, requesting credits and discounts. "Customers who spend $100 a month may actually be costing us $200 a month," says Salabi. "This was a significant finding—that some customers who spend less are actually more profitable."

Over nine months, Microcell saw results. "It was incredible," says Salabi. "Using SAS, we reduced the number of low-LTV customers by about half, from 25% to 12 or 13% while retaining high-LTV customers. We have a fixed budget— we stopped spending it on customers who did not warrant the investment and redirected funds to areas that better serve our best customers and our customer base as a whole."

Managing Customer LTV

During this period, Microcell conducted some change management in its operations to ensure effective linkage between analytical and operational units. "The key success factor was to integrate our knowledge of the profitability and defection risk of our customers in our daily operations," Salabi explains. "Now all of this customer intelligence is routed to our automated systems and front-line servicing, and we manage customer relationships accordingly."

Focus on profitable products, Microcell has also used SAS Activity-Based Management to analyze the costs and profitability of its products. "In some cases, it has shown that a product was not profitable despite insignificant volume," says Salabi. "This allows us to make product changes, find options that better serve customers, or simply withdraw a product from the market."

The combined use of SAS Enterprise Miner and the ABC solution has given Microcell a complete picture of its customer and product values and profitability. It has clearly identified its unprofitable customers and products, enabling the company to use its resources more effectively to serve customer needs, retain its higher-value customers, and sell its higher-margin products.

"We've had some customers who, while unprofitable because of excessive network usage, we wanted to keep," says Salabi. "We have begun to encourage them to use other products, such as long distance, voice mail, caller ID, and text messaging, which have higher profit margins. Basically, we move them up from being unprofitable to being profitable."

A Foundation for the Future

Microcell chose SAS Enterprise Miner for its diversity and value. "We didn't want a 'black box' type of solution where we throw in our data and it spits out some recommendations," says Salabi. "We very quickly realized that we needed a powerful modeling tool that could be used in every aspect of our marketing and financial management."

Salabi says the next step for his database marketing team will be to build a nonvoluntary churn model to predict which customers are most likely not to default on their bills. He believes SAS has the capacity and scope to grow with Microcell and his department.

"Realizing how quickly things change in this industry, what works today will not necessarily work tomorrow," Salabi says. "SAS is a great foundation that we can add to and that can evolve with us."

Salabi's work in customer segmentation and profitability has been recognized at the company's executive level for helping to develop Microcell's business and brand recognition during a period of intense growth and competition. "We've managed to keep our best customers through this whole process," Salabi says. "I think it shows a great deal of trust and confidence on our customers' part that they've stayed with us."

FINAL THOUGHTS

Technology is shrinking the global community. The two major forces that businesses currently must cope with are the rapid rate of technological change and increasing competition. The rate of change is likely to accelerate in the near future, led by further technological developments and increasing consolidation of technology vendors.

Unfortunately, most companies are, for the most part, still using traditional financial accounting and performance measurement methods that were developed centuries ago for an environment of arm's-length transactions using primarily tangible assets, such as buildings and equipment. The knowledge-based business environment that companies are developing today requires a new model and nomenclature.

There seems to be universal acceptance that the newer methods—activity-based costing, scorecarding, integrated planning and budgeting, and others—will provide a better way to manage performance. In his foreword to this book, Gary Cokins discusses why these methodologies have thus far been accepted slowly. I agree with Gary, and believe that over the next decade, these systems will become as widely accepted as cost accounting.

The cases in this book show that companies can use these ideas and find success. Technology should not be the limiting hurdle. Sadly, however, it often is. Usually the technology vendor becomes the scapegoat for failed implementations.

I believe that project teams and even technology vendors set unrealistic expectations, about the level of return they can get in the first year or two of implementing performance management systems. Managing performance is hard work. Whether you are still using a traditional financial system or you have embarked on a more progressive venture, learn from those who have done it in the past. Masters like Dr. Kaplan, Gary Cokins, Steve Player, and many others learned lessons and examples of how to implement and benefit from performance management. Why then do we keep repeating the same mistakes? Someone said to me once, "Maybe it is a maturation process that a company must go through to get buy-in, even though they know they are repeating past mistakes."

I think it is possible to get past the "fear of change" that seems to be a recurring theme in many of these implementations. There are many good things coming in the future in the area of performance management. Learn from these cases and the thoughts of the experts.

WHAT THE FUTURE HOLDS:

In the next few years, I foresee the integration of human capital and Business Intelligence into performance management systems.

Human Capital

Human capital represents the individual knowledge stock of an organization as represented by its employees.[1] Even though employees are considered the most important corporate asset in a learning organization, they are not owned by the organization.

William Hudson defines human capital as a combination of genetic inheritance; education; experience; and attitudes about life and business.[2] According to Nick Bontis, human capital is the firm's collective capability to extract the best solutions from the knowledge of its individuals.[3] Unfortunately, people's departure from the firm can result in the loss of corporate memory and hence can be a threat to the organization. Another school of thought believes that the departure of some individuals in a firm may be considered good, because it forces the firm to consider fresh new perspectives from replacement employees.

Bontis argues that human capital is important because it is a source of innovation and strategic renewal, whether it is from brainstorming in a research lab, daydreaming at the office, throwing out old files, reengineering new processes, improving personal skills, or developing new leads in a sales rep's little black book.[4] The essence of human capital is the sheer intelligence of the organizational member.

People are the driving factor in achieving performance in an organization. Future business leaders will require a comprehensive picture of how the workforce influences the performance of their organization. With this understanding, focus on financial measures will broaden as risk and opportunity—including credit, market, regulatory, organizational, and operational—are better understood and managed.

To understand how people influence organizational performance, business leaders must become better at monitoring workforce factors against short-term and long-term strategies. More information will be available for sound decision making. Calculated assessments, such as predictive analysis, will aid in understanding likely workforce outcomes, such as unplanned attrition, providing insight for planning, investing, and aligning resources to achieve desired corporate outcomes.

Business Intelligence

Today Business Intelligence (BI) involves making decisions that feed into operational systems. Typically data are extracted from operational systems, then integrated and loaded into data warehouses, where reporting and analyses are produced using BI tools. Some would call that classic Business Intelligence. This is not enough; it is really just measuring your business. It is not performance management.

Understanding and managing a business requires planning, analysis, and decision-making.

Companies today are dealing with these three requirements separately, but they must really be integrated. Typically, strategic planning currently is based on a stand-alone scorecard not linked to budgeting and planning applications; scorecards have a separate scorecard database holding only summarized data; there is no detail to allow executives and managers to drill down and find out why a problem has been flagged on a key performance indicator.

This is a good explanation of why many performance management–based scorecard applications have failed or not met expectations over the years. In addition to performance management, analysis is being done using analytic applications, reporting, and On Line Analytical Processing (OLAP) tools delivering front,- middle-, and back-office analytics based on summary and detailed data in data marts and data warehouses. In addition, production-reporting tools are working on other detailed databases to produce operational reports that support operational decisions. The combination of strategic and near–real-time operational analytics is what is needed to manage a business.

The future will offer objectives-driven business management using scorecards and dashboards at the strategic level. These scorecards will be integrated with BI tools and analytic applications that support business measurement at tactical and real-time operational levels.

BI projects must be tied to strategic, tactical, and operational business objectives. In addition, performance management, enterprise analytics, and operational

BI must be integrated into an overall BI framework. Portals and analytic application development tools are becoming key components of this framework.

In Chapter 5, Jonathan Hornby described the evolution of how companies consume information. Almost all of the companies described in this book are relatively low on the evolutionary model. A company's place in the evolution model could also be called their stage of maturity. These cases are a foundation to help organizations begin the process of moving up the ladder to a stage, as Hornby states, "where an organization can constantly innovate and through extensive use of analytics can predict which initiatives will succeed or fail with a high degree of confidence."

Use this book in full or in part. The cases have been chosen to provide examples of successful implementations across multiple industries:

- Manufacturing (discrete and process)
- Service (healthcare and finance)
- Public sector (defense and federal)
- Consumer packaged goods (manufacturing and distribution)
- Airline
- Energy and utility

There is no single way to model an organization. No one-size-fits-all methodology can be applied to an organization to guarantee successful performance management. Often there is a clash between the "new age" of costing outlined by academics and the reality of what must happen when companies get down to implementing a system. I have been asked why implementations of costing or performance management fail. In fact, someone suggested that as many as half of these projects fail. My response is simply that obviously the other half must be successful. Just as in the national media, often failures are highlighted and successes are not talked about. Take the time to learn from the experts. Do not repeat the failures and then chalk it up to a culture change. Be vigilant and be successful.

ENDNOTES

1. Nick Bontis, M. Crossan, and J. Hulland, "Managing an Organizational Learning System by Aligning Stocks and Flows," (*Journal of Management Studies*, 2001).
2. William Hudson,. *Intellectual Capital: How to Build It, Enhance It, Use It* (Hoboken, NJ: John Wiley & Sons, Inc., 2004).

3. Nick Bontis, "Intellectual Capital: An Exploratory Study That Develops Measures and Models," (*Management Decision*)36, no. 2 (1998): 63–76.
4. Nick Bontis, "Managing Organizational Knowledge by Diagnosing Intellectual Capital: Framing and Advancing the State of the Field," *International Journal of Technology Management*, 18, nos. 5/6/7/8 (1999): 433–462.

RESOURCES

Arkonas. Arkonas Corp. is a management consulting firm specializing in customer profitability. Its expertise is in the design and implementation of customer profitability systems. Its tools and techniques include:

- Economic-value added
- Cost of capital
- Activity-based cost tracing methodologies
- Customer segmentation
- Value proposition
- Product mix/profitability

CAM-I. CAM-I is a global, collaborative research not-for-profit organization, established in 1972 to support research and development in areas of strategic importance to industries. The focus is on advancing management and technical practices. CAM-I is an international of consortium companies including manufacturing companies, service industries, consultancies, government and academia, and professional bodies that have elected to work cooperatively in a precompetitive environment to solve management problems that are common to the group.

Its participative model produces value for members through:

- **Participative research.** By working together, the participants understand the journey—the best practice path.
- **Targeted intellectual efforts.** Each program targets results and produces implementable deliverables by its sponsors.
- **Human networks.** Develop and continue to share, challenge ideas, and learn long beyond the end date of the specific result.

CAM-I has two major programs to its credit:

1. Cost Management Systems (CMS). The CMS Program is the authoritative international body on organizational cost and resource management practices. The purpose of the CMS Program is to advance organizational cost and resource management practices internationally through collaborative development, standardization, and dissemination.

Interest groups associated with CMS are made up of thought leaders from industry, government agencies, consultancies, vendors, and academics from within the sponsor base who have a common interest in finding solutions to common problems. They work together in a precompetitive, collaborative environment to review the existent literature, resolve issues, develop conceptual models, and establish implementation techniques to further the cause of cost and resource management.

2. Process-Based Management Program (PBM). The PBM Program was launched in conjunction with the Advanced Technology Institute (ATI) in November 2004. Process management had been a focus in CMS since 1993, but the increasing importance of a process focus to organizations led to the creation of this new program. The initial focus will be the development of an implementation road map to help organizations become process based.

Institute of Management Accountants (IMA). IMA members are today's leaders, managers, and decision makers in management accounting and financial management. Its members are dedicated to continued professional development, to achieving the highest levels of professional certification, and to supporting each other in our commitment to professional excellence.

Globalization and standardization combined with more stringent financial reporting requirements means a continuum of change in practice, rules and regulations, ethics, and execution of accounting and financial strategy in all areas of operation. Members are the most prepared and the most proactive professionals in this changing environment. The future of the management accounting profession relies heavily on leadership and on dedication to continued professional development and to supporting and mentoring the leaders of tomorrow.

The success of IMA and its members depends on their commitment to:

- Continue to build value in IMA membership and certification.
- Provide programs and facilities to broaden and deepen its member population.
- Maintain relevant and stringent certification content.

- Assist local chapters in organization, education, communication, and recruiting.
- Increase international reach and support.
- Develop and support current and relevant professional education products.
- Expand its knowledge base through research to leverage new and existing assets.
- Demand and maintain the strongest ethics in all of its professional activities.

The Player Group. The Player Group, a performance management advisory firm, evolves leading-edge management concepts into action-oriented implementation plans and results. It brings deep experience and profound expertise to organizations seeking a better understanding of best practices. As cost management specialists, The Player Group helps measure and maximize return on investment.

Collectively, The Player Group has coauthored and edited six industry-leading cost and performance management books and served as a media resource for hundreds of articles. The firm has also led five global activity-based costing studies in conjunction with the American Productivity & Quality Center.

The Player Group has created unique communities of practice such as the Activity-Based Management Advanced Interest Group, comprised of a number of Global 1000 organizations that have been using advanced cost management techniques for a number of years.

Value Creation Group, Inc. This group was started at the suggestion of its clients, who were looking for skilled consultants and trainers who could solve their problems. They were tired of working with very large firms where partners sold the consulting assignment and junior staff performed the work. Clients wanted to work with people who had senior executives who had been in their shoes. They were tired of paying high consulting rates for junior people.

Although it creates value using a wide variety of techniques, each value creator specializes in only one or two techniques. They teach seminars, write books and articles, and have years of experience in their area(s) of expertise. This approach ensures you will obtain value creating, customized solution to challenges you are facing.

RECOMMENDED READING

Cokins, Gary. *Activity-Based Cost Management: Making It Work: A Manager's Guide to Implementing and Sustaining an Effective ABC System* (Chicago: Irwin, 1996).

Cokins, Gary. *Activity-Based Cost Management: An Executive's Guide* (Hoboken, NJ: John Wiley & Sons, Inc., 2001).

Cokins, Gary. *Performance Management: Finding the Missing Pieces (to Close the Intelligence Gap)* (Hoboken, NJ: John Wiley & Sons, Inc., 2004).

Cokins, Gary, Alan Stratton, and Jack Helbling. *An ABC Manager's Primer: Straight Talk on Activity-Based Costing* (Montvale, NJ: Institute of Management Accountants, 1993).

Hansen, Stephen C., and Robert G. Torok. *The Closed Loop: Implementing Activity-Based Planning and Budgeting* (Martinsville, IN: CAM-I Bookman Publishing, 2004).

Jennings, Jason. *Less Is More* (New York: Penguin Putnam Inc., 2002).

Kaplan, Robert S., and Robin Cooper. *Cost and Effect: Using Integrated Cost Systems to Drive Profitability and Performance* (Boston: Harvard Business School Press, 1997).

Kaplan, Robert S., and David P. Norton. *The Balanced Scorecard: Translating Strategy into Action* (Boston: Harvard Business School Press, 1996).

Kaplan, Robert S., and David P. Norton. *The Strategy-Focused Organization* (Boston: Harvard Business School Press, 2001).

Maxwell, John C. *The 21 Irrefutable Laws of Leadership* (Nashville, TN: Thomas Nelson Publishers, 1998).

McNair, C. J., and the CAM-I Cost Management Integration Team. *Value Quest* (Bedford,TX: CAM-I, 2000).

Miller, John. *Implementing Activity-Based Management in Daily Operations* (New York: John Wiley & Sons, Inc., 1996).

Niven, Paul R. *Balanced Scorecard Step-by-Step: Maximizing Performance and Maintaining Results* (Hoboken, NJ: John Wiley & Sons, Inc., 2002)

Player, Steve, and Carol Cobble. *Cornerstones of Decision Making: Profiles of Enterprise ABM* (Greensboro, NC: Oakhill Press, 1999).

Nair, Mohan. *Activity-Based Information Systems: An Executive's Guide to Implementation* (New York: John Wiley & Sons, Inc., 1999).

Nair, Mohan. *The Essentials of Balanced Scorecard* (Hoboken, NJ: John Wiley & Sons, Inc., 2004).

Turney, Peter B. B. *Common Cents: The ABC Performance Breakthrough* (Hillsboro, OR: Cost Technology, 1991).

RECOMMENDED WEB RESOURCES

www.arkonas.com
www.bettermanagement.com
www.bscol.com
www.cam-i.org
www.imanet.org
www.theplayergroup.com
www.sas.com
www.valuecreationgroup.com

GLOSSARY

Author's Note: Several of the terms in this glossary are from the *CAM-I Glossary of Terms*. Additional terms have been added to explain terms used in the book. For ease of use, some of CAM-I's "Choice of Terms" have also been included. However, where CAM-I separates them from their main glossary, I have chosen to include them within the body of this work for ease of use. The new terms are preceded by an asterisk to distinguish them from the original CAM-I terms. This material is used with the permission of CAM-I. The *CAM-I Glossary of Activity-Based Management*, Version 3.0, edited by Paul Dierks and Gary Cokins (Bedford, TX: CAM-I, 2000). CAM-I, 119 NE Wilshire Boulevard, Suite E, Burleson, Texas 76028, phone: 817-426-5744; fax: 817-426-5799, www.cam-i.org.

ABC Model

A representation of resource costs during a time period that are consumed through activities and traced to products, services, and customers or to any other object that creates a demand for the activity to be performed.

ABC System

A system that maintains financial and operating data on an organization's resources, activities, drivers, objects, and measures. ABC models are created and maintained within this system.

ABC/M Best Practices

As the actual practice of ABC/M has expanded and evolved, the identification and documentation of leading practices has become more important. The difficulty in executing an ABC/M application successfully is best evidenced by the high failure rate. Over the last few years, much work has been done to identify the critical success factors associated with ABC/M applications. Numerous articles and case studies have identified these as among the most critical areas for attention:

- Operational/strategic imperative
- Active executive buy-in and support
- Nonfinance ownership
- Effective project/change management
- Adequate resources and staffing
- Training and education
- Systems and reporting
- Integration and alignment
- Simplicity in modeling

Leading practices associated with specific areas identified above can best be found by reviewing individual company case studies. The American Productivity and Quality Center has documented and published a number of consortium benchmarking studies covering a broad variety of applications, companies, and industries. There are also several published ABC/M books containing significant case study material. These sources provide an excellent way to gain insight into the successes, failures, and lessons learned by experienced practitioners.

Activity

Work performed by people, equipment, technologies, or facilities. Activities usually are described by the "action-verb-adjective-noun" grammar convention. Activities may occur in a linked sequence, and activity-to-activity assignments may exist.

Activity Analysis

The process of identifying and cataloging activities for detailed understanding and documentation of their characteristics. An activity analysis is accomplished by means of interviews, group sessions, questionnaires, observations, and reviews of physical records of work.

Activity-Based Budgeting (ABB)

An approach to budgeting where a company uses an understanding of its activities and driver relationships to quantitatively estimate workload and resource requirements as part of an ongoing business plan. Budgets show the types, number of, and costs of resources that activities are expected to consume based on forecasted workloads. The budget is part of an organization's activity-based planning process and can be used in evaluating its success in setting and pursuing strategic goals. (*See* Activity-Based Planning.)

Activity-Based Cost Management (ABC/M) Model

Exhibit G.1 is a view of activity-based cost management. It depicts the key relationship between ABC/M and the management analysis tools that are needed to bring full realization of the benefits of ABC/M to the organization. ABC/M is a methodology that can yield significant information about cost drivers, activities, resources, cost objects, and performance measures. With data and information from an ABC/M system, an organization is provided the opportunity to improve the value of its products and services. But ABC/M should not be considered to be merely an improvement program; that may lead some employees to perceive it as a project-of-the-month fad. In the context described here, ABC/M is data reflecting how the organization is consuming its resources, and that data then become information that can be used as an enabler for inferences and decision support.

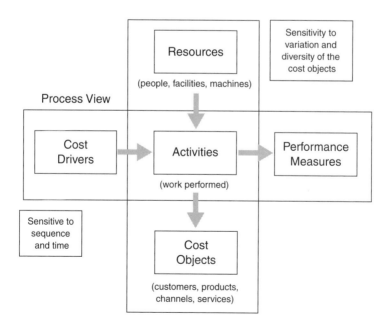

Derived From: The Consortium of Advanced Management International (CAM-3)

Exhibit G.1 Activity-Based Cost Management

Activity-Based Costing (ABC)

A methodology that measures the cost and performance of cost objects, activities, and resources. Cost objects consume activities, and activities consume resources. Resource costs are assigned to activities based on their uses of those resources, and activity costs are reassigned to cost objects (outputs) based on the cost objects' proportional use of those activities. ABC incorporates causal relationships between cost objects and activities and between activities and resources.

Activity-Based Management (ABM)

A discipline focusing on the management of activities within business processes as the route to continuously improve both the value received by customers and the profit earned in providing that value. ABM uses activity-based cost information and performance measurements to influence management action. (*See* Activity-Based Costing.)

Activity-Based Planning (ABP)

An ongoing process to determine activity and resource requirements (both financial and operational) based on the ongoing demand of products or services by specific customer needs. Resource requirements are compared to resources available, and capacity issues are identified and managed. Activity-based budgeting is based on the outputs of activity-based planning. (*See* Activity-Based Budgeting.)

Activity Dictionary

A listing and description of activities that provides a common/standard definition of activities across the organization. An activity dictionary can include information about an activity and/or its relationships, such as activity description, business process, function source, whether value added, inputs, outputs, supplier customer, output measures, cost drivers, attributes, tasks, and other information as desired to describe the activity.

Activity Driver

The best single quantitative measure of the frequency and intensity of the demands placed on an activity by cost objects or other activities. It is used to assign activity costs to cost objects or to other activities.

Activity Level

A description of how elastic or sensitive an activity is to changes in the volume, diversity, or complexity of a cost object or another activity. Product-related activity levels may include unit, batch, and product levels. Customer-related activity levels may include customer, market, channel, and project levels.

*Activity Module

The section of the model that organizes information about activities and their related costs. In modeling tools, these activities can be grouped into pools, and each pool can contain any number of other pools or activities.

Allocation

A distribution of costs using calculations that may be unrelated to physical observations or direct or repeatable cause-and-effect relationships. Because of the arbitrary nature of allocations, costs based on cost causal assignment are viewed as more relevant for management decision making. (*Contrast* with Tracing and Assignment.)

Assignment

A distribution of costs using causal relationships. Because cost causal relationships are viewed as more relevant for management decision making, assignment of costs is generally preferable to allocation techniques. (*Synonymous* with Tracing. *Contrast* with Allocation.)

Attributes

A label used to provide additional classification or information about a resource, activity, or cost object. Used for focusing attention and may be subjective. Examples are a characteristic, a score or grade of product or activity, or groupings of these items, and performance measures.

Attributes, Sustaining Activities, and Sustaining Costs

ABC/M practitioners rely on an item called "attributes" to attach "value" or "sustaining" characteristics to resources, activities, or cost objects. Attributes are user-defined, can be unlimited in number, are often subjectively assigned, but in no way do they affect the calculation of the ABC/M costs.

Many activities in an organization do not directly contribute to customer value, responsiveness, and quality. That does not mean those activities can be eliminated or even reduced without doing harm to the business entity. For example, preparing a required regulatory report certainly does not add to the value of any cost object or to the satisfaction of the customer, but it does have value to the organization because it permits the organization to function in a legal manner. In this regard, the business community needs to distinguish between activities that are:

- Not required at all and can be eliminated (e.g., a duplication of effort)
- Ineffectively accomplished and can be reduced or redesigned (e.g., due to outdated policies or procedures)
- Required to sustain the organization (i.e., the work is not directly caused by making product or delivering services through channels to customers), and therefore it may not be possible to reduce or eliminate the activity (e.g., provide plant security, compliance with government regulations, etc.)
- Discretionary, and can be eliminated (e.g., the annual employees' picnic)

ABC/M systems provide for distinguishing these activities either by tagging their costs as an overlay (i.e., attributes), or by including them in a "sustaining cost object" group, which separates these costs as not being involved with making or delivering a product or serving a customer.

Traditional costing does not provide any way for individual costs to be tagged or highlighted. Thus, aside from knowing the amount of a cost, organizations have little insight as to how costs in their products, costs of serving their customers, or costs in their business processes vary from each other.

But organizations interested in more than just computing costs—such as performance improvement—can use attributes as a grading method to evaluate activities that contribute to the output of goods or services. Attributes can be "tagged" or "scored" according to whether they are necessary, support critical strategic success factors, or are performed efficiently. Resources and cost objects can also have attributes attached to them, but activities have been the most popular ABC/M module for using attributes.

The costs that are attached to sustaining activities are sustaining costs. The makeup and disposition of these costs are closely related to the concepts embodied in several other important ABC terms: activity level, support or indirect costs, and the hierarchy of cost assignability. Key features of sustaining costs are:

- They cannot be directly traced to a final cost object.
- They are identifiable at various levels of an operation and thus are assignable to specific levels (i.e. product-level sustaining costs, facility-level sustaining costs, etc.).
- They are (probably) controllable at the level of their assignability.

The treatment of these costs varies considerably—but they cannot be ignored. Conversely, special efforts should be made to make people aware of them. How sustaining costs are treated can have significant and unanticipated effects. The primary concern in treating these costs lies in their reassignment. Sustaining costs can be allocated to either other activities or to cost objects—eventually becoming an undifferentiated cost of a cost object. Or they can be "kept aside" as a lump-sum amount that must, at some point, be covered by a form of contribution. In the latter case, they might end up being assigned to a sustaining-cost object, such as advertising, research and development, or regulatory costs.

In some organizations, identifying and isolating sustaining costs is viewed as an important aspect of making cost information relevant and actionable. For performance measurement purposes, sustaining costs are not assigned below the level of their control. Individual product managers are not held accountable for product-sustaining or organization-sustaining costs, yet product portfolio managers must ensure that prices cover all costs, including sustaining costs. Thus, sustaining cost can be "left out" for some uses and "put in" for others. When they are "put in," they are allocated where necessary; assignment cannot be made because of their indirect nature. The key in either case is to properly identify sustaining costs so that cost data can be developed that is appropriate for its intended use.

*Balanced Scorecard

A system that uses financial data, operational measures, customer satisfaction, internal processes, and the organization's innovation and improvement activities (indicators of future financial performance).

Best Practices

A methodology that identifies the measurement or performance by which other similar items will be judged. This methodology is used to establish performance standards and to aid in identifying opportunities to increase effectiveness and efficiency. Best-practices methodology may be applied with respect to resources, activities, cost objects, or processes.

Bill of Activities

A listing of activities required by a product, service, process output, or other cost object. Bill of activity attributes could include volume and/or cost of each activity in the listing.

Bill of Resources

A listing of resources required by an activity. Resource attributes could include cost and volumes.

CAM-I ABC Basic and Expanded Model Structures

The second version of the *ABC Glossary* (1991) included a set of illustrations of basic and expanded ABC and process view models that assisted in understanding the key concepts of activity-based costing and management (ABC/M). This section briefly describes these models. Subsequent sections will elaborate on them and point out advancements that have been made through them and the evolving role that ABC/M plays in the management of today's organizations.

CAM-I ABC BASIC MODEL

Exhibit G.2 presents the CAM-I ABC Basic Model—which subsequently became known as the "ABC Cross." It captures a summary of the transactions that occur during a period of time. It does not display the volatile peaks and valleys when transactions, activities or events occur within that time period. For example, it will not reveal if most of the expenses might have been booked in the last two weeks of the month.

The ABC Basic Model should be thought of as a template that can be adapted for various purposes. The model should not be thought of as a flow chart of an activity-based costing implementation plan or a flow chart of a business process. Exhibit G.2 is a very basic diagram that allows the reader to gain an understanding of fundamental ABC concepts and relationships.

There are two axes to the ABC Basic Model. The vertical one deals with the cost assignment view consisting of three modules and two generalized cost assignments. This view represents the calculation of the cost of cost objects (e.g., outputs, product lines, service lines or customers). It is basically a "snapshot" view similar to the income statement in a financial statement as a view of the business conducted during a specific time period. In this sense, the cost assignment view can be seen as the structure and rules by which cost assignment takes place for some specified time period—much like an income statement's "rules" for recognizing revenue and matching it with expenses. The time period may capture costs through the end of the month, a quarter, or any other period that may, or may not coincide with an accounting reporting periods. The cost assignment view reveals how resources and activities relate to cost objects.

The horizontal axis is a process view. A process is two or more activities, or a sequence of activities. The process view facilitates the calculation of the cost of

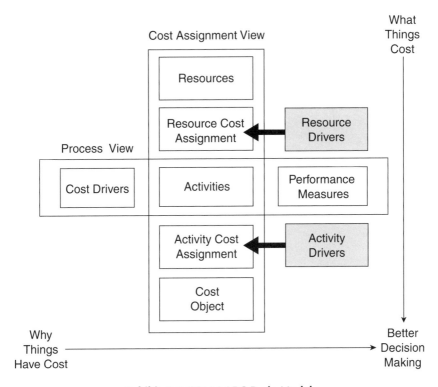

Exhibit G.2 CAM-I ABC Basic Model

business processes where activity costs belong to a process. This is also a "snap-shot" view for the same income statement period that reports what has happened/is happening. The horizontal axis describes the sequential or time-based relation-ships of how individual activities are sequenced with other activities in a process, and not how they relate to cost objects. This part of the ABC Cross Model reveals how activity costs are initiated by a high-order occurrence of an event, which is called a cost driver. The cost driver is the agent that causes the activity to exist and to utilize resources to accomplish some designated work. In this view the activity is a type of work center; each time a cost driver initiates work for the process, re-sources will be consumed and new outputs will result. Realistic performance mea-sures can then be established so that a tracking of activity and process results can be monitored and improvements made on a continuing basis.

The ABC Basic Model displays in a simple fashion that the activities at the in-tersection of the vertical and horizontal axis are integral to determining the cost of an organization's processes as well as the cost of its cost objects. In the model, the activity at the intersection schematically represents an individual activity—a very local view. But, from a global perspective, the vertical (cost assignment) and horizontal (process) views may consist of many activities that are networked together based on their relationships to resources, cost objects, and other activities.

CAM-I EXPANDED ABC MODEL STRUCTURE

Exhibit G.3 displays an expanded view of the ABC Basic Model. The expanded model also includes three modules—resources, activities, and cost objects—along with two broadly labeled cost assignment methods—resources to activities and activities to cost objects. Due to the simplistic presentation of the ABC Basic Model graphics, it may appear as if there is only a single cost assignment between each of the three modules. In practice, however, there are multiple cost assignments unique to each driver and intramodule cost assignments prior to the cost assignment exiting a module and entering the next one.

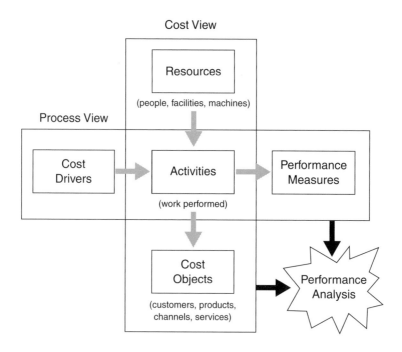

Derived From: The Consortium of Advanced Management International (CAM-3)

Exhibit G.3 Activity-Based Cost Management Model

Resources, as the top of the expanded ABC Model, are the capacity to perform work because they represent all the available means that activities can draw on. Resources can be thought of as the organization's checkbook since this is where all the period's expenditures are summarized. Examples of resources are salaries, operating supplies, and electrical power. Resources are traced to activities. It is during this step that applicable resource drivers are developed as the mechanism to convey resource costs to activities. A popular basis for tracing resources costs is the time (e.g., number of minutes) that people or equipment spend performing activities. (Note that "tracing" or "assigning" is preferable to the term "allocation." This is because many people associate the term "allocation" with the redistribution of costs that have little to no correlation between source and destinations; hence to some organizations overhead cost allocations are felt to be arbitrary and are viewed cynically.)

The activity module is where work is performed. It is where resources are converted to some type of output. The activity cost assignment step contains the structure and tools to assign activity costs to cost objects (or to other activities), utilizing drivers as the mechanism to accomplish this assignment.

Cost objects, as the bottom of the expanded ABC Model, represent the broad variety of outputs and services where costs accumulate. They are the persons or things that benefit from incurring activities. Examples of cost objects are products, service lines, distribution channels, customers, and outputs of internal processes. Cost objects can be thought of as: what, and for whom, work is done.

Once established, the vertical cost assignment view is useful in determining how the diversity and variation of things, such as different products or various types of customers, can be detected and translated into how they uniquely consume activity costs.

Activities also belong to processes. But, in contrast to the cost assignment view, the horizontal process view displays (in cost terms) the flowchart-like sequence of activities aligned with the business processes through time. As noted earlier, events or other influences which cause activities to be performed and fluctuate are formally called cost drivers. They appear in the expanded ABC Model in the first box of the process view—to the left of the cost assignment view. A cost driver, such as a sales or work order, is the trigger that causes an activity to utilize resources to product output. A sequence of activities is a process, and activity costs are additive along a process. Therefore, those activity costs can be accumulated into a total cost of performing the process.

In summary, the vertical cost assignment view explains what specific things cost, whereas the horizontal process view demonstrates why things have a cost, which provides insights to what causes costs and how much processes cost.

As organizations shift from a hierarchical (department) orientation to more process-based and cross-functional orientations, performance measures become more critical. The performance measures at the end of the horizontal process view are the evaluative criteria by which organizations can manage activities themselves and determine the efficiency and effectiveness of them. Many other nonfinancial performance measures exist (e.g., market share, level of customer satisfaction), as do many other financial performance measures (e.g., return on equity), but they are not calculated in the ABC system, which focuses on costs; however, these performance measures may use cost calculations from an ABC system or be referenced to other data in an ABC system.

Output information from the expanded ABC Model can also be thought of as the input to other applications. For example, ABC information becomes a valuable element for the increasingly popular "balanced scorecard" performance measurement system. Also, the metrics selected for performance measures show that a trend analysis could be used to identify candidate tasks for a continuous improvement program.

Capacity

The physical facilities, personnel, and processes available to meet the product or service needs of customers. Capacity generally refers to the maximum output or producing ability of a machine, a person, a process, a factory, a product, or a service. (*See* Capacity Management)

Capacity Management

The domain of cost management that is grounded in the concept that capacity should be understood, defined, and measured for each level in the organization to include maker segments, products, processes, activities, and resources. In each of these applications, capacity is defined in a hierarchy of idle, nonproductive, and productive views.

*Chart of Accounts

A systematically organized list of accounts representing the names and account numbers of an organization's expenses.

Constraint

A bottleneck, obstacle, or planned control that limits throughput or the utilization of capacity.

Cost Center

A subunit in an organization that is responsible for costs.

Cost Driver

Any situation or event that causes a change in the consumption of a resource or influences quality or cycle time. An activity may have multiple cost drivers. Cost drivers do not necessarily need to be quantified; however, they strongly influence the selection and magnitude of resource drivers and activity drivers.

Cost Driver Analysis

The examination, quantification, and explanation of the effects of cost drivers. The results are often used for continuous improvement programs to reduce throughput times, improve quality, and reduce cost.

Cost Element

The lowest level component of a resource, activity, or cost object.

Cost Management

The management and control of activities and drivers to calculate accurate product and service costs, improve business processes, eliminate waste, influence cost drivers, and plan operations. The resulting information will have utility in setting and evaluating an organization's strategies.

Cost Object

Any product, service, customer, contract, project, process, or other work unit for which a separate cost measurement is desired.

Cost Object Driver

The best single quantitative measure of the frequency and intensity of demands placed on a cost object by other cost objects.

*Cost Object Module

A structure that organizes information about the products, customers, or services that are the cost objects to which costs will be assigned. These cost objects can be grouped, and each center can contain any number of cost objects.

Cost Pool

A logical grouping of resources or activities aggregated to simplify the assignment of resources to activities or activities to cost objects. Elements within a group may be aggregated or disaggregated depending on the informational and accuracy requirements of the use of the data. A modifier may be appended to further describe the group of costs—that is, activity-cost pool.

Cross-Subsidy

The inequitable assignment of costs to cost objects, which leads to overcosting or undercosting them relative to the amount of activities and resources actually consumed. This may result in poor management decisions that are inconsistent with the economic goals of the organization.

Current ABC/M Practice

Objectives of ABC/M. In current practice the creation and use of ABC/M is generally found as an integrated part of an enterprise-wide attempt to meet its overall business objectives. Five business objectives frequently lead to the creation and implementation of ABC/M capabilities:

1. Profitability/pricing
2. Process improvement
3. Planning/budgeting
4. Strategic decision making
5. Understanding/management of costs

The ABC glossary helps to facilitate the use of a common language in addressing the critical business issues facing organizations today. As specific ABC/M applications to support these business objectives become more widespread and sophisticated, the use of consistent and well-defined vocabulary is critical to success.

Demonstrated Uses and Applications. Since the last update to the ABC Glossary in 1991, there have been significant changes in the application of ABC/M concepts in actual practice. Almost all applications in the early 1990s were focused solely on operational cost management in a manufacturing environment. Since that time, the use of ABC/M concepts has expanded to include applications that focus on enterprise-wide strategic issues. Applications in government organizations and service companies are now commonplace. Current ABC/M applications are increasingly likely to be found as part of an integrated business solution involving the financial or strategic management of an enterprise. Significant improvements in software options and the advent of client server hardware technology have facilitated and supported the overall expansion in the types and scope of current applications.

The following applications inventory was developed in January 2000 by CAM-I based on joint input from software vendors, ABC/M consultants, and industry practitioners. This listing demonstrates the expansion of ABC/M concepts in terms of both the scope and type of application. The updated ABC Glossary is intended to serve as a resource across this entire spectrum of current ABC/M applications.

- Product/Service Profitability Analysis
- Distribution Channel Profitability Analysis
- Product Mix Rationalization
- Supporting Intercompany Charge-Outs on Shared Services
- Product Pricing
- Acquisition Analysis
- Moving or Replicating Operations
- Project Management
- Cost Driver Analysis
- Cost of Quality
- Activity Attribute Analysis
- Activity-Based Planning and Budgeting
- Defining Accountability of Responsibility for Activities
- Forecasting
- Evaluating Outsourcing
- Customer Profitability Analysis
- Market Segment Profitability Analysis
- Estimating/Bidding on Customer Work
- Support, Focusing or Quantifying Improvement Initiatives
- Life Cycle Costing
- Business Process Modeling
- Operational Cost Reduction
- Strategic Cost Reduction
- Consolidated Operations Analysis

- Process-Based Costing
- Capital Justification
- Resource Allocation
- Activity-Based Performance Measurement
- Internal Benchmarking
- External Benchmarking

Direct Cost

A cost that can be directly traced to a cost object because a direct or repeatable cause-and-effect relationship exists. A direct cost uses a direct assignment or cost causal relationship to transfer costs. (*See also* Indirect Cost; Tracing.)

Driver

Probably no term, other than "activity," has become more identified with activity-based costing than "driver." The problem is that it has been applied in several ways with varying meanings. The broader, more encompassing "cost driver" is a root cause of an organization's need to perform activities, and it is something that can be described in words but not necessarily in numbers. For example, a storm would be a cost driver that results in many cleanup activities and their resulting costs. In contrast, the "drivers" in ABC/M's cost assignment modules are more local in scope; integral to the work performed; and must be quantitative, using measures that apportion costs. In the ABC/M cost assignment view, there are three types of drivers, and all are required to be quantitative:

1. Resource drivers: trace resource costs to activities.
2. Activity drivers: trace activity costs to cost objects.
3. Cost object drivers: trace cost object costs to other cost objects.

An activity driver, which relates an activity to cost objects, must be stated as a quantity (measured or estimated) because it apportions or "metes out" the cost of the activity based on the unique diversity and variation of the cost objects that are consuming the activity. It is often difficult to understand whether use of the term "activity driver" is related to a causal effect (input driver, such as "number of labor hours") or to the output of an activity (output driver, i.e., "number of in-voices processes" or "number of gallons produced"). In many cases, this is not a critical issue as long as the activity driver traces the relative proportion of the activity cost to its cost objects.

In this glossary the term "cost driver" is used as a larger-scale causal event that influences the frequency, intensity, or magnitude of an organization's activities (i.e., workload) and therefore influences the amount of work done and the overall cost of the activities. As mentioned, this version of a cost driver is not necessarily a quantified measure; it can be described in words. For example, a sales promotion can be a cost driver for substantial increases in the activities of a company's order fulfillment process. The amount of effort taking orders for examples, segmented by teenagers versus senior citizens would require an activity driver (i.e., number of orders placed due to promotion) to calculate the proportional costs to customers in each segment.

As mentioned, in the cost assignment view, the term "driver" is prefix-appended in three areas. The first deals with the method of assigning resource costs to activities—called a resource driver. The second deals with the method of assigning activity costs to cost objects—called activity driver. The third—a cost object driver—applies to cost objects after all activity costs have been assigned. (Note that cost objects can be consumed or used by other cost objects.) Older, less effective terms, such as first- and second-stage driver, unfortunately continue to be used to describe items identical to these currently more accepted terms.

By limiting the use of the word "driver" to four clearly defined areas—cost driver, resource driver, activity driver, and cost object driver—we hope to prevent misinterpretation or misuse of the term. And we believe that restricting the definition of cost driver to one more general meaning will facilitate its understanding.

*Driver Quantity

The measure of the cost assigned to a destination resource, activity, or cost object.

Enterprise-Wide ABM

A management information system that uses activity-based information to facilitate decision making across an organization.

*Fixed Cost

An indirect cost that remains constant; an expenditure or expense that does not vary with volume level of activity.

Hierarchy of Cost Assignability

An approach to group activity costs at the level of an organization where they are incurred or can be directly related to. Examples are the level where individual units are identified (unit-level), where batches of units are organized or processed (batch-level), where a process is operated or supported (process-level), or where costs cannot be objectively assigned to lower level activities or processes (facility-level). This approach is used to better understand the nature of the costs, including the level in the organization at which they are incurred, the level to which they can be initially assigned (attached), and the degree to which they are assignable to other activity and/or cost object levels, that is, activity or cost object cost, or sustaining costs.

Indirect Cost

A resource or activity cost that cannot be directly traced to a final cost object since no direct or repeatable cause-and-effect relationship exists. An indirect cost uses an assignment or allocation to transfer cost. (*See* Direct Cost; Support Costs.)

*Key Performance Indicator (KPI)

A short list of metrics that a company's managers have identified as the most important variables reflecting mission success or organizational performance; a proxy measure of the success of part of an organization, or a manager of that part; a type of indicator, with the difference that the future of the unit or person depends on achieving a satisfactory figure.

Life Cycle Cost

Product life cycle: The period that starts with the initial product conceptualization and ends with the withdrawal of the product from the marketplace and final disposition. A product life cycle is characterized by certain defined stages, including research, development, introduction, maturity, decline, and abandonment. Life cycle cost is the accumulated costs incurred by a product during these stages.

*Objective

An explicitly defined and measurable statement that an organization defines to help the organization manage performance and achieve its strategies or goals.

Pareto Analysis

An analysis that compares cumulative percentages of the rank ordering of costs, cost drivers, profits, or other attributes to determine whether a minority of elements have a disproportionate impact. For example, identifying that 20% of a set of independent variables is responsible for 80% of the effect.

Performance Measures

Indicators of the work performed and the results achieved in an activity, process, or organizational unit. Performance measures are both nonfinancial and financial. Performance measures enable periodic comparisons and benchmarking.

Process

A series of time-based activities that are linked to complete a specific output.

Profitability Analysis

The analysis of profit derived from cost objects with the view to improve or optimize profitability. Multiple views may be analyzed, such as market segment, customer, distribution channel, product families, products, technologies, platforms, regions, manufacturing capacity, and so on.

*Resource Consumption Accounting (RCA)

A dynamic, integrated, and comprehensive cost management system. RCA combines German cost management principles with activity-based costing (ABC). This combination involves features that achieve a significant improvement over other cost management systems.

Resource Driver

The best single quantitative measure of the frequency and intensity of demands placed on a resource by other resources, activities, or cost objects. It is used to assign resource costs to activities, and cost objects, or to other resources.

Resources

Economic elements applied or used in the performance of activities or to directly support costs objects. They include people, materials, supplies, equipment, technologies, and facilities. (*See* Resource river; Capacity.)

Support Costs

Costs of activities not directly associated with producing or delivering products or services. Examples are the costs of information systems, process engineering, and purchasing. (*See* Indirect Cost.)

*Strategy

A statement, defined by an organization, that describes an organization goal.

*Strategy Map

A visual representation of a company's strategies and strategic goals. It usually shows the four perspectives of the balanced scorecard in four layers, with learning and growth at the bottom, followed by business processes, customer satisfaction, and financial results (or mission value in the case of nonprofits). Activities to achieve strategic goals are mapped as "bubbles" linked by cause-effect arrows that are assumed to occur. Sometimes called strategic map.

Surrogate <item> Driver

A substitute for the ideal driver, but closely correlated to the ideal driver, where <item> is resource, activity, cost object. A surrogate driver is used to significantly reduce the cost of measurement while not significantly reducing accuracy. For example, the number of production runs is not descriptive of the material disbursing activity, but the number of production runs may be used as an activity driver if material disbursements correlate well with the number of production runs.

Sustaining Activity

An activity that benefits an organizational unit as a whole, but not any specific cost object.

Target Costing

Calculated by subtracting a desired profit margin from an estimated or a market-based price to arrive at a desired production, engineering, or marketing cost. This may not be the initial production cost but is one expected to be achieved during the mature production stage. Target costing is a method used in the analysis of product design that involves estimating a target cost and then designing the product/service to meet that cost. (*See* Value Analysis.)

Tasks

The breakdown of the work in an activity into smaller elements.

Tracing

The practice of relating resources, activities, and cost objects using the drivers underlying their cost causal relationships. The purpose of tracing is to observe and understand how costs are arising in the normal course of business operations. (*Synonymous* with Assignment. *Contrast* with Allocation.)

Unit Cost

The cost associated with a single unit of measure underlying a resource, activity, product, or service. It is calculated by dividing the total cost by the measured volume. Unit cost measurement must be used with caution as it may not always be practical or relevant in all aspects of cost management.

Unit of Driver Measure

The common denominator between groupings of similar activities. For example: 20 hours of process time is performed in an activity center. This time equates to a number of common activities varying in process time duration. The unit of measure is a standard measure of time such as a minute or an hour.

Value Adding/Non–Value Adding

Assessing the relative value of activities according to how they contribute to customer value or to meeting an organization's needs. The degree of contribution reflects the influence of an activity's cost driver(s).

Value Analysis

A method to determine how features of a product or service relate to cost, functionality, appeal, and utility to a customer (i.e., engineering value analysis). (*See* Target Costing.)

Value Chain Analysis

A method to identify all the elements in the linkage of activities a firm relies on to secure the necessary materials and services, starting from their point of origin, to manufacture, and to distribute their products and services to an end user.

INDEX